SPY vs. SPY

SPY VS. SPY

Stalking Soviet Spies in America

RONALD KESSLER

DAVID & CHARLES
Newton Abbot   London

British Library Cataloguing in Publication Data
Kessler, Ronald
    Spy vs Spy, stalking Soviet spies in America.
    1. United States. Soviet anti-American espionage. Incidents
    I. Title
    327.1'2'0973
    ISBN 0-7153-9337-5

First published in the USA by
Charles Scribner's Sons,
Macmillan Publishing Company,
New York.

Printed in Great Britain
by Billings & Son, Worcester
for David & Charles Publishers plc
Brunel House   Newton Abbot   Devon

Contents

Acknowledgments

The people who helped the most to make this book possible would not want to be singled out for thanks. They are listed with others in the author's notes, and they have my appreciation.

My editor, Edward T. Chase, brought tremendous enthusiasm to the project, for which I am grateful. My agent, Julian Bach, shaped the idea for the book and provided wise counsel.

My wife, Pamela Kessler, gave me helpful suggestions during the preparation of the manuscript, participated in major decisions, and accompanied me to Czechoslovakia.

She and my children, Greg and Rachel Kessler, make it all worthwhile.

Introduction

At 10:58 A.M. on February 11, 1986, a short man wearing a fur hat, a black overcoat, baggy pants, and an angelic smile stepped across the white line that bisects Glienicker Bridge, the 420-foot span joining East Germany with West Berlin.

For nearly nine years, Anatoly Shcharansky, now known as Natan Sharansky, had been imprisoned by the Soviet Union. His offense was his open defiance of the government when it refused to let him emigrate to Israel. Since his incarceration, the United States had made repeated efforts to negotiate his release—all to no avail. That is, until the U.S. had someone important enough to trade for him.

Half an hour after Sharansky stepped into the West, another man and his wife strode over the same white line in the opposite direction. With his mustache and fur-lined coat, Karl F. Koecher looked like a fox. His wife, Hana, wore a mink coat and high white mink hat. Blond and sexy, with incredibly large blue eyes, she looked like a movie star.

Press accounts that day described Koecher as a member of the Czechoslovak Intelligence Service who had worked for the CIA from 1973 to 1977. Because of the shroud of secrecy surrounding his case, very little else was known about him.

The CIA had wanted it that way. After all, Koecher was the *only* spy known to have penetrated the CIA on behalf of the KGB. He had continued as a CIA contract employee until the FBI arrested him and his wife in 1984. In intelligence circles, Koecher is known as one of the most important spies in U.S. history.

Together with his wife, he orchestrated a phony defection from Czechoslovakia in 1965 and developed a "legend" or cover story to conceal his spying activities in New York and Washington. He obtained a job as a CIA translator and analyst in 1973, managed to meet his Czech and KGB handlers at safe houses in Austria and Zurich, and continued to pass classified documents to the Czechs and

3

the KGB until the FBI caught up with him after twenty years of spying.

All told, it was a remarkable feat, and the Soviets showed their appreciation by trading him for the most prominent Soviet dissident of all time.

But there was more to the Koecher case than that:

• Koecher gave his Czech handlers and the KGB details of dozens of "top secret" CIA operations targeted at the Soviets and U.S. allies alike. He supplied them with classified CIA documents, lists and photographs of CIA employees in the U.S. and overseas, and names of U.S. government officials who might be blackmailed into cooperating with the Soviets.

• One of the CIA documents Koecher gave up compromised Aleksandr D. Ogorodnik, a Soviet diplomat in Moscow who was a key CIA asset. Upon being confronted by the KGB, Ogorodnik committed suicide by swallowing a poison pill hidden by the CIA in his Mont Blanc pen.

• The Koechers led still another secret life—that of swingers who attended spouse-swapping parties, orgies, and free-for-alls at sex clubs like Plato's Retreat. Many of the parties were attended by other CIA employees; Koecher passed their names along to the KGB for possible recruitment.

• Koecher flirted with pretending to become a double agent—while employed by the CIA, he approached the FBI and offered to spy on the Czechoslovak Intelligence Service.

• In a bizarre twist, New York FBI agents, together with a CIA official, eventually obtained Koecher's confession using blatantly illegal methods: making promises that they never intended to keep and threatening the personal safety of Koecher and his family. Secretly, Justice Department officials reprimanded the FBI for disregarding all guidelines governing confessions, and the FBI's Office of Professional Responsibility censured the agents. Nevertheless, the key agent responsible for the case is now one of the headquarters officials in charge of training other FBI counterintelligence agents.

Just over a year after the historic trade on Glienicker Bridge, I interviewed this mole and his wife for five days in Czechoslovakia. Making no secret of the fact that he is a spy, Koecher told me no Soviet intelligence officer had ever agreed to be interviewed by the Western press before. While ego certainly played a part, he explained why he had agreed to this:

"Even if it comes out principally hostile, I can only gain by talking to you," he said. "It will certainly be somewhat less hostile simply because it was not really as described in the publicity. A serious writer for the sake of his own prestige would try to do an honest job."

With my wife, Pamela Kessler, we toured Prague and its restaurants, ate wild pheasant and deer sausage, visited the Old Jewish Cemetery that dates to 1439, stopped at Franz Kafka's grave in the New Jewish Cemetery, saw the concert hall where Mozart performed, and viewed Czech art at the National Gallery. One day we drank slivovitz, a strong plum brandy, in the Koechers' new home, walked in the woods, and sampled Hana's cooking.

All the while, Koecher and I taped and photographed each other while we probed each other for hidden agendas. I learned how Koecher had checked me out before I arrived and why he became convinced my wife was an undercover FBI agent. He discussed their swinging activities and all the changes in their lives now that they are in Czechoslovakia, barred from ever again entering the U.S. He told me why he feared being kidnapped if he enters a Western country again. Koecher spoke, too, of his Jewish heritage, how his mother had hidden her Jewish ancestry to escape persecution during the Nazi occupation of Czechoslovakia, and how his grandparents were killed in a Nazi concentration camp. I even met Koecher's eighty-eight-year-old mother, who had lived for twenty years in the belief that her only child had genuinely defected.

Most of all, Koecher talked about what he referred to as his "career" as a spy, why he chose it and likes it, and his experience in the U.S. as an "illegal"—a foreign intelligence officer who enters a country under false pretenses, with no overt tie to that intelligence service or the country that operates it. He also revealed new details about the information he passed to the Czechoslovak Intelligence Service.

In all, the interviews spanned sixty hours, with twelve hours on tape.

It was remarkable that the Czechoslovak Intelligence Service, which works closely with the KGB, had trusted Koecher enough to allow him to be interviewed. But what was most striking was the similarity in language and outlook between this premier spy and the FBI counterspies I had come to know during equally unprecedented interviews over the course of a year.

As a *Washington Post* reporter for fifteen years, I had done many stories on the FBI—critical ones during then–FBI director J. Edgar Hoover's reign and more favorable ones lately as the bureau, under William H. Webster, became a highly professional, sophisticated organization.

I had never done a story about spying until *Regardie's,* a Washington business magazine, approached me in July 1986 to do a piece on how the FBI caught a Soviet spy just expelled from the U.S.

Most people think the CIA catches spies. That's a basic misconception. While the CIA engages in spying, the FBI engages in counterspying—tracking, identifying, and neutralizing spies. Since everything about the FBI's counterintelligence work is classified, the FBI almost never talks about it, and then only in controlled interviews at headquarters.

Yet within several weeks of getting the magazine assignment, I was allowed to interview FBI counterintelligence case agents—the counterspies who actually follow Soviet intelligence officers, run double agents, and engage in undercover work to catch spies. With them, I visited "dead drops" where double agents controlled by the FBI had left classified documents for Soviet spies, toured the FBI's counterintelligence facilities at the Washington field office, and saw the Soviet establishments that are the FBI's targets. While out with two FBI agents, I even saw a Soviet spy as he was leaving his apartment in Arlington, Virginia.

"Ah, maybe you should look to your left," the agent driving the FBI car had said as we drove out of the parking lot of a building where several Soviet spies lived. "He spotted us when he walked out to the car. He was the gentleman crossing the parking lot."

"Now you're on a surveillance," the other agent said. "He'll think you're an FBI agent, because he's going to see you with me and [the other agent], and he's going to say, 'I've got another one identified, boss. It's another one they've got. But I don't understand; they've got three in the car.' "

I later found out that the approval to give me so much access had all been a mistake. Dana E. Caro, then the special agent in charge of the Washington field office, had approved the interviews, but James H. Geer, assistant FBI director in charge of the intelligence division, had disapproved them. As head of the FBI's entire counterintelligence effort, Geer was in charge, but Caro sometimes thought he was. Through a misunderstanding at headquarters, the interviews had started before the word of Geer's decision made its way to the

Washington field office. Since the interviews had already begun, Geer let them continue.

When the *Regardie's* article appeared, I was told Geer and Webster thought it accurately portrayed counterintelligence work, but a key FBI counterintelligence official claimed it gave away so many secrets that it had severely damaged the FBI. If I had learned anything from doing the article, it was that each FBI official has a different view of what should be disclosed. While everyone agreed that items like names of undercover agents or codes should remain secret, each had a different perception of what information could be useful to the other side. Since everything about the FBI's counterintelligence program is classified, anyone could claim that secrets had been disclosed without authorization.

In a memo, the key FBI counterintelligence official called for an administrative inquiry—the FBI's term for a noncriminal investigation—to determine who had said what to me. The fact that the article prominently featured agents with whom he had had conflicts did not help. Yet his reaction represented a view held by many FBI officials: that the FBI's counterintelligence program should never be discussed with the press. Others tended to take a more flexible attitude. Recognizing that the Soviets already knew a lot about the FBI's methods anyway, they felt that publicity could help deter would-be spies.

Geer put the memo away, and when I later met with him in November 1986, he laughed about the consternation the article had caused. Nevertheless, while he claimed the FBI would cooperate in the preparation of the book, he decided that no more interviews could be conducted with case agents.

". . . We are unable to allay our concerns to protect sources and techniques, and in some cases identities, in this important area," he explained in a letter.

His ruling had little effect on the book. During the interviews already conducted, I had gathered much more than could be used for an article. Many FBI counterintelligence agents, Justice Department officials, and former FBI officials came out of the woodwork to help. I could still interview headquarters officials. And I was able to interview former double agents, convicted spies, and others with firsthand knowledge of the cases in this book.

In the end, my FBI sources were so current that they told me the FBI knew, through surveillance of the Czechoslovak Embassy in Washington, about my trip to Prague before I took it.

"We figured you had either gone over to the other side or were doing something for the book, and we knew you hadn't gone over to the other side," one agent said.

A book has never been done on the FBI's counterintelligence program, and few books have been written on the FBI's nonclassified criminal investigations. One reason is the FBI's insistence that everyone in the bureau must share credit—a throwback to the days when Hoover's name alone appeared at the beginning of every FBI press release.

A former deputy chief of the FBI's Soviet section summed up this attitude in declining to be interviewed for the book:

Certainly, individual accomplishments are recognized and rewarded within the organization, but I know of no human endeavor that so exemplifies the words "team effort" than does the successful counterintelligence operation. From the lowliest clerk to the highest executive, all make their individual contributions upon which the success of an operation depends. To glorify in print selected individuals not only reveals their identities to the enemy and therefore may adversely affect future operations, it can also adversely affect the *esprit de corps* of the rest of the team and thus do even further damage.

The idea that publicity damages team spirit would be news to a Joe Theismann or a Pete Rose. And the point about disclosing agents' identities ignores the fact that the FBI routinely discloses the names of counterintelligence agents in court filings. While spies always work undercover, counterspies may or may not require anonymity, depending on the case.

More to the point, books need to focus on people to make them interesting. For that reason, *Spy vs. Spy* focuses on one FBI counterintelligence squad and some of its members to tell the story of the entire counterintelligence effort and the recent spy cases.

Interviews in prisons with convicted American spies provide the inside story from the traitor's point of view. Finally, the interviews with Koecher give the other half of the story—the view of the FBI's efforts from the Soviet perspective.

Because it leaves no footprints, espionage is one of the most difficult crimes to uncover. Yet the business of catching spies affects profoundly the American way of life. If done well, it protects our freedoms by keeping us strong. If done poorly, it can impinge on our liberties just as surely as a takeover by a foreign power.

1

A Rule Is Broken

The Southwest Freeway leaves behind the Washington Monument, the White House, and Washington's other symbols of power. It hovers above apartment houses and riverside marinas with their fishing boats and stalls redolent of crabs and shrimp.

The freeway leads to South Capitol Street and Washington's all-black neighborhood of Anacostia. At the first intersection is Skyline Inn, a motel filled by busloads of tourists from Iowa. A right turn, then a left, and the driver is on Half Street.

Framed by junkyards and fields of weeds, Half Street is a rutted road crisscrossed by railroad tracks like canals on Mars. At the end of the road, just before the muddy Anacostia River, is a Potomac Electric Power Company plant. Across the street from the power plant is a building constructed so cheaply that the din of its air-conditioning system drowns out the hum of Pepco's generators.

This is the FBI's Washington field office, 1900 Half Street SW, the home of CI-3, a crack FBI counterintelligence squad so secret that only the CIA, the NSA, and Soviet spies know about it.

The squad's quarters are on the eleventh floor. Near the front of the squad room is a bulletin board where hang a yellowing "Eat Bertha's Mussels" sign and a postcard with a picture of a girl in a bikini.

Arranged in twos and threes and facing front, thirty metal desks squeeze into the brown-carpeted, twenty-five-by-forty-foot room. The noise from a public address system paging agents alternates with the "beep, beep, beep" of Clyde, a robot that delivers mail.

But it was quiet the night of October 21, 1985, when, at eight-thirty, Special Agent Michael D. Grogan, a forty-year-old member of the CI-3 squad, walked into the office of his boss, William P. O'Keefe. Grogan's hair was thinning at the top, and his sideburns were turning gray. His eyes perpetually squinted, as if he were looking into the sun at a baseball game. His boss, O'Keefe, had a high forehead, a Roman nose, blue eyes, and skin as fresh as a twelve-year-old's.

"Bill, you're not going to believe this," Grogan started.

Just off the squad room, O'Keefe's office overlooks the Anacostia River. Grogan sat down by a wall map of the U.S. that shows what parts are restricted to Soviets—about 10 percent of the country. Some of the areas have been declared off-limits simply because the Soviets have put similar areas off-limits to Americans in Russia. Russians can enter some cities—like Tucson—only via airplane, because the surrounding terrain is restricted to them.

What Grogan had to say was not something that would have shocked the average person. It was a breach of etiquette, true, but not something that Miss Manners would have frowned on.

It was a breach of *spy* etiquette.

And to appreciate this, you have to be, like Grogan, an FBI special agent assigned to track Soviet spies in Washington—a member of an elite, secret squad of agents who focus on the best and most aggressive spies in the business. You have to spend your days and nights following them until you have a working knowledge of what's accepted and what's not, what's in the rule book and what's beyond the pale.

As an FBI counterspy, Grogan had seen the Russians brazenly knock on the doors of military men at night asking for secret documents. He had witnessed them soaking up information at hearings of the Senate Armed Services Committee. He knew that on any given night they were swarming like locusts through northern Virginia, "trolling" for new American spies in bars and restaurants. And he knew that, very often, they successfully recruited Americans to become traitors to their country.

That was to be expected. That was the Soviets' job, and they did it well. So long as they followed the rules, Grogan even admired the Russians for their professionalism, just as lawyers may admire their opponents in the courtroom. And that was why this particular breach of etiquette galled him.

Grogan told O'Keefe he learned about the incident from Yogi, the FBI code name for a high-ranking Air Force officer who had been approached by a Soviet to spy for Russia. Yogi had played along with the Russian, Colonel Vladimir Makarovich Ismaylov, and he had reported the contact to the Air Force in May 1985. He then agreed to become a double agent, pretending to be a spy but in reality controlled by the FBI and the Air Force's Office of Special Investigations. While the FBI has primary jurisdiction in counterintelligence investigations, each of the military services has its own investigative branch that looks for spies within their agencies.

By August 1985, Yogi and Ismaylov had exchanged coded post-cards meant to signify that Yogi was ready to be a player—to commit treason for Russian lucre. Nothing happened at first. Then, on October 21, at seven-fifteen in the morning, Yogi was driving to his office at the Pentagon. It was a rainy, wretched day, the kind that mysteriously ties up traffic from Baltimore to Richmond. Yogi was inching along Telegraph Road in Alexandria, Virginia, listening to oldies on WXTR-FM. He could have made better time walking.

As he slowly passed Telegraph Video at Farmington Drive, he heard a knock on his passenger window. Through beads of water, he saw a beefy, forty-three-year-old six-footer, with thinning brown hair, lined forehead, mustache, and long sideburns—the same Soviet he'd met in a bar five months earlier.

"Let me in," Ismaylov said in his guttural accent.

Yogi's heart was pounding. He was dressed in his military uni-form, and the people in the traffic jam around him could be his neighbors, his friends, or the Air Force chief of staff. And a spy attached to the Russian Embassy was accosting him in broad day-light.

In role-playing sessions at the Ramada Hotel in New Carrollton, Maryland, the FBI and the Air Force's OSI had taught Yogi how to behave with Ismaylov. He was always to remember that he was supposedly betraying his country and could be tried for espionage and sent up. He should therefore feign apprehension when the Soviet asked for "top secret" documents. But Yogi needed no coaching now.

Without thinking, he opened the door and let Ismaylov in.

"How are you?" Ismaylov asked pleasantly.

Yogi mumbled an answer but was thinking about what would happen if he were kidnapped. He was one man against the Soviet Union. Would he ever see his family again?

Ismaylov told Yogi to take a right and drive toward the Penn Daw Shopping Center three quarters of a mile to the south. When they arrived, he handed Yogi a raincoat. The two men got out and walked around, pausing to look in the window of Crown Books.

As they walked, Ismaylov briefed Yogi on the types of documents he wanted. Ismaylov was not shy. Ostensibly, he was a diplomat, an assistant air attaché with the Soviet military office. But he had an undercover role as well. Ismaylov was a member of the GRU, Russia's most aggressive spy agency.

Unlike the KGB, which seeks economic, political, military, and scientific information, the GRU, or Chief Intelligence Directorate of the Soviet General Staff (*Glavnoye Razvedyvatelnoye Upravleniye*), focuses only on military secrets. Of the roughly two hundred Soviet diplomats in Washington believed by the FBI to be spies, a third of them are members of the GRU.

The GRU is like a rogue elephant, Phillip A. Parker, formerly deputy assistant FBI director for operations in the intelligence division, told me. "They run around doing things the KGB wouldn't," he said. "They are rude, crude, and crass. They believe anybody can buy an American for the right amount of money."

The most famous GRU officer was Colonel Oleg Penkovsky, a Soviet double agent whose information helped President Kennedy face down the Soviet Union during the Cuban Missile Crisis of 1962. Petr Ivanovich Ivashutin, a man with a receding hairline and a large pug nose, has headed the GRU out of Moscow since 1963.

More often than not, when expulsions of Soviets are announced, they are clandestine GRU operatives. Yet, unlike the more well-known KGB, the GRU has managed to stay out of the public eye.

Ismaylov told Yogi he wanted only documents that dealt with America's most sensitive military projects—the Strategic Defense Initiative, Stealth technology, the Cruise missile, and the Trans-atmospheric vehicle, a combination airplane and missile that would take off from runways but travel from the U.S. to Europe in half an hour. At their next meeting, Ismaylov said he would brief Yogi on where to deliver the documents. For his trouble, Ismaylov handed Yogi a down payment of $4,000 in twenty-dollar bills—not bad for an hour of his time.

By the time he arrived at the Pentagon, Yogi was shaking. When he was with Ismaylov, the adrenaline suppressed his fear like a heavy blanket on a cold day. Now the reality hit him: he could be accosted anytime, anywhere, by a Russian espionage agent. Each time, he would have to dissemble. If the Russians ever discovered that he was a double agent, he could be killed.

Yogi dialed the number he had been given in case he needed an emergency meeting with his handlers, Grogan of the FBI and OSI Special Agent Michael D. Scott. Since everything about his role was classified, Yogi was never to discuss it on the phone or even tell his wife—a restriction that would later create problems at home. Instead, he was to arrange to meet with Grogan and Scott at an Air Force base—the one place where Ismaylov could not follow him.

That night, Yogi met with Grogan and Scott, a thirty-six-year-old agent with a bulldog face, and told them what happened. When Grogan returned to his office, O'Keefe was waiting for him. A veteran of twelve years of tracking spies in Washington, O'Keefe, thirty-eight, was as shocked as Grogan and Scott had been.

Very simply, by jumping into Yogi's car in rush-hour traffic, Ismaylov had breached the intricate skein of rules that govern the way the spy game is played.

It's a fast-paced game, played in Washington on a court that includes the Washington Monument, Capitol Hill, Georgetown, the bars of Virginia, and the country roads of Maryland—anyplace not specifically declared off-limits to Soviet diplomats because of military or research facilities.

On one team are the Russian diplomats and employees believed by the FBI to be undercover spies—about a third of the more than five hundred employed by components of the Soviet Embassy in Washington. Helping them are Americans who commit treason, usually for money.

Arrayed against them and against spies from other countries are the FBI's counterintelligence agents—more than half the five hundred agents assigned to the Washington field office, plus thousands of other agents assigned to each of the FBI's fifty-nine field offices and four hundred resident agencies.

Their uniforms may vary, but for the most part the players use vehicles that both sides easily recognize. All Russians attached to the embassy drive cars with red, white, and blue diplomatic plates coded "FC" to mark them as Soviets. Driving without the plates is strictly prohibited, and rental cars cannot be used without special permission of the State Department. For the most part, the Soviets follow the rules. Only employed "illegals" like Karl Koecher with no overt connection to the Soviet bloc go without their assigned markings.

"They're really good citizens except when it comes to committing espionage," said FBI Special Agent J. Stephen Ramey, a former counterintelligence agent who is now in charge of the FBI's counterintelligence budget.

The FBI, for its part, uses vehicles that are as easily spotted by the Russians as the Russian vehicles are by the FBI. Unless the FBI is conducting undercover surveillance, its agents drive full-size, four-door sedans that come in drab colors that nobody with a sense of style would select for himself.

The object of the game, of course, is to shoot as many secret documents back to Moscow as possible. The FBI expects the Russians to spend their time here spying, just as it knows some Americans based in Moscow engage in spying. The Soviets, in turn, expect the FBI will wiretap, bug, and shadow them as long as they are here—an impression the FBI likes to exploit.

In a few cases, the attention has come in handy. After the Soviet Union shot down a Korean airliner in 1983, FBI agents trailing Soviet intelligence officers on a tour of the South saved their lives when irate locals threatened the Soviets with handguns. The Soviets sent the agents a letter of thanks. At other times, the Soviets spend hours "dry cleaning" themselves to make themselves "black"—free of FBI surveillance. Before accosting Yogi on Telegraph Road, for example, Ismaylov devoted two hours to turning into dead-end streets, speeding up to seventy miles per hour, then slowing to five miles per hour, in an effort to make sure he was not being tailed.

Although the FBI agents are armed, so long as the quarry is Russian spies the game is not necessarily dangerous. Protected by diplomatic immunity, the Soviets cannot be charged with a crime, and so have no need to defend themselves: beyond some minor scuffling, they have never been known to attack an FBI agent. Nor does the FBI harass the Russians unless they egregiously breach the rules. One Russian, for example, insisted on speeding around Washington. On two occasions, four FBI cars surrounded his car as it was moving, forcing him to slow down. He quickly got the message.

If the FBI catches a Russian diplomat spying, the worst that can happen is that he is ejected from the game. Declared *persona non grata* by the Department of State, he is returned to Russia and cannot play in the U.S. anymore. After a delay of several months, play starts again when the Soviets send in a substitute.

If a Russian makes a particularly clever play, his FBI opponent may privately tip his hat to him.

"The Russians are very good. I have a lot of respect for them," Robert B. Wade, deputy chief of the FBI's Soviet counterintelligence section, told me.

On the other hand, if a Soviet intelligence officer engages in a clumsy or foolhardy act, as Ismaylov did, the agent feels he should be thrown out of the spy game.

For Americans engaged in espionage, for Soviet spies without diplomatic immunity, and for "illegals" without any overt connection to the Soviet Union, the stakes are higher. They can be sent up for life, and they are often armed and dangerous. What's more, a Soviet intelligence agent caught spying for the U.S. can expect to be killed.

When they graduate from training school, GRU and KGB officers are subjected to a particularly gruesome sight: a movie of a turncoat KGB officer being raised and lowered by a crane into a blast furnace, his screams finally stifled as he is lowered a final time into the 2,000-degree flames.

Since 1985, the Soviets have executed six of their own for spying for the U.S., apparently because they had been compromised by former CIA employee Edward Lee Howard, according to FBI sources.

Central to the way the game is played is the belief shared by both sides that intelligence officers—whether they are Soviets working for the KGB and GRU or Americans working for the CIA—are patriots in the eyes of their own countrymen. But Soviets who spy against the Soviet Union, and Americans who spy on America, are seen by spies from both sides as contemptible traitors—even if they are helping that side. Thus, the two governments never intervene to win the freedom of a foreign national imprisoned for spying for the other side, while intelligence officers from their own side are routinely swapped.

"If somebody offers genuine intelligence information, nobody would say no," Karl Koecher told me. "But you don't have too much respect for a person like that, or at least you reserve comment. It doesn't require much cunning. He's got it and he sells it. There's a moral aspect to it. He doesn't do it for something he believes in or believes he should defend, and he probably doesn't think he is risking as much. He simply believes it's a cinch. So he's a sort of thief. I wouldn't consider an intelligence officer, even if he steals, a thief, any more than you would consider a soldier on the battlefield a murderer. Killing other people is abominable; so is stealing. But under very special circumstances, at least in our culture, it becomes acceptable."

It was always so. The American revolutionaries were far more outraged at Benedict Arnold, who offered to give up West Point and its gunpowder in exchange for £20,000, than they were at Major

John André, the British officer who negotiated the sellout. Arnold was one of their own; André was a Brit. Nevertheless, André was executed. Arnold managed to escape to England.

At any moment, a counterintelligence case may turn into a criminal case when the government elects to prosecute spies who do not have diplomatic immunity. From 1966 to 1975, there were no successful federal prosecutions for espionage. But since 1975, the Justice Department has brought indictments in forty-nine cases. Only one resulted in a verdict of not guilty. Another two cases were prosecuted in the military courts.

CI-3 agents were responsible for five of the cases and participated in most of the other major ones, including the arrest of retired Navy warrant officer John A. Walker Jr. and other less-publicized cases that were nearly as damaging to U.S. security.

For all the increased emphasis on prosecutions, CI-3 counterintelligence agents devote only an estimated ten percent of their time to cases that lead to prosecutions. Most often, they are quietly trolling—watching their opponents, dangling decoys in front of them so they can't engage in productive spying, learning how they operate, and trying to recruit them to the American side. Every decision entails balancing the benefit against the harm of revealing what the FBI knows or provoking the Soviets into retaliating against U.S. spies in Moscow. And every decision requires weighing what the FBI's role should primarily be—a law-enforcement agency that catches spies or a counterintelligence agency that tries to learn as much as possible about the opposition.

In that regard, the FBI is under constant pressure—pressure from within the intelligence community to become more like spooks, from the courts to become more like cops, and from individual members of Congress to go in either direction.

The game is played in secret. Until now, the way the FBI goes about tracking spies—as well as the Soviet view of it—has never been told. Each CI-3 agent has clearance to see "sensitive compartmented information," a level beyond "top secret." Practically everything a counterspy does is classified. Even the number of agents assigned to FBI counterintelligence work—more than a third of the FBI's 9,220 agents—is kept secret.

In fact, most Americans do not realize that the FBI—as opposed to the CIA—has responsibility for catching spies in the U.S. Nor is the FBI interested in letting people in on the secret. The current head of the intelligence division, Assistant FBI Director James Geer, is an affable Tennesseean who keeps such a low profile that his name rarely appears in the news media. The references include only two four-paragraph stories run by United Press International when his appointment was announced in September 1985.

On his wall is a quotation from *Light of Day* by Eric Ambler: "I think if I were asked to single out one specific group of men, one category as being the most suspicious, unbelieving, unreasonable, petty, inhuman, sadistic, double-crossing set of bastards in any language, I would say without hesitation the people who run counterespionage departments."

In ninety percent of the cases, expulsions for spying are not publicized either. After all, both sides are doing it. Like nuclear warheads, each diplomatic spy in one country is delicately balanced against a spy in the opposing country. Publicity may prompt more expulsions or—worse yet—upset delicate diplomatic negotiations between Russia and the U.S.

Just as Soviet and U.S. pilots sometimes shoot at each other, or enter each other's territory, without either side acknowledging that an incident occurred, neither country wants to take a chance on letting outside referees step in. As long as everyone plays by the rules, why have spectators? In that sense, the spy game mirrors relations between the two superpowers, which bluster publicly while privately exchanging soothing words.

The arrest of Nicholas Daniloff, Moscow correspondent for *U.S. News & World Report,* only illustrates what can happen when a skirmish erupts off the field, creating an uproar that neither side wants. KGB agent Gennady Zakharov, caught red-handed in New York on August 23, 1986, was not wearing his invisible shield: his position at the United Nations did not come with full diplomatic immunity. He was supposed to cultivate intelligence sources but not pick up secret documents. Because he had no immunity, he was subject to being tried for espionage, prompting the Soviets to grab Daniloff in an effort to win Zakharov's freedom.

When expulsions are publicized, it is with a purpose—to convey a certain message to the "bad guys."

Before Michael Grogan decided he wanted to become a special agent for the FBI, he aspired to be a priest. His father, an Army counterintelligence officer, wanted him off the streets of Chicago and enrolled him in a Catholic seminary when Grogan was fourteen. For ten years, first in Wisconsin and then in Florida, Grogan studied in seminaries.

In retrospect, Grogan found it hard to understand why he had wanted to be a priest. In the evenings, there was "grand silence," when Grogan was forbidden to speak until Mass the next morning. He could watch only two television shows, *Paladin* and *Maverick*. Sometimes, he ate dinner with grouchy priests. But Grogan wanted a wife and children to have dinner with. Occasionally, he still slips and refers to the seminary as the "cemetery."

Yet the solitary, regimented life and the endless probing of the mysteries of theology taught him patience—just the thing for studying the serpentine movements of a spy.

Leaving the seminary, Grogan taught English and Latin at a Catholic high school in Miami. He also coached basketball, football, and baseball. The fathers of several of his players were FBI agents, and they impressed him as well-spoken and physically fit. When they asked if he wanted to join the FBI, he jumped at the chance.

By now, Grogan had married an Irish, red-haired woman, also the product of Catholic schools—Patricia King. He knew he could not feed a family on his annual teacher's salary of $5,500.

Grogan entered the FBI in 1971 and was sent to Baltimore. Assigned to what was then known as domestic security work, he kept an eye on doddering members of the Communist Party USA—men in their seventies who watched television all day.

After a year, he was transferred to Columbia, South Carolina, and then to the resident agency at Myrtle Beach. He hoped to make his career there. Living costs were low, the beach was pristine, and to occupy him there were lots of bold bank holdups to solve. What Grogan liked most was that he was his own man, assigned to a stretch of coastline that was his responsibility.

Beneath Grogan's soft-spoken manner, trim, five-foot, ten-inch frame, suits from Sears, and shuffling gait is a fiercely competitive spirit. The family room of his comfortable, split-level home in Fairfax, Virginia, overflows with 150 trophies won by him or teams he has coached in every game that uses a ball. He talks slowly, deliberately. Yet his chin gives it all away. It's a Rock of Gibraltar chin, jutting scrappily into the world.

In Myrtle Beach, he was recognized for the fugitives he caught and the holdups he solved. He acquired a reputation as an agent who never lets up.

"I just think that whatever you're going to do, you have to do it all out," he would tell his older son, Michael.

Soon, he got a call that he was being transferred to Washington.

Grogan's initial assignment was in the counterintelligence side of the field office, which accounts for more than half the agents in the office and is funded by a generous budget that is classified. By the early 1970s, the FBI's emphasis had shifted from "security" cases focused on domestic radical groups to "counterintelligence" work aimed at foreign spies, a distinction that former FBI director William H. Webster often hammered home: "We certainly don't have enough agents to keep track of every citizen of this country, nor do we want to investigate the activities of lawful organizations without predication for doing so," he has said. "Rather, our focus—indeed our strategy—must be on the intelligence operatives themselves and the identification of those who have come here with intelligence commissions. . . . I believe that in a free society this is the only way we can function without turning ourselves into a police state."

Through a headquarters program, Grogan was trained in counterintelligence work and later received further instruction from the CIA. As a new agent, he had fifteen weeks of intensive training at the FBI Academy at Quantico, Virginia. His Soviet opponent, the GRU agent, receives three years at the secret Soviet Military Academy in Moscow.

Grogan was assigned to track Bulgarians, but he felt they were only lackeys for the Soviets. In fact, many American spies recruited by the Bulgarian, Czech, Polish, and Hungarian intelligence services are "tasked"—directed—by Soviet agents.

Grogan wanted to be closer to the action. After a brief stint on the criminal side, he transferred to CI-3. Very shortly, he found himself at the epicenter of the FBI's secret war on Soviet spies.

Throughout the country, there are 4,250 diplomats, commercial officials, and other representatives from Communist countries. Some 2,100 of them come from the Soviet Union and other Warsaw Pact countries. The FBI believes that thirty percent of them are intelligence officers or spies.

Predictably, the FBI's biggest counterintelligence force is in Washington, which has the greatest number of Soviet officials and the most sensitive targets from a national security standpoint—the CIA, Capitol Hill, the Pentagon, and the National Security Agency. Because of the United Nations and its Soviet contingent, New York is second, followed by San Francisco, which has a Soviet consulate. Chicago is third because it has the consulates of several Soviet bloc countries.

In all, the Washington field office has twenty counterintelligence squads—CI (for counterintelligence) one through twenty. The squads, each consisting of up to thirty agents, are evenly divided between those focusing on Soviets and those that track spies from Soviet bloc countries, the People's Republic of China, and the rest of the world. The FBI's Soviet squads each have their specialty. CI-2, for example, watches KGB agents in the KGB's KR section—the Soviet internal security force that wiretaps, bugs, and follows other Soviets to make sure they have not become double agents. CI-4 watches the KGB at the Soviet Embassy.

In 1983, CI-3—known as "GRU Busters"—was split into two squads. Now CI-6 follows GRU officers who are not in the military office. The roughly thirty members of CI-3 focus only on GRU officers assigned to the embassy's military office.

No one really knows why the Soviets—or the Americans, for that matter—need a military office as part of their diplomatic representation. Ostensibly, the military attachés—split about evenly among Soviet Army, Navy, and Air Force representatives—gather publicly available information about the U.S. military and represent the military at receptions.

In fact, all of the approximately thirty attachés in the military office are members of the GRU, bent on uncovering as many U.S. military secrets as possible.

The Soviet military office is a handsome, four-story residence at 2552 Belmont Road NW, just around the corner from the Islamic Temple on Massachusetts Avenue. Assessed at $916,659, the brick building has apartments on the top floor so it can be manned twenty-four hours a day. Tacked to a wall on the second floor are photos taken of CI-3 squad members.

To Grogan and the other members of the CI-3 squad, the Soviet military office is "SMO." While they have never been inside it, members of the squad spend more time around it than they do at their own homes.

Grogan knew that because the U.S. is an open society, the deck was stacked against him from the start. The GRU can gather bushels of information just by reading the latest leaks in *The Washington Post* or attending a public hearing on military spending on Capitol Hill.

U.S. military attachés assigned to the Soviet Union, in contrast, have a nearly impossible task—to find out as much as they can about the Soviet military through overt means. As a rule, the CIA uses State Department employees rather than the military as cover.

"In the Soviet Union, you can't photograph roads or bridges, even if you're a Soviet," said Lieutenant Commander James R. Kirkpatrick, a Navy intelligence officer who recently returned to the Pentagon after serving two years as a military attaché in Moscow. "Here you can see a ship being launched at Newport News on TV, or pick up *Aviation Week* and see a photo. There it would be unthinkable. Here you can go to congressional hearings on the military. There you couldn't put your nose in the Politburo. You'd be dead."

The greatest source of information was the military parade in November, when new weapons occasionally were displayed.

"When they got a new head of the navy, we would have to read it in the military paper, *Red Star*. That would make our day. You can't find out who is the head of their equivalent of the Marine Corps," he told me. "Here you can look up in the Department of Defense phone book how we're structured. Even the local phone company directory has it," he said.

Because the Soviet military office is the first listing in the District of Columbia phone book under "Soviet Embassy," it is often the first place a would-be spy calls. So, because it watches SMO, CI-3 gets some of the more highly publicized espionage cases that begin with telephone calls or visits to Soviet establishments.

In other cases the squad uses intricate cover stories: an FBI agent posing as someone else; informants or defectors; reconnaissance aircraft; technical help from the CIA and NSA; and ruses so crafty that they would be edited out of spy fiction as being too unbelievable.

Once a month, an FBI supervisor meets over lunch with the head of the KGB's Directorate K, the internal security police, to discuss mutual problems. At restaurants like Danker's, Harvey's, and the Mayflower Hotel dining room, chosen alternately by the two men, they exchange information meant to make each other's jobs easier.

Ostensibly, the purpose of the meetings is to go over security concerns: the U.S. government is responsible for protecting all embassies here, and the Soviets are often the target of demonstrations and terrorist plots. In addition, there are incidents within the embassy that need to be explored. For example, in January 1984, the

Soviets refused to allow the District of Columbia medical examiner to view the area where Evgeniy Gavrilov died in the embassy. An autopsy revealed that a rope or belt had been tightened around his neck, but without viewing the scene of death, no verdict could be given on whether it was a suicide, accident, or murder.

But the meetings range well beyond the protection of the embassy. The KGB man may complain that the FBI has been tailing one of its agents excessively. The FBI man may explain the reason: the KGB agent spat on an FBI agent or gave him the finger, or the Soviets have been tailing a U.S. diplomat in Moscow excessively. Very often as a result, the surveillance in Moscow is removed, at least for the time being.

Sometimes, the FBI man tries to score points by letting the Soviet know that a walk-in spy has a history of mental illness and suicidal tendencies.

"Sometimes we do it just to make the point we know about it," said an FBI counterintelligence agent.

In the same vein, the KGB man may claim over lunch that an overzealous FBI agent was caught breaking into an apartment without authorization.

"They'll say you have a bad FBI agent. He was caught in someone's apartment. There are some things they perceive as negative that might have been fully approved on our side," the agent said.

While these claims may be true, both sides also introduce disinformation meant to start the other side on a wild goose chase.

Very often, CI-3 sends double agents into the Soviet military office offering classified information. The FBI then purports to arrest them, just to teach the Russians to be leery of walk-ins.

To help it along, CI-3 uses special FBI support groups and squads skilled in installing tiny video cameras in devious places, wiring a car for sound on short notice, or translating Russian.

Agents who go undercover—perhaps to fool the Soviets by acting as double agents—are responsible for getting their cover stories down and changing their appearance. They might grow beards and tint their hair. Each agent must get his own American Express card, telephone listing, and apartment, all under a phony name. CI-3 has one agent in charge of cover stories. He has a supply of twenty-five phony licenses from motor vehicle bureaus to hand out as needed. He also keeps track of cover stories so the agents don't wind up giving conflicting stories. For example, if one agent says he works for Boeing Corp., the FBI would not want a second agent to make the same claim. The first thing the Soviets would do is ask the purported spy about the other bogus employee; the agents wouldn't necessarily know each other's cover story.

Nor is the squad above using sex as a come-on. Currently, at least one female member of the squad is involved in operations referred to in spycraft as "honey pots." This entails compromising married GRU officers sexually so they will work for the U.S.

In the past, CI-3 has used extremely attractive young American women as double agents, just as the opposing intelligence services use attractive females. There was, for example, the case of Jennifer Miles, a sexy, twenty-six-year-old South African who was recruited by the DGI, the Cuban intelligence service, to work in Washington. Miles was a tall blonde, so shapely that men could not believe what they saw. But women liked her, too. She was sweet, ladylike, effervescent. She became enamored with the goals of the Cuban Revolution, and when she went to Cuba on vacation in 1968, the DGI recruited her as an unpaid agent. Her code name was Mary.

Miles's method was to sleep with as many State Department and White House aides as she could, to try to get them to reveal informa-, tion. Just by chance, in the summer of 1969, the FBI found out about her activities. She had left a report for her handlers in a crevice at the base of a wall next to an apartment building in Jackson Heights, Queens, New York. Just after she left, the superintendent of the building finished trimming flowers on top of the wall. When he dropped his shears, he saw the package. After reading it, he called the FBI. While her name was not on the document, the FBI concluded that the author of the report was probably a young unmarried woman, a member of a club called the English-Speaking Union, and an employee of a British Commonwealth country. By checking the club's membership list, and matching names of employees of British Commonwealth embassies, the FBI deduced that the author of the document was Miles.

Soon, the FBI was bugging her studio apartment on Wisconsin Avenue in Washington and began counting her beaus: the bureau stopped at one hundred. She never learned any secrets, but when she began dating White House aides, the FBI confronted her and she confessed. She was allowed to return to South Africa without any other action being taken against her.

Other investigations don't go as well, like the case of Edward Lee Howard, a disgruntled former CIA employee who cunningly slipped out of an FBI surveillance net and flew to Moscow, taking the agency's secrets with him. Or the Koecher case, where the lack of due process almost certainly would have resulted in the dismissal of the charges against him.

Many attempts at fooling the Soviets simply fail. The Soviets know that any would-be spy offering them secret information may be an FBI plant, and they treat walk-ins to their embassy in Washington with suspicion. Other cases fail because of lack of cooperation from U.S. intelligence agencies. Sometimes they balk at giving up secret documents that may be needed to convince the other side that an FBI double agent is a genuine spy. In one case, the agencies refused to hire a CI-3 double agent so that the Soviets would think the agent had secrets to offer.

Yet other CI-3 operations have managed to cripple some of Russia's most valuable spies and—just as important—would-be spies. CI-3 is credited with cracking the case of Thomas P. Cavanagh, who attempted to give the Soviets detailed blueprints showing how to build the Stealth fighter plane. His is one of six cases identified by the Senate Select Committee on Intelligence as the most damaging, or potentially damaging, to the United States.

In some instances, CI-3 has apprehended GRU spies from other countries when they were visiting the U.S. For example, CI-3 agents obtained a confession from Dieter Felix Gerhardt, a South African Navy commodore who gave the GRU NATO military and computer codes. During his naval career, Gerhardt had access to most of NATO's electronic intelligence, almost all of the surveillance information pouring out of a secret underground communications center called Silvermine, and secrets of NATO military and computer codes, including when and why the codes were changed.

After obtaining his confession, CI-3 agents shipped him off to South Africa, where he was sentenced to life in prison.

Very often, CI-3 helps out other squads involved in other major cases, as it did during the apprehension of former Navy warrant officer John A. Walker Jr. O'Keefe, the special agent in charge of CI-3, directed Walker's arrest at a motel in Rockville, Maryland. Prior to that, CI-3 agents helped track Walker as he dropped "top secret" information in the woods of Maryland. CI-3 also helped investigate Koecher.

Because of the cases and informants it has developed, CI-3 is considered one of the best squads in the FBI.

When O'Keefe first called Grogan into his office in September

1984, the former seminarian was a seasoned counterintelligence agent. Yet his work was so complex and involved so many close calls that he constantly looked to the more experienced O'Keefe for guidance.

O'Keefe was descended from a line of policemen in Sioux City, Iowa, an agricultural town where corn and beans are grown and cattle are raised. His grandfather and uncle successively headed the police department there, and his father, Frank O'Keefe, was assistant chief.

While in high school, O'Keefe set the local quarter-mile speed record drag-racing in his Pontiac GTO, and worked as a bouncer in a bar.

After majoring in Russian history and political science at Briar Cliff College in Sioux City, O'Keefe took the tests to become a policeman and passed. But his father urged him to apply to the FBI because of the higher salaries and better career opportunities. In 1971, he became an FBI clerk and quickly was promoted to special agent. In 1974, O'Keefe was transferred to "the other side of the house"—the counterintelligence side of the Washington field office. He was assigned to CI-3.

At first, he thought his career had taken a nosedive. In the past, counterintelligence work had been associated with older agents who had retired at their desks. The counterintelligence program was often confused with what the FBI used to call domestic security cases—a ragtag collection of investigations that, under former FBI Director J. Edgar Hoover, often had more to do with political beliefs than violations of laws.

Not that the opposition thought of the FBI as lax. In a training lecture delivered in the early 1950s, GRU Lieutenant Colonel Ivan Y. Prikhodko warned that the bureau runs a "severe counterintelligence regime" marked by "constant surveillance." In 1957, Reino Hayhanen, a defected KGB officer, told the FBI that Moscow had told him the FBI follows Soviet diplomats so thoroughly that the Soviets have difficulty spying in the U.S. For that reason, he said, the Soviets had sent Colonel Rudolph Abel to New York to work as an "illegal," with no ostensible ties to Moscow.

After six months on CI-3, O'Keefe decided he liked foreign counterintelligence work better than criminal work. Because a counterintelligence matter may turn into an espionage investigation, he still got to do criminal work. Yet, like most counterintelligence agents, he found tracking Soviets to be more intellectually stimulating than breaking down doors and apprehending bank robbers. There was always so much to learn about the Soviets and about spycraft from defectors, double agents, courses, other intelligence agencies, and the popular press. The Washington field office had a spy library second only to the CIA's. A growing percentage of CI-3 agents spoke Russian. To O'Keefe, as to many other counterintelligence agents, it seemed counterintelligence work put more emphasis on brains than brawn.

In 1984, after nine years as a "brick agent" working the streets on CI-3, O'Keefe became squad supervisor. As such, O'Keefe had developed a reputation as a hard-ass—a man who expects production from his agents. He believed some agents thought they could retire at their desks. If their reports failed to show that they had followed all leads and were getting results, O'Keefe had them transferred to other squads or cities.

"If you don't produce, you're gone," O'Keefe told his agents.

On Ismaylov's first tour of duty in the U.S., from 1976 to 1980, O'Keefe was one of the agents assigned to watch him. Now O'Keefe had learned from headquarters that Ismaylov was coming back for a second tour. It was his turn to assign an agent to watch him.

Besides checking miscellaneous tips and leads relating to the GRU, each agent in the CI-3 squad gets one or more GRU agents to watch. During his first tour here, Ismaylov had developed relationships with a number of Americans he tried to recruit as spies. His FBI file now filled three file drawers. From his own experience with him, O'Keefe knew that Ismaylov was an aggressive spy. Now he told Grogan he had just gotten word that Ismaylov was coming back for a second tour. It was his turn to assign someone to track him. To watch him, O'Keefe—known as "Specs"—had wanted a particularly vigilant agent.

Putting his leg up on his desk, O'Keefe told Grogan, "Ismaylov is coming back. He was a good one. Do you want to take a shot at it?"

"Yeah," Grogan said. "As a matter of fact, I got some things in mind."

Unlike some agents who sit back and conduct surveillance, Grogan constantly came up with tricks for "neutralizing" his opponent—catching him in the act so he could be deported, or taking up his time with phony leads. The only problem was that FBI headquarters did not always approve his plans. He never knew if it was because headquarters knew *more* or *less* than he did.

Many CI-3 agents thought headquarters purposely held up approving their ideas just to show who was boss. Within the FBI, counterintelligence is directed by Division Five. On the FBI's organization chart, both Division Five and Division Six—the criminal investigative division—report to the executive assistant director for investigations, who reports to the FBI director.

For unknown reasons, Division Five is known as the intelligence division. In fact, it does counterintelligence. Some agents thought the reason it was misnamed was that memos addressed to "CID"—for counterintelligence—might get mixed up with mail addressed to the criminal investigative division.

Division Five, known as INTD, is headed by Geer, the assistant director for intelligence. Under him are two deputy assistant FBI directors, one in charge of operations and one in charge of administrative matters. Under them are chiefs of three sections—one dealing with Soviets, one concerned with all other intelligence services, and a third unit that provides technical support and does research.

Once agents transferred to headquarters, they often seemed to take the attitude that only they knew what was best for the field, and no decision should be made without their concurrence. In that respect, counterintelligence work was more confining than criminal work. A criminal agent might have dozens of cases ranging from the theft of $150 from a bank teller's window to a major Mafia case. Headquarters would have no interest in the lesser cases, leaving agents free to pursue them as they thought best. In the Soviet area, every case was important, and there was far more scrutiny from the forbidding J. Edgar Hoover FBI Building on Pennsylvania Avenue.

"The feeling is, headquarters is the enemy," a CI-3 agent told me. "Sure they approved it [whatever idea worked out] because it was a darn good idea. When something is disapproved, they say, 'There they go again, those dirty bastards.'"

Said a former FBI Washington field office official, "Headquarters should provide oversight and liaison. Instead, there's an ego battle. They feel they're God. The truth is that they're a hindrance. They question everything."

From the perspective of headquarters officials, the agents in the field often see only a corner of the total picture. A new White House peace initiative, an expulsion of a U.S. diplomat in Hungary, or another spy case in San Francisco might have some bearing on how a case in Washington should be handled.

Yet the best headquarters officials see their role as helping the agents in the field rather than trying to control them.

"They're there to support the field," said one headquarters official. "Nobody likes headquarters, because you're not supposed to."

Grogan found that people like O'Keefe knew how to negotiate the mine fields that could blow up one of his proposals, even if it meant circumventing certain headquarters officials. This, and a brash, roguish style, had earned O'Keefe the enmity of some headquarters officials. Yet he always managed to find a rabbi who appreciated the fact that he got results.

While the FBI workday is 8:15 A.M. to 5:00 P.M., Russian spies don't work office hours. So usually Grogan is in the office by 6:00 A.M., looking over correspondence and reports. At night he hangs out in places frequented by Soviets, sometimes befriending them, then breaking off the relationship. Sometimes they give him gifts, like bottles of Stolichnaya vodka.

Besides tracking spies, Grogan teaches firearms and defensive tactics at the FBI Academy at Quantico, Virginia, and helps recruit new agents. With the two hours of overtime pay he is allowed each week, he clears about $50,000 a year.

His wife teaches children with learning disabilities in the Fairfax public schools. Because of his schedule, the Grogans often wind up eating dinner with their two young sons, Kevin and Michael, at McDonald's or Popeye's Famous Fried Chicken. While Patricia doesn't fret much about his safety, she does worry that he has to drink too much when his work takes him to bars.

Early on, Grogan was amazed at how forward the GRU could be. They seemed to think that all Americans cared about was money. After all, didn't Wall Street run the country? Yet he knew that, occasionally, money will buy a spy. In spite of the increased number of arrests, Grogan felt that for every spy the FBI catches, there could be another spy the FBI does not know about.

If there were any question about that, one had only to compare the Soviets' first space shuttles with those lofted previously by the U.S. They were copies, stark evidence of a spy the FBI never caught.

"Espionage is going on every day," a senior Justice Department official said.

When Grogan was assigned to a particular GRU agent, he tried to find out everything there was to know about him. He knew that the GRU competes with the KGB to provide Soviet leaders with the juiciest intelligence about missiles and weapons systems. It scared him to think that if he took his eye off a Russian, he might scurry off with secrets that could cause billions of dollars in damage to the country and quite possibly result in the American side losing a war.

"This is no game. This is for real," he commented to O'Keefe one time when he learned the types of sensitive information the Russians were trying to get.

Sometimes, he would make pretext calls—"Antonio's Pizza calling"—just to assure himself that an agent assigned to him was in his office. Like many of the CI-3 agents, he found protecting the U.S. security a more compelling priority than catching criminals.

Yet there was only so much he could do. He was always walking a tightrope between Moscow and Washington. If he became too pushy, the Soviets might complain, retaliate against Americans in Moscow, become even more crafty, or change the rules.

The trick was to strike the right balance between overt surveillance and surreptitious snooping, to know when to concentrate on his man and when to work other cases, to recognize when he should pass, punt, or take a trip to the water cooler.

Besides catching GRU intelligence officers in the act of spying, Grogan wanted to divert their attention with decoys. If he could get them to expend time directing double agents, they wouldn't have any time for fruitful spying. Through more overt surveillance, Grogan hoped to make his target think he was always being followed.

"If I know what he's doing sixteen hours a day, he'll start seeing the FBI in the woodwork the other eight hours," another CI-3 agent said.

Just as important, Grogan sought to recruit GRU agents to his side, a sensitive point because the State Department frowns on the idea of recruiting foreign diplomats. Ostensibly, they are diplomats, not spies.

"The State Department would go crazy if it knew about it," a CI-3 agent said. "The State Department wants us to give them a kiss."

The fact that any arrest of a Soviet has to be cleared through political channels never failed to irritate Grogan and other CI-3 agents.

Explained an FBI official: "The State Department will say, 'Now isn't a good time to arrest anyone; arms reduction talks are going on.' So we have to wait two months until the talks are over. Meanwhile, Igor is goofing off. We want to pop him. We have to keep him under surveillance until the talks are over. If the talks don't bother the Soviets [who continue to spy], why should it bother us?"

Like a man encountering a pretty woman in a supermarket, Grogan wanted to watch his subject first. By watching, he could detect signs that his quarry might be susceptible to recruitment. In much the same way, a British intelligence officer noticed that GRU officer Penkovsky seemed to spend a lot of time by himself, indicating his disaffection, when Penkovsky was stationed in Ankara, Turkey. Several years later, when Penkovsky was transferred back to Moscow, the British assigned Greville Wynne, a British businessman and former intelligence officer, to try to develop him. What the British didn't know is that Penkovsky had already tried to pass messages to U.S. intelligence authorities but had been spurned. When Wynne approached him, he readily agreed to become a mole for the West and met with British intelligence officers in London in April 1961.

Once he felt that his subject might be open to such an overture, Grogan moved in closer to test his subject's reaction without setting himself up to be rejected.

After Soviet leader Leonid Brezhnev died in 1982, for example, Grogan left a condolence note on the windshield of one of the GRU officers he was assigned to watch. He signed it "Mike."

As Grogan watched, the Soviet read the note and broke into tears. To Grogan, his reaction meant he might be amenable to overtures by Americans. Someday, he might become an "agent in place"—a defector who works for the American side as a double agent.

Occasionally, Grogan goes undercover, perhaps taking an apartment next to a Soviet spy's apartment and pretending to work for a computer firm. To cultivate the Soviet, he might throw a large party at which every other guest—male and female—is an incognito FBI agent.

Other encounters are less well rehearsed. One evening, Grogan and a partner were following two GRU officers who appeared to be lost. After trailing them all over northwest Washington, Grogan pulled up to their car and asked if he could help.

"Do you know where [a certain pizzeria] is?" one of them asked.

Grogan gave them directions and continued following their car. When they pulled into the restaurant lot, Grogan pulled in, too. When they got out of the car, he and his partner got out. As they walked toward the restaurant, the two FBI agents started walking there, too.

Seeing four men coming toward her, the hostess asked, "Table for four?"

"Yes," Grogan said.

For two hours, they ate pizza and drank beer, talking about their children and life in America. For those two hours, the battle lines between the two superpowers didn't exist, at least not in the pizza parlor.

Very few CI-3 agents have the view that Russians are evil people. Most of them realize that the Soviets are doing their jobs and are patriotic, that they have trouble with their bosses and worries about their kids, just as the FBI agents do. Some CI-3 agents have even entertained thoughts of someday having a particular Soviet as a friend. It's a form of objectivity that was encouraged within the FBI, even if at other times FBI agents referred to their opponents as SOBs.

"I have no animosity toward the GRU," O'Keefe has said. "They do their job, and they do it well. But I'm going to beat their ass."

Indeed, Soviet intelligence agents and their FBI counterparts are more similar than not in outlook, training, and their perceptions of their jobs and the world.

"If you overlay their [the GRU's] manuals on ours, there isn't that much difference," an FBI source who has seen the "top secret" documents said. "The requirements, reporting to headquarters, documentation of expenses are all pretty much the same."

Grogan was one of those agents who could admit that the Soviets were human, and in doing so, he hoped that his sympathetic attitude would help him recruit one.

This was the ultimate prize, a counterspy's greatest accomplishment. With a recruit, the FBI could learn everything it ever wanted to know about how the opposition operates—what it is trying to find out, who its agents are, what Americans are helping them, what kinds of electronic wiretaps and bugs it has in place, and how to counter the threat without letting on that the FBI has cultivated a mole.

In fact, the FBI and CI-3 agents in particular have penetrated the Soviet intelligence apparatus in Washington. At times, when CI-3 agents find out about a Soviet operation, it is because of information originally obtained from double agents recruited by the FBI.

With the hope that he would one day make such a recruitment, Grogan gave the Soviets in the pizza parlor his card. He hasn't yet heard from them. But recruitment is just one way he and other CI-3 agents neutralize their opponents.

2 *Laying the Bait*

Anyone entering the brick office building at 6845 Elm Street in McLean, Virginia, an upper-class suburb of Washington, D.C., has to pass by Suite 107.

Located on the ground floor, it is enclosed on two sides by glass. It commands a view of both the front and rear entrances to the building. Invariably, people looking for the offices of their doctors or dentists drop into Suite 107 to ask directions.

So Dr. Armand B. Weiss, the president of the company that occupied the suite, was not at all surprised when his staff told him a visitor wanted to know about the books displayed on a rack in his office. As head of Associations International Inc., Weiss had a curious job. He managed the offices of dozens of professional engineering and scientific societies—organizations like the International Society of Parametric Analysts and the Washington Operations Research/Management Science Council. Much of the consulting work done for the Pentagon was carried out by the members of Weiss's organizations. Weiss himself is an economist who has written sixty technical papers on defense subjects.

Heavy-set and balding, Weiss, forty-nine, was working at his desk on the afternoon of December 23, 1980, when a staff member told him a visitor wanted to buy a book he had seen through the glass windows. Called *Force-on-Force Attrition Modeling,* it was a slim gray volume that outlined a method for determining how opposing forces can get the upper hand in battle. The staff member had already explained that the book was not for sale; the books are published by the members of Weiss's organizations and have to be obtained through them, he told him. But the man was insistent, and the employee took him to see his boss.

"Look," Weiss told him, "you'll have to buy it from the Operations Research Society of America, which put it out."

32

"But I need it right away," the man said, pulling out his wallet. "I will pay you. How much it cost?"

Weiss noticed a big wad of bills. The visitor was wearing a sports jacket and tie. He had an accent which Weiss could not immediately place. Otherwise, there was nothing unusual about the man. Weiss's main interest was getting him out of the office so he could get back to work.

"It's not for sale," Weiss repeated, motioning with his hands to signal that the conversation was over. "Go buy it from them."

But the visitor was not going away. He thrust twenty dollars at Weiss. Weiss realized the only way to get him out of his office was to give him the book. He made up a price—$18.65—and fished in his pocket to give the man his change. But the visitor said Weiss should keep it, and declined a receipt.

Strange, Weiss thought.

Now the man was looking over the other books in Weiss's bookcase.

"I notice you have military books," the man said. "I have interest in military subjects. What else you have?"

Weiss told him he not only manages the offices of professional organizations but often prints their publications for them. As a result, he has access to hundreds of publications on the military, hot off the press.

"You mind I come back, maybe in few weeks? I'm interested in what else you've printed," the visitor said.

"Not at all," Weiss said, pleased that the man was finally leaving.

Two weeks later, the man showed up again. This time, Weiss did not argue when he gave him ten dollars for several more publications. The man seemed friendlier than before and obviously wanted to strike up a relationship.

"Where do you work?" Weiss asked.

"A little research firm; it's here in Washington," he said.

"What do you do?" Weiss asked.

"I have interest in military studies," he said. "My staff, we're not big enough to keep up with all the material. Please, can you let me know when new titles are coming out?"

"How will I let you know?" Weiss asked.

The man took a scrap of paper from Weiss's desk and wrote in uneven block letters: "Yuri Leonov, 2552 Belmont Road NW, Washington, D.C. 20008."

Leonov told Weiss there was no point in listing his telephone number. "Messages for me always getting lost. Better I come to see you," he said.

Weiss looked at the paper and looked at Leonov. From the name, it was obvious that the thirty-nine-year-old man was a Russian. Looking closer, it now appeared to Weiss that the man's clothes were foreign. But the address meant nothing to him. As far as Weiss knew, the only Soviet establishment in Washington was the Soviet Embassy on Sixteenth Street NW. He did not know that 2552 Belmont Road is the address of the Soviet military office.

Less than a week later, Leonov dropped in a third time. This time, he said he was an air attaché at the Soviet Embassy and had been a MiG-21 fighter pilot. The two men began discussing airplanes. Then Leonov asked Weiss a highly technical question about a radar system that Weiss had worked on. The radar system was classified, and very few people knew that Weiss had even worked on it.

"I can't tell you that; it's classified information," Weiss told him.

Leonov immediately changed the subject, commenting on the beautiful weather. But that night, Weiss began thinking. Leonov was with the Soviet Embassy. He had asked a question that showed intimate knowledge of a classified project. Even Weiss's staff did not know that Weiss had worked on the radar system. Yet Leonov knew.

Working on defense matters in McLean, the headquarters of the CIA, Weiss has a number of friends employed by the spy agency. In fact, he had previously been out to CIA headquarters for an award ceremony for one of his friends. After a speech, his friend got a plaque, a medal, and a check. At the end of the ceremony, Weiss looked on incredulously as a security officer approached his friend and removed the medal and the plaque, leaving him with only the check. Covert agents are not supposed to have anything in their possession identifying them as CIA agents.

The day after his last encounter with Leonov, Weiss ran into his friend at Rodef Shalom, the temple in Falls Church, Virginia, where they both are members. He told his friend about the Russian and asked him what he thought.

"What's his name?" the CIA man asked.

"Yuri Leonov," Weiss said.

"He's a spy," the CIA man said.

Weiss later learned that Leonov was in fact a member of the GRU, the most aggressive Soviet spy agency. Somewhere in his career, the CIA man had run into him.

"What should I do?" Weiss asked.

"That's simple," the CIA man said. "Call the FBI."

Weiss had other things to do and put off calling. But two days later, working late in his office, he remembered the conversation with the CIA man. At 10:00 P.M. he picked up the phone and dialed the number of the FBI field office in Alexandria, Virginia.

When Weiss told the duty officer about the encounter with Leonov, the man sounded unimpressed, as if he had already heard that night from three hundred other people who thought they had met spies. He took Weiss's telephone number, and Weiss thought that would be the end of it.

The next morning at nine, Weiss got a call at his office. The caller identified himself as Special Agent William P. O'Keefe of the Washington field office of the FBI. Overnight, the message had been teletyped from the Alexandria field office to the Washington field office, where the mailroom found Leonov's name on an index of foreign agents. Next to Leonov's name was his case number. Under the FBI's filing system, case numbers begin with a code denoting the violation or type of investigation under which the case falls. In Leonov's case, the code was 105 for "Soviet." In all, there are more than two hundred code numbers. Number 65, for example, is "espionage." In Leonov's case, the code was followed by "A," for a first priority investigation, usually of a known intelligence officer. Other categories are for foreign workers who are not agents and for individuals suspected of being agents. The final six digits are assigned consecutively as each Soviet enters the United States. If they leave the U.S. and then return for a second tour, they are assigned the same file number.

The mailroom had routed the message to the CI-3 squad. As he was the agent assigned to watch Leonov, the message ended up on the desk of O'Keefe, who had not yet been promoted to head CI-3.

"Did you call the FBI last night?" O'Keefe asked.

"Yes," Weiss said.

"Did you report that you met somebody?" he asked.

"Yes," Weiss answered.

"Was his name Leonov?" O'Keefe asked.

"Yes," Weiss said.

"Well, I'd like to come out and talk with you about that," he said.

"Fine," Weiss answered.

Weiss thought it would take an hour for O'Keefe to drive to McLean from Washington. But two minutes after he hung up the phone, O'Keefe was in his office. He had called from a pay phone outside a luncheonette in the lobby of the office building.

O'Keefe introduced his partner, Donald Young. The FBI likes two agents to go out on sensitive interviews because, in a criminal investigation, two witnesses are better than one. In a counterintelligence case, the second agent may think of questions that the first agent had not thought of.

Everyone in CI-3 has a nickname. A native of Mississippi, Young, a tall, lean agent with a brown mustache that reveals a ready smile, had acquired the nickname "Fish." The name was variously ascribed to a dissertation he once gave fellow agents on catfish, or the fact that his mustache makes him look like a catfish.

O'Keefe displayed his credentials for Weiss, and after a few minutes of chitchat, put his briefcase on Weiss's black-topped, oversize desk. He pulled out an eight-by-ten glossy photo of Leonov dressed in military uniform, then another one showing a side view.

"Is this the man?" O'Keefe asked.

"Yes, that's him," Weiss answered.

O'Keefe looked at Weiss for a few seconds, then smiled.

"Now would you like to see a photo of him with you?" he asked.

"I'm glad I called you first," Weiss said, grinning back.

To Weiss, it seemed Kafkaesque. First he had met up with a Russian spy. Now the FBI was telling him they knew about it all along.

"Would you like to know how we knew?" O'Keefe asked.

"Sure would," Weiss said.

O'Keefe told him that the Soviets had twice visited Weiss's office before Leonov nonchalantly asked about the book in the window. The first visit was by two other Soviet intelligence officers. Trying to make themselves "black"—free of surveillance—they had twice passed homes or cars occupied by other Soviets at prearranged times so the Soviets could look out and see if the intelligence officers were being followed. From pay phones, the intelligence officers called the lookouts or relay points to find out if anyone had been following them. The surveillance detection route, as it is called, had been planned on a timing sheet so the Soviets would arrive at Weiss's office at prearranged times.

O'Keefe did not say how the FBI had been able to follow the GRU officers. But Weiss later learned the bureau can attach homing devices to their cars or watch them from single-engine surveillance aircraft. In addition to using agents to tail Russian spies, the FBI frequently uses members of its Special Support Group (SSG), called simply G's.

Since the late 1970s, the FBI has used G's to supplement agents' surveillance in counterintelligence cases. Lower-level civil servants, they are housewives, students, and retired people recruited because of their ability to blend into the background. Most earn $15,000 to $20,000 a year, compared with the average $50,000 annual salary of an agent.

In doing their work, they are aided by special FBI devices like binoculars attached to gyroscopes so they can follow cars more easily from moving vehicles.

After the two Soviet intelligence officers entered Weiss's office building, the G's saw one of the officers ride the elevator to the third floor, then return to the marble lobby and peer in Weiss's windows. The other officer checked out the lobby. A week later, Leonov did the same thing, parking his car at Tysons Corner Shopping Center several miles away and taking a bus to the center of McLean, then walking six blocks to Weiss's office. Like the first officer, he rode the elevator up and down before finally pretending to have just noticed Weiss's suite.

O'Keefe told Weiss the FBI knew Leonov was a spy but could do nothing about it unless agents caught him in the act.

"Would you like to help?" he asked.

In Richmond, where he was born, Weiss had been an Eagle Scout and later a scoutmaster. As the president of his temple, he had been concerned about the oppression of Jews in the Soviet Union. And he had always enjoyed spy movies and shows, particularly *Mission Impossible.*

"Sure," he told O'Keefe. "Sounds like fun."

Thus Weiss became a double agent, pretending to work for the Soviets but in reality controlled by the FBI. Over the next two and a half years, he would meet with Leonov two dozen times—probably more than any other double agent dealing with the Soviets. Because he thought it would worry her, he never told his wife about his other two lives. Over time, his role would wreak havoc with his mind as he tried to sift truth from fiction, never quite sure if he was being set up by the FBI or the Russians, always fearful that the Soviets would kill him for his duplicity.

But for now, Weiss was excited about his new adventure, and he pumped O'Keefe with questions when they met again at Charley's Place, a restaurant two blocks from his office in McLean.

O'Keefe told him never to call him from his office or home. Instead, he should use a pay phone. When he called, he was to identify himself only by his middle name, Berl, which was to be his code name. If he needed FBI help quickly, he was to call a seven-digit number. There was no need to say anything. Once the number was dialed, an alarm would sound at the FBI field office and summon agents to his office.

The next time Weiss heard from Leonov, the Soviet suggested having lunch at Evans Farm Inn, a gingerbread restaurant in a pastoral setting practically in the backyard of the CIA. Weiss went to the pay phone in a far corner of McLean Shopping Center to tell O'Keefe about the lunch date. When he heard where they were to meet, the agent chuckled.

"He'll never meet you there," he said. "That's a big hangout for CIA people. After he checks with his bosses, he'll probably meet you at the door and suggest that you go someplace else."

Weiss promised to tell O'Keefe what happened at the lunch, but O'Keefe said that wouldn't be necessary.

"We'll be listening," he said.

"Are you going to wire me?" Weiss asked.

"No, but we'll be listening," O'Keefe said.

"You don't even know where we'll be sitting," Weiss protested.

"We'll know," O'Keefe repeated. "I can't tell you how. We'll be there. If I told you where, you'd either keep looking at the person or looking in the opposite direction. Either way, it would make Yuri suspicious."

Leonov showed up at the inn on Chain Bridge Road at noon. Weiss thought the Soviets must be reading from a different script than the one used by the FBI, because Leonov did not suggest a different restaurant. They went down to the Sitting Duck Pub on the lower level, where a fire was crackling in the fireplace. The two set at a table before a window. Both men ordered cheeseburgers.

As he placed a red napkin on his lap, Weiss looked around the room. He saw eleven diners who looked like FBI or CIA people and who seemed to be watching them.

After chatting about his two teenage children, Leonov told Weiss he would like to continue getting documents from him.

"I will pay you well," he said.

Weiss agreed to continue his help.

As they walked out of the restaurant, past the horses from an abandoned merry-go-round, Weiss offered to give Leonov a lift.

"No, no," he said. "You have to go back to work."

To try to throw off surveillance, Leonov always parked his car at the shopping center at Tysons Corner and took the bus back and forth to see Weiss. Before returning to his car, he would browse through Bloomingdale's, stopping to look but never buying anything.

Weiss, meanwhile, thought a young woman was tailing him as he left the restaurant to return to his office. He took down her license number and gave it to O'Keefe. At their next meeting, O'Keefe told him the woman was a CIA agent who may have been curious about who was meeting with Leonov. While the CIA is supposed to leave investigations within the U.S. to the FBI, the agency occasionally strays over the line.

Weiss began to tell O'Keefe what Leonov had said at the restaurant, but O'Keefe already knew.

"Which one of those eleven people was an FBI agent?" Weiss asked him.

"None of them," O'Keefe said. "There were eleven CIA agents in there. Most of them knew who Yuri was but didn't know who you were."

"How did you find out what was said?" Weiss asked.

"Did you notice the young couple at the table behind you?" O'Keefe asked.

Weiss had noticed them only because they had been all over each other, kissing and hugging and obviously very much in love. They were about twenty-one years old. Weiss would have picked the waiter, the busboy, or the cashier before he would have guessed that the two young people were FBI agents.

O'Keefe told Weiss the agents had listened to the entire conversation.

At their next meeting two weeks later, Leonov gave Weiss a shopping list of publications he wanted. It consisted of titles of papers cut from Defense Department bibliographies pasted on sheets of paper. In pencil, Leonov had placed double check marks next to the titles he was particularly interested in—publications ranging from *A Model for the Study of High Energy Lasers in a Space Defense Role* to a *Catalogue of Wargaming and Military Simulation Models.*

Each time Weiss gave him the documents, Leonov handed him white envelopes containing $200. It never occurred to him that Leonov might be skimming money from the payments before he gave them to Weiss, but the FBI suspected that he was because the going rate was higher.

By this time, Weiss had come to think of both Leonov and O'Keefe as friends, even younger brothers. Weiss would tease Leonov about his job, and Leonov would admit that he would much rather return to being a fighter pilot. At other times, the two men discussed politics. Yet Leonov never told him where he lived. He had an apartment at 5550 Columbia Pike in Arlington, Virginia, but told Weiss he lived in Washington.

There was no pattern to Leonov's visits. Sometimes he visited every two weeks, and sometimes months went by before he showed up. When that happened, Weiss worried that he had been found out, or that he was not doing a good job. He also worried that he would say the wrong thing when he was with Leonov, showing more knowledge of him than he was supposed to have.

O'Keefe had told him the date of Leonov's birth, for example, and when the Soviet happened to show up on his birthday, Weiss was about to say, "Happy . . . " when he caught himself.

Besides cash, Leonov occasionally brought gifts of Johnny Walker Scotch or Stolichnaya vodka. While Weiss enjoyed the Scotch, O'Keefe and Young drank the vodka. They seemed to get a kick out of investigating him while drinking his booze.

Weiss came to think O'Keefe must be bugging his office, because twice he had muttered to himself, "I wish O'Keefe would call," and the FBI agent would call later in the day. When Weiss asked O'Keefe about it, he said the FBI was not conducting any surveillance of him.

But one evening, Weiss was working late again when he began to feel that someone was watching him. Occasionally, a shadow seemed to move across his office, as if someone were lurking outside the glass windows.

At 2:30 A.M., Weiss walked to the men's room near the entrance. As he stood at the urinal, he heard panting. Very cautiously, he stooped down and looked under the stalls. There were two shoes on the floor. Apparently, the person on the toilet seat was out of breath.

Weiss decided the best thing to do was to leave quickly. As he walked out the door, he heard a shot.

"Oh, my God! I've been shot," he thought.

As his dying act, he decided to lunge at his assailant and dig his fingernails deep into his skin, leaving a clue as to who had murdered him.

He swung around, and no one was there.

"I've just been shot, and I don't feel anything," he thought. "Am I dead?"

Then, at his feet, he saw a spotlight that had fallen from the ceiling. He realized that when the bulb fell, it popped, sounding like a gunshot.

Weiss never found out who was in the bathroom, but he was sure someone had been watching him. Was it the Soviets? Was it the FBI? It was only the beginning of a series of events that led him to wonder if he was losing his mind.

By now, O'Keefe was becoming impatient. Over the course of a year, Leonov had gotten hundreds of documents from Weiss, but since none was classified, the FBI could not arrest him. O'Keefe decided that Weiss should show the Soviet some classified papers just so he would know that Weiss could get them.

For the purpose, O'Keefe gave Weiss three documents marked "secret." All three related to the M-X missile system, which Leonov was particularly interested in. In fact, the documents were not really classified. The FBI had placed classification stamps on them at O'Keefe's request.

The next time Leonov showed up, Weiss had the three documents spread out on his desk. Weiss motioned toward them and showed Leonov the titles of two of them: *M-X/RES Methodologies for Estimating Electrical Energy Loads for the M-X/RES System* and *M-X Environmental Technical Report.*

Leonov did not ask for the documents. Rather, he asked Weiss to turn the pages of the reports so he could glance at each page. It seemed he did not want to get his fingerprints on them.

The bait would soon work.

3 *The Swinging Mole*

In early 1982, the counterintelligence squad that handles Czech matters in the FBI's Washington field office got wind of Karl Koecher's activities on behalf of the Czechoslovak Intelligence Service and the KGB, which generally operate together. Conducting routine surveillance of Czech intelligence officers, the FBI discovered that the Czech agents were having "brush contacts" or "brief encounters" with a man of slight build who had a graying mustache, an angular chin, and close-cropped brown hair. He wore glasses, weighed 150 pounds, and stood five feet, ten inches tall.

Tailing him, the FBI determined that the man who was passing documents to the Czech agents was Karl F. Koecher, a forty-year-old Czech who had become a naturalized U.S. citizen in 1971.

Delving into his background, agents from the Czech squad, CI-3, and other counterintelligence squads discovered that he had become a full-time CIA employee in 1973 and continued to be a contract employee of the agency. His then thirty-eight-year-old wife, Hana, had emigrated to the U.S. with him. It was not long before the FBI found that the attractive, blue-eyed blonde was part of the spy team, filling "dead drops" for her husband and making "brush contacts"— brief encounters with Czech agents to pass information or documents. Moreover, the FBI was astonished to find that Koecher in the early 1970s had almost become a double agent for the FBI.

The multiple discoveries sent shock waves through the FBI's Division Five, misnamed the intelligence division.

Over the years, the CIA had repeatedly been racked by "mole scares"—a persistent belief that foreign intelligence agents had somehow penetrated the agency. The late James J. Angleton, the avuncular genius who headed CIA counterintelligence until the mid-1970s, routinely claimed the agency was full of moles but never developed any evidence to support the claim.

Quite clearly, several CIA employees had gone over to the other side after leaving the agency. In 1977, David H. Barnett, a former CIA agent stationed in Indonesia, sold the Soviets details of one of the CIA's most successful undercover operations, code-named "HA/BRINK." In 1978, William P. Kampiles, a former CIA employee, sold a "top secret" technical manual on the KH-11 "Big Bird" surveillance satellite to a Soviet agent in Athens. After the CIA fired him in 1983, Edward Lee Howard apparently got revenge by unburdening himself to the KGB about the CIA's Moscow operations.

But so far as anyone could prove, the KGB had never succeeded in implanting a mole within the CIA—someone who could supply information upon request while still employed by the agency. Someone who, moreover, had joined the agency with the intention of infiltrating it and reporting to the other side.

No one had done it, that is, until Karl Koecher came along.

Koecher's case is thus a classic spy success story, one that earned him multiple decorations from the Czechoslovak Intelligence Service and the KGB. He was the prototypical "illegal," an agent of a hostile intelligence service who infiltrates another country's intelligence service without ever appearing to have any ties with his original employer.

There was a lot about Koecher that didn't make sense. Presumably, a spy whose mission in life is to remain undetected would lead the most prosaic, unblemished existence imaginable for fear of attracting attention. Not so Karl Koecher. To his friends, employers, and the students he taught when he was a professor, he presented himself as being a virulent anti-Communist. So seething was his apparent hatred for the rulers of his homeland that he tried to blackball tennis star Ivan Lendl from buying an apartment in his East Side building in New York—simply because Lendl came from Czechoslovakia.

To some of his friends, Koecher seemed to be Jewish, but some thought he was an anti-Semite. On job applications he claimed to be Roman Catholic.

In fact, Koecher told me, his mother is Jewish while his father was Catholic. From a religious point of view, he said, he is an atheist.

Yet Koecher seemed more emotional when talking about his Jewish heritage, particularly the fact that his mother had to hide her Jewish ancestry to escape persecution during the Nazi occupation of Czechoslovakia.

In his interviews with me, Koecher said his mother's parents were executed in a concentration camp. He said he wrote to the Holocaust research center in Israel to get the record of his grandparents' death but never got a reply.

Perhaps, he suggested to me, the impression that he was anti-Semitic arose from his remarks about American Jews failing to come to the aid of Holocaust victims, or maybe it was the fact that he does not support Israel as a homeland for Jews.

When we toured a Jewish cemetery where Franz Kafka is buried, Koecher provided yarmulkes but declined to pose next to his tombstone while wearing one.

Koecher spoke four langauges and earned a Ph.D. in philosophy from Columbia University, but some thought he embellished his credentials by claiming another doctorate in physics from a university in Prague.

He was arrogant and had a violent temper that manifested itself when he was with his wife—whom he occasionally hit—and with strangers. A physical fitness buff, he worked out daily at the Young Men's Hebrew Association (YMHA) on Ninety-second Street, where fellow members recall his outbursts vividly.

"He once threatened the porters because they had put Lysol on the floor. He thought the fumes would hurt him," said Kurt Chang, one of the members.

When he found a window had been left open just a crack in the winter, "He went berserk. He yelled, he screamed, he threatened," said Herbert Strauss, another member.

Charles Bronz, the health director of the YMHA, said Koecher "once grabbed a barbell and dropped it" on the foot of another member who had kept him waiting to use some weights.

"Thank God one end hit the ground before it hit his feet," he said.

"I blew up at people because I believe if you want people to do something, you have to be very forceful," Koecher later explained to me. "I provoke resentment, particularly in lower-class people. I guess I have an elitist attitude sometimes. If you dress in a certain way and speak in a certain way, you classify yourself as an upper-class person. This is immediately not liked."

As for the complaints at the YMHA, Koecher said, "They thought I wasn't Jewish but German. The accent they didn't like. They also didn't like the fact I was probably the best-dressed person there. One guy tried to harass me. I would try to do bench presses. I warned him three or four times. I dropped the weight near him, not on him."

"He can be impatient and angry," Hana Koecher conceded to me.

Perhaps the most unusual behavior for a mole wanting to remain under deep cover was Koecher's penchant for swinging. At least once or twice a week, Koecher and Hana had one or two couples over for dinner, or went to their homes, to swap spouses for sex. While they had a wide circle of friends for the purpose, the Koechers also participated on a regular basis in larger sex parties and orgies in Washington and New York. They frequented a nudist colony in New Jersey, along with Plato's Retreat and the Hellfire, two sex emporiums in New York that were open to anyone who could pay the price of admission. Occasionally, they brought one of Hana's female relatives along to Plato's Retreat when she came in from Europe.

On the side, they each had separate affairs going, and Karl dabbled as well in answering personal ads placed by single women.

In retrospect, Koecher's exotic lifestyle and peccadilloes, his outbursts and seeming instability, were not outlandish but rather brilliant. For who would suspect that a master spy would be so peculiar and perplexing? And how does one extract truth from one who appeared to be an enigma even to himself? Sometimes it seemed Koecher must be schizophrenic, for how else could he so convincingly pass himself off as someone he was not? Indeed, if one were to sum up the secret of Koecher's success, it would be that he came across as being everything a spy is not supposed to be.

Much about Koecher will always remain hidden, wrapped in layers of deceit that even he could not unfold if he chose to. While he admitted in 1984 to doing incalculable damage to the CIA and its assets, the FBI is convinced that the full story will never be told. The fact that he was considered by the Soviets to be important enough to trade for Sharansky attests to that. But from still-secret FBI interviews and electronic intercepts, interviews with the Koechers' friends and former employers, copies of the couple's diaries, letters and job applications, and interviews in Prague with the spy couple themselves, it is possible to gain some idea of who Koecher is and how he managed to fool the CIA.

In developing a "legend" to conceal their activities, "illegals" typically adhere to most of the facts from their past so they won't become confused, omitting only those details that would point to their true allegiance. So it was with Koecher. Undoubtedly, the résumé that he submitted to the CIA in 1972 was true as far as it went—it simply failed to state that he joined the Communist Party in 1960 and that, in 1962, the Czechoslovak Intelligence Service began training him to get a job with the CIA.

According to that résumé, along with interviews with former employers and employment and naturalization applications, Karel Frantisek Köcher was born on September 21, 1934, in Bratislava, the third largest city in Czechoslovakia. Located near Austria at the southern tip of the country, Bratislava is the capital of Slovakia, which combined with two other countries, Bohemia and Moravia, to form Czechoslovakia in 1918.

Koecher's father, Jaroslav, was a postmaster who died of a stroke in 1970. His mother, Irena, was a store manager. Karl was their only child.

When Karl was five, the family moved to Prague, where he attended the English Grammar School. The family lived in an apartment on a main thoroughfare where Karl's mother still lives.

That same year—1939—Hitler dissolved Czechoslovakia. Jews were supposed to wear stars, but Koecher's mother managed to hide her ancestry, Koecher said.

"There were certain problems during the war because she was of Jewish descent," he said. "My mother never reported as a Jew, never wore a star. Basically she managed to hide it until the end of the war. There was then no time to do anything about it. They started to investigate. She claimed she was half-Jewish, but she wasn't. She was submitting papers. She would have been deported but by then the war was over."

In addition to her parents, two of her brothers died in concentration camps, Koecher told me.

Koecher joined the Boy Scouts, becoming a patrol leader. But he was sickly, contracting pneumonia and bronchitis once a year. Staying in a tent full of mosquitoes didn't help, and he quit in 1948, when the Communists seized power in advance of scheduled elections.

The following year, he became a licensed tour guide and began writing for local publications. His first published article, sold to a syndicate, was about the Jewish ghetto in Prague.

Koecher attended the French High School, graduating in 1953. He was admitted to Charles University, which was founded in 1348, where he studied mathematics and physics, along with required subjects like the history of the Communist Party in the U.S.S.R., foundations of Marxism-Leninism, and military training. He earned an M.S. in general physics in 1958.

In college, he began to jog at night. He told me he thought everybody would think he was crazy if he did it during the day.

During his last year in college, and for a year after he graduated, he attended the Prague Academy, where he studied film theory and script writing. At the same time, he worked part-time as a writer for Czechoslovakia Television in Prague, specializing in educational programs and news of science and industry. Briefly, he also taught science and math at Vocational High School for Mechanics.

Koecher enjoyed teaching and in 1961 became an assistant professor of mathematics at the Czechoslovakia Institute of Technology in Prague.

In 1962, Koecher began working for Czechoslovakia Radio in Prague.

"The way I got the radio job was a producer, knowing my Jewish background, said there is a Jewish fiddler who has played in some of the best bars in Prague. He said why don't you talk to him and maybe it would be a story. I got acquainted with the fiddler. Prague sold arms to Latin America. These people would meet in the bar and do business, and he would play for them. He would know high-class prostitutes, con men, everyone. He started telling me things I just couldn't believe." Koecher wrote the story and got the job.

It is here that his cover story begins to differ from what he later confessed to the FBI. On several résumés and job applications in the U.S., Koecher claimed his "biting" commentary about life in Czechoslovakia got him in trouble with Communist authorities. He said he was ordered to work for a year at a factory to "reshape" his opinions. When he refused, he claimed, he was fired, and was forced to get a job as a night watchman at a construction site.

But in statements to the FBI that were confirmed with a lie-detector test, Koecher admitted that he had willingly joined the Communist Party two years earlier, and that a friend from the art academy named Liska had introduced him to officials of the Czechoslovak Intelligence Service. In 1962, according to his later statement, the Czech service and the KGB assigned him to become a CIA mole.

At a party in 1963, Koecher met Hana Pardamcova, a nineteen-year-old translator who was also a member of the Communist Party. Born in Tabor, Czechoslovakia, on January 8, 1944, she was the daughter of Josef Pardamcova, a plant manager who was born in

Austria and was a member of the Communist Party. Her mother, Marie Pardamcova, was a broadcasting engineer.

Five feet, two inches tall, warm and outgoing, Hana was a fair-skinned blonde with thinly arched eyebrows over light blue eyes. She was more socially adept than Karl and probably just as smart. After knowing each other three months, they married on November 22, 1963. It was a civil ceremony in the Gothic town hall, built in 1367 and rebuilt in 1561.

Koecher laughed at the idea he had to get approval from the Czech Intelligence Service to marry Hana.

"If you're a wise man, you marry someone who would follow you anywhere," he said. "She had everything."

"Karl was a whole new world—an intellectual challenge," Hana told me. "I hadn't met anyone like that before."

According to his résumé, Koecher spent the next two years as a lecturer at the Prague Planetarium and as an editor at the State Publishing House for Technical Literature. Most likely, he spent most of his time being trained by the Czechoslovak Intelligence Service in communicating secretly, detecting surveillance, and foiling lie detectors.

After his three years of training, the Koechers defected to Austria while visiting Hana's uncle on September 11, 1965. They entered the U.S. as immigrants on December 4, 1965.

Living briefly in West Nyack, New York, with a Czech artist, Koecher did free-lance assignments for Radio Free Europe. To build his résumé, he moved to Bloomington, Indiana, on a fellowship to study the history and philosophy of science at Indiana University's graduate school.

Asked to describe his reasons for applying for the fellowship, he wrote, "During my studies of physics in Czechoslovakia, I had encountered many problems connected with the philosophical interpretation of the physical laws, and being not satisfied with the official explanation that could be found in the Soviet textbooks given by lecturers from the Department of Marxism-Leninism, I tried to find more penetrating answers on my own. . . . All this had aroused my interest in the philosophy of science, as well as in the history of science, since those two fields cannot exist one without another. I would be very happy if I could now have access to the information I always wanted to get, and to work in this field."

In 1967, while still attending graduate school, Koecher applied for a full-time job with Radio Free Europe. On his application, he noted that after the Communists took power in Czechoslovakia in 1948, he joined the Communist-affiliated Czechoslovak Union of Youth because he had no choice. Asked to amplify his past affiliations, he wrote a four-page letter detailing his alleged difficulties with the Communists from the age of eleven.

"I made some derogatory remarks about the Soviet Union," he claimed. "I merely repeated what my father was saying at home. I was expelled from the school. I have saved the letter announcing this to my father, and I still have it," he wrote.

Ironically, he explained to Radio Free Europe that while Hana had joined the Communist Party, he could vouch for the fact that she never showed Communist tendencies.

"I have to say that I have never thought of her association with the Czechoslovak CP—and to the best of my knowledge neither did she—as other than an entirely perfunctory membership. After all, if she were really a Communist, she would hardly have married me . . . ," he wrote.

Koecher gave somewhat differing versions of why he had not served in the Czech military. To Radio Free Europe, he said he was "cold" toward the required military courses at Charles University and was therefore barred from taking the final exam in military science. If he had passed, he would have become a reserve officer in the Czech army, he said.

To the CIA, he said, "Rejected for military service in the Czechoslovak Armed Forces in 1958; the latter rejection secured by complaining of nonexistent ear troubles and because of utter unwillingness to served in the Czech armed forces."

He said he passed the military science courses but was rejected for military service because of his frail health.

In October 1967, Radio Free Europe hired him as a consultant to the Czech desk at $10,000 a year. There, he developed and wrote programs for Czech listeners. He also began passing along information he picked up to the Czech Intelligence Service, according to what he later said.

Koecher moved back to New York, where Hana worked first as a laboratory assistant and later as a diamond grader for Harry Winston Inc. and Trav Inc. Fluent in Russian and French as well as English and Czech, Koecher occasionally translated books and articles on a free-lance basis as well.

Still, the extra income—and the fact that the couple had no children—were not enough to account for their affluent lifestyle.

They lived at 300 West Fifty-fifth Street and took vacations all over the world.

According to their visas, they spent three weeks in St. Lucia and Martinique in the Caribbean in August 1966. Beginning in June 1967, they spent several months in France, Switzerland, Austria, Italy, and West Germany. In 1968, they spent several months in France, Germany, Austria, Italy, Spain, and Portugal.

Later, Koecher would tell the FBI he received regular remuneration from the Czech service and a bonus of $20,000 so he could buy their cooperative apartment in New York.

Now that he was living in New York, Koecher transferred from Indiana University to Columbia University. In applying, he wrote that he wanted to "work on problems concerning the differences between the dialectical materialism and Western interpretation of modern science."

Koecher's professors included Zbigniew Brzezinski, who later became President Carter's national security adviser, at Columbia's Research Institute for Communist Affairs.

"He's a fast talker, fast thinker, but is very superficial," Koecher said of Brzezinski. "Sometimes giving names to things makes it sound like you discovered things."

He had more respect for Loren Graham, then a history professor at Columbia, who described Koecher as a "bright student."

"He wrote a dissertation on Soviet ideology and science," said Graham, now professor of the history of science at the Massachusetts Institute of Technology. "He was quite anti-Soviet, but not in a simplistic way. He liked to analyze the Soviet system and what kind of flaws there were in it. There was nothing that would make one think he was a spy."

Another professor, Dr. George L. Kline, considered him thoughtful, sensitive, and industrious. Kline met Koecher in 1956 in Prague, when Koecher was assigned to him as an official guide. Later, Koecher often asked Kline for references and did translations for him.

At one point, he told me, Koecher invited him to attend "pot" parties with them, but he declined. He wondered how the Koechers could go on trips to Europe and the Caribbean on their salaries, but Koecher always had some explanation.

In September 1966, when Kline was in the philosophy department at Bryn Mawr College, Koecher wrote to him that he and Hana had had a wonderful time in the Caribbean. "It cost us all the money we had saved but we do not regret it in the least," he wrote. On May

6, 1967, Koecher wrote to Kline that he was flying to Paris in July. "I took a part-time job here to meet all the expenses connected with our travel plans," he said.

When Kline told Koecher about a friend of Kline's daughter who was being threatened by a snubbed boyfriend, Koecher remarked, "Well, you know, we hear about crises like that from friends, but our lives are very unexciting. The only excitement we see is in the movies."

"Let's say that I was carrying Soviet studies so I could really understand the way Americans working on issues connected with the Soviet Union think," Koecher later told me. "What is the image they have of the Soviet world? That was a special position that gave me special contacts. I learned the mental barriers between the two cultures, which is incalculably valuable. It certainly is appreciated here."

While still attending classes at Columbia, Koecher became an assistant professor of philosophy at Wagner College, a liberal arts institution located on an eighty-six-acre campus on Staten Island, New York. His starting salary in February 1969 was $11,800 a year.

When joining the faculty, as required by the college, he signed an "oath of allegiance" to the Constitution of the United States.

In 1970, Columbia awarded Koecher a Ph.D. in philosophy and a certificate from the Institute for Communist Affairs. The following year, he applied to become a naturalized citizen.

When he did not hear from the Immigration and Naturalization Service for several months, Koecher wrote the service that he had forgotten to list on his application the fact that he had received a ten-dollar fine for speeding in New York.

"I realize that the speeding violation itself is hardly of such a nature that it could affect the naturalization procedure," he wrote, "but I would like to make sure that my failure to report it is not looked upon as an attempt to conceal the requested data from your examiner."

It was a typical gesture designed by Koecher to engender trust. When he had not heard anything about his application for six months, he made another characteristic move—he complained, openly and aggressively.

Referring to the delay, Koecher wrote to Bella S. Abzug, then a member of Congress from the 20th District of New York: "I have to admit that I feel very bitter about it. My record for the five and a half years I have lived in the U.S. is, in my opinion, spotless. I got my

Ph.D. from Columbia University while working for Radio Free Europe in New York City and later teaching. In my RFE broadcasts and as a teacher, I tried to serve this country as well as I could, and I think that this is a fact which can be very easily established."

Abzug said she has no recollection of the matter.

The immigration authorities granted Koecher's application in September 1971. Apparently because of questions about her former membership in the Communist Party, Hana did not become a U.S. citizen until the following year.

"Needless to say, I am happy to have my naturalization certificate," Koecher wrote to his friend Kline on September 29. "It's like formally marrying someone with whom you lived happily for years."

By 1972, Koecher was ready to carry out the assignment he had received ten years earlier. He was an established member of the U.S. academic community with a special interest in Soviet affairs. He could list impressive references from well-respected scholars in the field. And anyone who checked with his employers or friends would find he was violently anti-Communist.

When Koecher applied to the CIA in April 1972, he signed a form warning that he would be subject to "a time-consuming [investigation] which, in addition to loyalty and security checks, includes evaluation of competence, physical and emotional fitness, and availability of a suitable position at such time as employment may be offered."

Not to worry. Koecher passed the FBI's background investigation and, on October 30, 1972, took a CIA lie-detector test. Asked during the test if he had ever been a member of the Communist Party, he said he applied in 1959 to get ahead in his career in Czechoslovakia but had been turned down.

He passed the test. Later, during the FBI's investigation, polygraph experts noticed that Koecher had given some signs of deception.

"Koecher's lie-detector results were misinterpreted by the CIA," a source said.

Koecher boasted to me that he knew how to pass.

"They asked have you worked for the Communist Party or the opposition. I really don't believe in the machines. You concentrate during the lie-detector test. You just believe in what you're saying. We don't use them here."

On the other hand, Koecher later flunked an FBI lie-detector test.

On November 1, 1972, Koecher tendered his resignation to Wagner College, giving as his reason the "highly attractive offer of a position with the U.S. government." The resignation was effective on November 1, 1972.

"I shall always keep in good memory Wagner as a place where I found my first opportunity to take an active part in American academic life and where I had met so many wonderful young people as my students," he wrote.

Koecher became a CIA translator with "top secret" security clearance on February 5, 1973. His salary was $10,000 a year, a slight reduction from his salary at Wagner.

Koecher was assigned to AE/SCREEN, a cryptonym for a translation and analysis unit in the CIA's Soviet section. From a rented building in Rosslyn, Virginia, he translated reports or tapes dictated in Russian or Czech by CIA informants. He also translated and analyzed intercepted conversations. Because of his knowledge of science and engineering terms, he was given some of the most sensitive material the CIA had.

While Koecher was neither a case officer nor a CIA official at the center of operations, all of the material he translated was collected clandestinely. He was therefore in a position to learn, either directly or through inference, about CIA operations, agents, and sources of information, including identities of assets overseas and locations of electronic bugs and wiretaps. His "cover" in his CIA job was that he was a Pentagon employee.

Characteristically, three weeks after he began work, Koecher complained that the job was not up to his abilities.

"My present position is by no means one that would require a Ph.D.," he wrote in a memo to his superiors. "I am interested in intelligence work, and I want to stay with the agency and do a good piece of work. But I also think that it would be only fair to let me do it in a position intellectually far more demanding than the one I have now. . . ."

Presumably in response to his complaints, Koecher later was asked to write evaluations of the people whose words he translated and to write evaluations of other Soviet and Czech diplomats and government officials. As an analyst, he was in a position to seek additional "top secret" materials to help in his evaluations. After two years with the agency, he was making $12,000 a year.

While working at the CIA, Koecher lived in an apartment at 3100 Manchester Street in Falls Church, Virginia, while Hana remained in New York, where she now worked as a diamond grader and salesperson for Savion Diamonds Inc., a wholesaler in New York's diamond district.

On weekends, the couple commuted to see each other, to pass classified CIA documents, and—in those pre-AIDS days—to attend sex parties. One of their haunts, according to its organizer, was Virginia's In Place, an elite private club organized in 1972 by a suburban Virginia real estate man who was bored with his wife.

For the purpose, the man told me he rented a spacious home in Fairfax, Virginia, just minutes from Koecher's office in Rosslyn across the Potomac River from Washington. The home had a large, circular driveway and four tall, white pillars in front. During the week, it was occupied by an older, single man who agreed to maintain it in exchange for not paying rent. On weekends, it was the scene of sex parties that usually took place on Friday and Saturday nights but could occur whenever two or more couples converged there at the same time.

Anyone on a list of some two hundred couples could attend, as well as their friends. Besides a prohibition on drugs, the only rule was that everyone bring a spouse or date. More than three-fourths of the couples were married.

When the couples arrived, they paid a fee of twenty dollars, which covered drinks and the cost of renting and maintaining the house. Usually, couples paired off at the bar in the living room to the right as they entered the house. Typically, they would have sex on mattresses laid out on the floors upstairs, in walk-in closets, or downstairs in the recreation room.

Most of the couples engaged in group sex, which often followed the bunny hop. They would dance in a line and then fall into various positions on the floor, the organizer told me.

A double bed in the recreation room was a popular location. A couple would begin making love on the bed, followed by a second or third couple, joined by others who participated from the perimeter in sex acts with those on the bed.

Some of the partygoers preferred one partner at a time but many partners throughout the night. One woman decided to take on each of the twenty-one males at the party one evening but succeeded in making it with only nineteen.

Occasionally, there were special events, announced by a flyer sent to those on the mailing list. "The Merrie Month of May is upon us," said one, "and we have big plans for your pleasure. If you haven't yet realized it, this is Leap Year. That means the girls do the choosing. In honor of this old and honored tradition, VIP is holding a Sadie Hawkins Day Night on May 8th. Girls bring your mates or dates, and then make your selections as the evening progresses."

There would be animated conversation when the sex got old.

"You can't screw all the time," one of the former guests told me. "There's a lot of talking and observing. It's like your fantasies except that everyone is not sexually aroused all the time. You'd have two girls and one guy and two guys and one girl and three or four guys and one girl or vice versa."

The partygoers included the usual assortment of movers and shakers one would expect at a party in Washington—a member of Congress, a woman who worked in the White House, a GS-16 from the Commerce Department. At least ten of the partygoers at the In Place, including Koecher, worked for the CIA.

CIA security directives say unusual sexual conduct is to be avoided because of the possibility for blackmail. To this day, many of the CIA people are sensitive about their involvement. But that didn't keep them from going, and the CIA never found out about the parties.

To the uninitiated, this may seem strange. How could an organization as super-secret and sensitive as the CIA allow its officers to attend orgies? The answer is that the CIA in reality can be an undisciplined place, where a former drug user was hired to go to the Moscow station and where people like Edwin Wilson could engage in criminal conduct under the agency's mantle.

The organizer of the Virginia sex parties recalls seeing the Koechers on several occasions. Often, Koecher sat on the sofa in the living room and talked while Hana amused herself downstairs.

"I remember him because he used a few Czech words, and I would tell his accent; my late mother-in-law was part Czech," he told me. "We got talking, and he said he was Czech. He was sitting on the sofa while his wife was partying. She was a very attractive girl and a very active young lady. She was doing group things."

Because of all the activity, neighbors complained about the parties to Fairfax police. Apparently thinking the club was a house of prostitution or a drug den, the police set up roadblocks one night and took license-plate numbers. After interviewing some of the guests, the police decided whatever was going on was none of their business. But the fact that the license-plate numbers had been recorded would later turn out to be a problem for the participants.

After several years at the Fairfax house, the club moved to another home in Clifton, Virginia, owned by a State Department official who was temporarily assigned overseas. When he returned, he found out about the parties. Spurred on by his wife, he sued the organizer, and his lawyer began taking the depositions of people whose license-tag numbers had been taken down by the police at the previous party place.

"Did you ever take your clothes off at any of these parties?" the plaintiff's lawyer, Lawrence D. Huntsman, asked one of the females who had attended the parties.

She squirmed and tried to duck the question, asking her lawyer if she had to answer. The lawyer advised her she could take the Fifth Amendment, but only if her answer would incriminate her.

"At the parties?" she hedged. "And you are saying that I shouldn't take the Fifth?" she asked her lawyer.

After more back and forth, she answered, "Yes."

Soon thereafter, the suit was settled out of court, and the party-goers breathed a collective sigh of relief.

Koecher himself denies going to Virginia's In Place but admits going to nudist colonies, Plato's Retreat and the Hellfire in New York, and the Swinging Gate and Capitol Couples in Washington.

The Gate, as it was called, had a reputation for steamy parties. Located in a large country house in Jessup, Maryland, it was outfitted with wall-to-wall mattresses, black lights, a "tent room" with billowing parachutes, and a sauna and utility room, where all manner of sex acts were performed. So famous was the Gate that porn stars from New York sometimes drove down from New York to join in the parties.

Members of Capitol Couples met on Saturday nights at the Exchange, a bar where the club's organizer worked. The couples paired off for sex parties at one another's homes or at hotel suites rented by the organizer. When the organizer took new jobs at other bars, the club moved with him.

"Ah, yes," said the organizer when asked about the Koechers. "I remember them quite well. I found them an interesting couple. He was a professor. She was a diamond merchant. Strikingly beautiful. Warm, sweet, ingratiating. Incredibly orgasmic. I went to bed with her several times.

"But I thought Karl was a bit strange. I thought he took some kind of special drug. He was always naked at the parties. Usually people keep their clothes on at least some of the time, but he was always walking around naked. And he always had an erection. The women he was with said he was a terrible lover, very insensitive. His wife was everything he wasn't."

The fact that CIA officials attended these and other sex parties with the Koechers gave rise to a theory within Washington's Metropolitan Police Department that the Koechers were picking up intelligence secrets in the course of their swinging. The department passed on several leads in the case to the FBI—including a photo taken by a guest of Hana having sex with four men at a swingers' party.

In fact, while sexual liaisons can be compromising, they do not necessarily elicit really damaging information. John Profumo, the British war minister, apparently gave no secrets to Christine Keeler, the attractive call girl who simultaneously carried on affairs with Profumo and GRU officer Eugene Ivanov in 1962. Profumo's affair, and the fact that he lied about it to the House of Commons, led to his resignation in June 1963.

At first, the Marine Corps thought Sergeant Clayton J. Lonetree and Corporal Arnold Bracy had let the KGB run wild in the Soviet Embassy in Moscow in early 1986 in return for the sexual favors of two comely Soviet women. While Lonetree had become involved with a Soviet woman, he never allowed any Soviets into the embassy.

In Koecher's case, the evidence suggests he had ample opportunity in his job to obtain classified material directly rather than through sexual liaisons.

To some extent, Koecher said, the parties were useful in picking up information.

"Even knowing that somebody attends parties like that—maybe a GS-17 in the CIA—is interesting stuff," he said. "Or you just pass it on to someone else [another intelligence officer] who takes over. That's the way it's done."

But for the most part, they went to the parties because they enjoyed them. The parties were no more important than any other source of information, Hana said. As if explaining how she collects cookbook recipes, she said art exhibitions were "another way. Maybe once a week we would do it. We always like interesting things. These people [CIA and other U.S. officials] are very interested in art. We were interested also."

Meanwhile, Koecher was trying to ingratiate himself with the

FBI. The first attempt was in November 1970, when he was having difficulties getting his citizenship approved. As usual, the web of deceit he wove was intricate.

Koecher called the FBI and said a Czech agent was trying to recruit him to spy for Czechoslovakia. When the FBI interviewed him, he said the man was Vesek Kralik, the first secretary of the Czechoslavak Embassy in New York and an agent of the Czech Intelligence Service. The FBI told him to play along, reporting each contact to the FBI. After a year, Koecher told the FBI that Kralik had said U.S. authorities were aware that the two had been in contact and he should flee to Czechoslovakia for his own safety.

The FBI recommended that he break off contact with Kralik at that point, and Koecher said he did.

In July 1973, Koecher, who was now working for the CIA, called the FBI again to report that Kralik had shown up unannounced at his New York apartment. He said he asked him to take a walk with him.

In a written report on the alleged meeting, Koecher told the FBI, "VK [Kralik] expressed regret at the interruption of our contacts in 1971, saying it was their mistake. After displaying interest in personal matters, he asked me where I work and who is my superior. I told him I work as an analyst for the Department of the Army, that my office is in the Pentagon, and that my superior is Colonel Brauer. VK said he hopes I will be willing to cooperate with him, and made a number of promises in return for unconditional cooperation: money in U.S. dollars as well as in Czech currency, the latter deposited in my name in Prague, visits to Czechoslovakia, medical care, an important position after I return, and possibly even party membership."

Koecher later told the FBI he was noncommittal. Kralik suggested they meet again at 9:00 P.M. on August 3 at Stouffer's at 666 Fifth Avenue. In the event either of them could not show, Kralik said they should meet the following day at the same place.

Kralik did not show up, Koecher told the FBI, nor did he show up the next day. But on the alternate day he saw two men who appeared to be watching him from across the street, according to his memo to the FBI on the meetings.

What Koecher did not say was that Kralik was then Koecher's Czech case officer, as he later admitted to the FBI. The approach to the FBI was nothing but a ruse to enhance his standing in the U.S. intelligence community. If it had worked, Koecher could have become a double agent, feeding the FBI phony information on behalf of the Czechs and reporting back to his case officer on the kinds of information the FBI wanted to know.

If only because the FBI and CIA never use each other's personnel as double agents—too messy—the effort failed. Beyond that, the FBI, like the Soviets, views any walk-in with a jaundiced eye. If the FBI seeks out an individual to play double agent, it is more likely he can be trusted. On the other hand, a person who comes in and offers his services may be a set-up. The CIA is far more likely to take a chance with a walk-in overseas.

Koecher displayed special sensitivity about this episode during my interviews with him.

"What was calling the FBI all about?" I asked him.

"Ahh," he said, clearing his throat. Long pause. "Ahh, ahh. What do I say about that? You're right, I did call them. However, I really don't know very much what happened. What I know is from the papers [FBI reports] I read. They do seem to claim that I tried to maybe offer them cooperation or something. I did try to make that impression around my naturalization hearing. That was about the extent of it."

"Why did you do that?"

"Oh, certainly to help me. But the impression I got from the papers was that they were trying to discredit me with respect to the Czech service or pretend I had been working for them for some time."

"But the guy you mentioned who approached you was Kralik from the Czech Embassy," I said.

"That's what they say he was. I don't know what he was."

"But he was also your case officer in the operation?" I asked.

In very soft tones, Koecher said, "I can't really say." Smiling, he said, "I wouldn't discuss any case officers."

Why was Koecher so sensitive about this phase of his secret life? I later asked an FBI agent involved in the case and got an interesting answer.

One of Koecher's CIA assignments was to translate reports from Aleksandr D. Ogorodnik, a key CIA asset in Moscow, and to write an evaluation of him. In 1974, while serving at the Soviet Embassy in Bogotá, Colombia, Ogorodnik had made contact with the CIA. Over a period of twenty months, after he was transferred to the Global

Affairs Department of the Soviet Ministry of Foreign Affairs in Moscow, he provided the CIA with microfilm of hundreds of classified Soviet documents, including reports from Soviet ambassadors.

The information was so valuable that it was circulated, in summary form, to the White House, the National Security Council, and the State Department.

The KGB caught Ogorodnik photographing documents in 1977 and arrested him. As recounted by John Barron in *KGB Today,* Ogorodnik confessed immediately, saying he was prepared to pay the price for acting on his political beliefs. He agreed to give a full written account of his activities on behalf of the CIA and after preliminary questioning, his interrogators led him to a desk and gave him a pen and paper.

"By the way, for some years, I have written with the same pen, a Mont Blanc," he said. "I think it's on top of my desk. If one of your people happens to go near my apartment in the next few days, I'd like to have it."

The KGB delivered the pen, which contained poison carefully concealed there by the CIA. He opened it, swallowed a pill, and died within ten seconds.

When asked how he was able to get the Ogorodnik reports out of the CIA, Koecher said, "I didn't necessarily have to bring documents out. I wouldn't say I have an absolutely fantastic memory, but I would say in the short term it's almost photographic. There was no need to take the Ogorodnik document out."

He added, "There were spot checks to look in my attaché case. But they wouldn't search me. You probably could carry things out, but it would be risky. Of course, the documents would have to be missing. Somebody could find out."

If CIA officials suspected Koecher of leaking Ogorodnik's identity to the KGB, they gave no sign of it. The CIA recently declined to comment on any aspect of the Koecher case.

On February 10, 1975, Koecher left full-time CIA employment but continued as a contract employee based in New York. He was given more demanding tasks, including writing a paper on Soviet leaders and how they make decisions.

William J. Colligan, the CIA official who gave him the assignment, recalled that the work Koecher turned in was "highly abstract. The paper needed work."

Now that Koecher was doing contract work in New York, he decided to buy a cooperative apartment there. In October 1975, he and Hana applied to buy apartment 1 2-B at the Park Regis, a luxury building at 50 East Eighty-ninth Street. The price for the two-bedroom apartment was $40,000. Koecher later admitted asking the Czech Intelligence Service for the full amount. The Czechs gave him $20,000, calling it a bonus.

Among the Koechers' neighbors in the building were comedian Mel Brooks, actress Anne Bancroft, and Tommy Tune, the dancer and actor. Later, Koecher would stand for election to the board of the co-op, saying he was a consultant and expert on building security. When there was a dispute over whether he had won, he demanded to see the ballots, and when he was refused, he threatened to get his gun. On another occasion, he punched a resident of the building during a dispute in the garage, where he and Hana kept their blue 1974 BMW.

With time on his hands, Koecher responded to singles' ads.

"Well," he wrote to one woman, "I am a professional man, over forty (forty-two to be more precise, Ph. D., working as an independent political analyst for the U.S. government), and I happen to wish a voluptuous, vibrant brunette. Maybe we can have lunch or a drink somewhere and find out more about each other?"

Besides working for Savion Diamonds as a diamond grader and salesperson, Hana was trying to make a go of it on her own, selling pendants and earrings wholesale through Novissa Corp., a company jointly owned by the Koechers and Savion. Both Savion and Novissa operated out of Suite 707, 30 West Forty-seventh Street, a cramped office behind a light blue door in the diamond district.

While Koecher described himself as the president of Novissa, he in fact had no role in the company, according to Joseph Savion, owner of Savion Diamonds. Eventually, Hana made $20,000 a year in salary from Savion Diamonds. She rarely earned any profit from Novissa.

Hana later admitted that the diamond business served as an excellent cover for her work as a courier for the Czechoslovak Intelligence Service. She secreted CIA documents in cigarette packs and gave them to Czech agents in Prague and other cities, on visits she made at the tail end of trips to the diamond centers of the world.

Affectionately calling him "Bombisku," she would send her husband postcards from Tel Aviv or Antwerp with imprints of her lips on the back, signing them "Bombinka," "Hanka," "Ziza," or merely "wife." Occasionally, the messages conveyed a hint of jealousy.

"Greetings, darling," she wrote in Czech from Tel Aviv. "Today,

I came home at six and your letter was waiting here for me. Immediately I feel better. I'm drying my hair now and nobody is helping me with it. I hope that you don't get your hair cut by 'somebody.' . . . I kiss you."

After arriving in Bombay, she wrote, "Take care of yourself. I'm sorry that you're not missing me like I do you. H."

Like Karl, Hana had several faces. One was the bright, sophisticated woman who took full advantage of New York's cultural events, painted and read when Karl was away, and gained the trust of her employers in a business where trust is all-important.

"She was a great saleswoman. Everybody on the street loved her," Joseph Savion, who employed her for ten years, said.

In New York, according to her diaries, she shopped at Bloomingdale's or Lord & Taylor, exercised at home, sewed Koecher's pants when they needed repair, ran in Central Park, played tennis, watched movies on television, went to the Guggenheim, made cabbage strudel and plum pies, and dined out at the Cattleman or the Russian Tea Room. Occasionally, she went to McDonald's.

Together, they went to nudist camps; drank slivovitz, a plum brandy popular in Eastern Europe; sunbathed in Miami; had cocktails at the Playboy Club; spent weekends with other swinging couples in Cape Cod or the Hamptons; and took vacations in St. Croix, Paris, Zurich, and Mexico. Occasionally, Karl took cocaine during sexual romps and experimented briefly with other drugs.

One Christmas, the Koechers attended a CIA office party. Karl later admitted sending photos taken at the party to the Czech Intelligence Service.

"Somebody took them [the pictures]," he told me. "Anybody could have them. That's a fact. How you manage to take pictures and if you manage to take them, these are again very secret," he said.

Hana's other face was the woman from Prague, insular, and subordinate to a husband who heaped physical and verbal abuse on her. When FBI agents began bugging the couple's apartment and car and Hana's business, they were appalled at what they heard. If Hana brought the paper in and began reading it before Karl did, or misplaced a coffee cup, or adjusted the blinds the wrong way, he would blow up at her and sometimes hit her.

By 1979, Koecher's contract work with the CIA was drying up. He got a job as an assistant professor at the Old Westbury College of the State University of New York in Long Island. In his résumé, he said he was employed from 1973 to 1975 by the "Department of the Army, Washington, D.C."

According to Philip A. Camponeschi, who was then chairman of the humanities department, he was released after a year because of disputes with other faculty members over his anti-Communist positions.

In October 1979, Koecher applied for a job as an intelligence operations specialist with the National Security Agency.

"He is a broadly cultivated and attractive human being, at home in current fiction (which he reads in several languages) as well as in the plastic arts, drama, and cinema," George Kline wrote of him in a letter of reference.

He apparently never got the job.

In June 1980, Koecher wrote to a friend in Washington who was with the CIA. Explaining that he had not been given tenure at the university because of opposition from "radicals" on the faculty, he said, "One thing I wonder about if, by any chance, you would have any idea whom I could talk to in order to explore if there might be some opportunity for me with the old firm. Watergate times are gone, and there may be again some need for people like me."

By 1982, when the FBI began watching him, Koecher was again doing contract work for the CIA. The FBI notified the CIA, which quietly cut him off from classified information. But because they trusted him as a longtime CIA employee, officials in other sensitive agencies continued to deal with him, giving him documents and other information that they thought would help him in his work for the U.S. government.

4 *The Dangle*

Meanwhile in Washington, things were getting out of hand at the Soviet military office. Spies were strolling in with classified documents to sell as if they were hawking T-shirts at a football game. What's more, the Soviets were accepting them. To O'Keefe, it seemed the attitude at SMO was, "Hey, even if a wacko comes in, talk to him. It's more information than we've had before."

O'Keefe felt it was time to teach the Soviets an object lesson. There were three schools of thought on this. Some FBI counterintelligence agents thought the best way to do their job was to arrest more Soviets—the "bust their ass" school. Another camp felt it was more useful for double agents to string out relationships with Soviet spies over many years. That way, the FBI would learn more about how the GRU and KGB operate—where their dead drops are, what they are interested in, and how they go operational (intelligence lingo for spying). Over time, a Soviet officer might return to the motherland, and a new officer might take responsibility for the same double agent. According to a third school of thought, these goals are fine, but the most valuable achievement is developing a relationship with a Soviet intelligence officer and recruiting him in place, turning him into a double agent.

If O'Keefe had to be put in any of these camps at that time in his career, other CI-3 agents thought it would probably be in the "bust their ass" school. Realistically, some Soviets would never be developed as agents in place. While it helped to have long-term relationships, over time the FBI might have to give up more information than it received. By teaching the Soviets a lesson, O'Keefe felt he could make them more cautious and make the FBI's job easier. Very often, after an expulsion, the replacement is younger and not as regimented; therefore, a younger replacement may be a better target for recruitment by the FBI. On the other hand, he could be better than his predecessor. What's more, it often takes the GRU two years to replace an agent. The GRU does not keep a stock of agents at the ready in case they are needed to replace one who is expelled. More recently, O'Keefe has tried to blend these three approaches.

For his purpose, O'Keefe decided he would send in a double agent and catch the Soviets at their own game. He needed someone with a convincing background—someone with access to classified information but who also fit the profile of a spy. Usually, that meant a desperate man—someone with a severe financial problem, or perhaps a man whose wife had just found out about his girlfriend.

To find the right person, O'Keefe had been calling Washington defense firms and "think tanks" in the spring of 1982, asking if they would cooperate in a counterintelligence matter involving Soviets. O'Keefe had called seventeen firms, and none would go along. He couldn't blame them. There was a certain amount of risk involved. If the operation backfired, it could besmirch their reputations in the defense community. If it succeeded, there was nothing in it for them. Then again, few people wanted to take the risk of walking into Soviet territory.

After seven weeks of making fruitless calls, O'Keefe found himself chatting with John L. Stine, the forty-year-old security officer for the Washington office of Riverside Research Institute. Originally part of Columbia University, Riverside is a nonprofit research organization based in New York. Its annual income, primarily from contracts with the Defense Department, is $13.3 million. It works on everything from the Strategic Defense Initiative, known as Star Wars, to ballistic missiles.

Assuring him it did not involve a criminal matter, O'Keefe asked Stine to meet with him. Stine knew better than to press him for the subject on the phone. For twenty years, he had been in the Navy, specializing in intercepting communications. In his last tour, he worked for the communications center of the Defense Intelligence Agency. From talking to CIA and FBI people, Stine knew all about the fiasco at Mount Alto, the location the State Department had chosen for the new Soviet Embassy complex, and how it had compromised telephone calls in Washington.

O'Keefe and his partner, Don Young, or "Fish," met with Stine at his office at 1701 North Fort Myer Drive in Arlington, Virginia.

Stine's office was part of an inner partitioned area within Riverside's seventh-floor suite. Because of the classified work there, the inner sanctum had no windows. Double walls enclosed it. The walls were heavily insulated and fortified with a steel plate.

O'Keefe immediately liked Stine. He had a deep reassuring voice and a relaxed manner that tended to put people at ease. He had bushy brown hair and, at two hundred pounds, didn't quite fill out his six-foot, four-inch frame.

"I can't go into any details at this point," O'Keefe told him, "but we need an employee with access to classified information."

Stine showed him résumés of several employees who might be willing to cooperate, including a few women. Meanwhile, he asked his superiors for approval but ran into immediate resistance. Riverside dealt with practically every component of the defense establishment, from the Army's White Sands Missile Range to the Strategic Defense Initiative Organization. Any one of them could raise an eyebrow at the idea of becoming involved with the Soviets. Even if Riverside were collaborating with the FBI, Defense Department bureaucrats might wonder if the company really had something going with the Russians. In the government, anything controversial is suspect.

After getting negative responses all the way up Riverside's organization chart, Stine finally met with Lawrence H. O'Neill, the institute's chairman and president, at the organization's headquarters at 330 West Forty-second Street in New York.

"Hell, yes, we'll do it," O'Neill said.

O'Neill took Stine to the office of the institute's executive vice president to tell him Stine would be cooperating with the FBI. But the fact that Stine had gone over the heads of his immediate bosses would later create severe difficulties for him.

Meanwhile, O'Keefe had been thinking that Stine himself would make an ideal candidate for the job he had in mind. They were on their way to becoming friends, and O'Keefe was starting to trust him. In the delicate relationship between a double agent and his handler, nothing is more important than trust. At the same time, O'Keefe felt Stine could play the part of a spy. He was a bachelor with a smooth style. He drank Scotch and water at lunch, chain-smoked Kools, and frequented singles bars. Ever since his high school days in Sioux City, Iowa, O'Keefe had been known as a lady's man, too—a debonair man-about-town who liked to hang out at R.J.'s Tavern on Twentieth Street in Washington, where the buxom barmaid knew him and his FBI friends.

To O'Keefe, who was divorced, Stine's lifestyle was appealing, and they often exchanged tips on the subject of women.

For his part, Stine had been thinking that he might like to help

O'Keefe. As they discussed possible candidates, he blurted out, "How about me?"

Stine already had a "top secret" security clearance, but O'Keefe asked him to fill out a form listing his background so the FBI could check him out further. While the background investigation dragged on, O'Keefe began the lengthy procedures necessary for freeing up classified documents that Stine could give the Soviets as feed material—information that would establish him as a valuable spy. In FBI lingo, O'Keefe was preparing a "dangle."

O'Keefe had to obtain approval not only from FBI headquarters but from the Defense Department agency that prepared the documents, and from a special Pentagon board that rules on matters of classification. In any given month, the FBI passes this so-called feed material not only to the Soviets but to the Bulgarians, the Chinese, the Cubans, and the Czechs, among others. Dummy information will not do. Worldwide, the Soviets collect all the information they get from all types of sources and put it into a computer. It has to match up. If a document says a secret project is being developed in Africa, and a satellite shows the area is desert, the double agent who passed the information could be in jeopardy.

To make sure he had enough approved documents, O'Keefe submitted a list of classification numbers for thirty documents, when he really only needed five or six. That way, even if most of the requests were rejected, he would still have enough to give Stine when he walked into SMO. Most of the documents had been done for the Defense Advanced Research Project Agency on methods for detecting bombing targets. All were stamped "secret."

Before he could pass them to the Soviets, Stine had to be trained to play the part of a Soviet spy. Half a dozen times, O'Keefe, Young, and several other agents met with him after work behind the cranberry-red curtains in a room at the Key Bridge Marriott in Rosslyn, not far from Stine's office. With the room darkened, a Russian-born agent presided at one end of a table and quizzed Stine.

"Why do you want to do this?" the agent asked him over and over again in a Russian accent.

Each time, Stine told his listeners the story O'Keefe had concocted—he owed $50,000 to a bookie and was desperate for cash. The story could not be penetrated, either by the Soviets or the FBI.

"How much access do you have?" the agent would ask.

Stine would say that any new documents that come into Riverside pass through his office. But once they are filed, he cannot obtain them without the consent of a second security officer. He and the other officer each know only a portion of the combinations needed to open the vaults where the papers are stored.

In fact, Stine had access to everything at Riverside. He could have turned on the copying machines at night and duplicated everything in the place. But the FBI didn't want the Soviets to think they could obtain anything they wanted from him.

In the room at the Marriott, O'Keefe and the other agents critiqued Stine's performance. After the first sessions, Stine, O'Keefe, and some of the other agents retreated to the Madhatter Bar at Eighteenth and M streets NW. O'Keefe drank a Miller Lite, and Stine had his usual Scotch and water. Like stereotypical spies, they never took off their trench coats. But otherwise they looked like men having a friendly drink after work—rather than counterspies plotting to foil the Soviets.

When the documents were approved for use in the operation, O'Keefe told Stine to copy them on Riverside's copying machines. And he warned that no one else's fingerprints should appear on them. That proved to be a tall order. In Riverside's reproduction room, everyone seemed to be yearning to help Stine. Secretaries grabbed finished copies out of the collator for him or tried to help him stack them in piles. As soon as the secretaries left, he tossed the copies into the classified trash bin, which was marked with a red stripe, and started over.

O'Keefe said that the best time for Stine to walk into SMO would be Thanksgiving Day, November 25, 1982. As a security officer, Stine would be expected to know that the FBI watches the Soviet establishments. It stood to reason, too, that he would figure fewer agents would be watching on Thanksgiving. The Soviets would appreciate the extra bit of caution.

The night before, O'Keefe and Stine met at the Key Bridge Marriott for one last interrogation. O'Keefe thought he was being too flip about his assignment. Stine explained that that was how he reacted to pressure: he made light of things. Then they repaired to the Madhatter. A woman with her blond hair in barrettes gave Stine the eye, but Stine had more important things to think about. O'Keefe wanted him to have a hangover the next day, so he would appear more desperate to the Soviets.

The next morning at 9:00 A.M., Stine walked through the lobby of the Marriott to meet O'Keefe once more before he went to SMO.

On the way to the elevator, he ran into a waitress he knew, and they chatted. In O'Keefe's suite, Stine rinsed his mouth with liquor and put on a disguise—gray tint for his hair, a brown handlebar mustache, an Irish walking hat, and green-tinted aviator glasses. The disguise was to show the Soviets that he was a genuine spy and was trying to avoid being spotted by the FBI.

As Stine walked out through the lobby, he again ran into the waitress. He was wearing the same tan parka as when he entered the hotel. But this time she walked right past him. He smiled to himself.

Stine took a Virginia cab to K Street in Northwest Washington. Then he got out and took a D.C. cab. It was 10:00 A.M. The sky was overcast. As he walked in front of a station wagon parked in front of SMO and into the building, an FBI agent shot a blurred surveillance photograph of him strolling through the gate.

Stine walked into a foyer. To his right was a Russian clerk behind a glass partition.

"Can I help you?" the clerk inside the booth asked.

"I want to see an Air Force officer," Stine said.

The clerk opened a wooden door electronically and handed Stine a visitor registration card.

"Fill this out, please," he said.

The clerk showed Stine to a parlor to the left of the front entrance.

"Someone will be with you in a few minutes," he said.

Stine was glad for the opportunity to sit down. His legs were shaking. He looked around. The entire place had the air of an aging bachelor's quarters, he decided—threadbare furniture, musty, not at all inviting.

He played with the card and decided not to fill it out. A real spy would not list his name, address, and the purpose of his visit on a piece of paper.

Another Soviet came in. He was five feet, eight inches tall and had pasty, fleshy skin, blue eyes, and short reddish hair graying at the temples. He introduced himself only as Nick. Later, Stine would learn the Soviet was Lieutenant Colonel Vyacheslav Pavlov, an assistant air attaché and GRU officer.

"Can I help you?" he asked.

The adrenaline began coursing through Stine.

"I'm here to do some business with you," he said.

"What type of business?" the Soviet asked.

"I work for Riverside Research Institute," Stine said, lighting a Kool. "I'm the security chief there. I have access to a number of classified documents."

"I am diplomat," he said. "I don't engage in this type activity."

Over and over again, the agent conducting the mock interrogation had made the same protest. It was up to Stine to convince him that he knew better.

"I know you are," Stine said, "but I have information that I'm going to sell you. I want to talk to you, in private."

Pavlov got up and escorted him into another, smaller room to the right of the front entrance. It had a cocktail table and a small table with an old radio on it. Pavlov tuned it to a rock station and turned the volume up. Stine realized the Soviet wanted to make sure he couldn't be taped.

Stine bragged about his access to "top secret" documents on Star Wars, ballistic missiles, lasers, and methods for separating real targets from decoys.

Pavlov repeated that he was a diplomat, but he seemed to be listening more intently. "Please, I have to leave the room for a minute," he said.

Stine didn't have a feel for whether this was a good sign or a bad one. Impulsively, he pulled out three of the documents he had tucked under his belt beneath his sweater. The top document was stamped "secret."

"Here," he said, and handed the documents to the Russian.

Pavlov's eyes lit up. He started to leave, clutching the documents.

"Just a minute," Stine said. "You might as well have the rest of them."

Stine hauled out another three documents which he had hidden in the small of his back. This time Pavlov smiled broadly. He took off.

Ten minutes later, Pavlov was back. Apparently having made copies of them, he returned the documents to Stine.

"How many documents do you have access to? Do you have problems entering? Copying? Are there alarms?" he wanted to know. Then he asked Stine to tell him about himself.

Stine mentioned his debt to the bookie, then began reciting his background. Pavlov gave him a piece of paper and asked him to write it down, apparently because he was afraid of being bugged.

Over the next several hours, the Soviet asked for the tag number of his car, his home address, and his previous addresses. When he asked for identification, Stine handed him his driver's license, which Pavlov took with him and apparently copied.

At one point, Stine pulled off his mustache. Pavlov appreciated the disguise.

Pavlov was particularly interested in the fact that Stine was a bachelor.

"In Washington, you can pick up all the girls you want in a bar. You can take them home and to bed and never see them again," Stine told him, playing the part of a rakish spy.

Pavlov, who was married, seemed to relish Stine's stories.

Stine was thirsty and asked for a glass of water. Pavlov brought him a glass, holding it by the edges. It was obvious to Stine that he wanted Stine's fingerprints. From time to time, Pavlov continued to excuse himself and leave the room, apparently shuttling back and forth between Stine and the Soviet's bosses.

Stine said he had to go to the men's room but was concerned that someone would see him. Pavlov stood guard in the hall and signaled when it was safe for Stine to walk across the hall into the bathroom.

At 3:30 P.M., Stine asked for a drink. Still holding the glass like it was a bomb, Pavlov brought him brandy. Stine was not a brandy or cognac drinker and thought the stuff tasted horrible. But, acting the part of a desperate man, he choked it down. Later, he joked that it was one of the hardest things he had to do that day.

Pavlov returned from one of his apparent visits to his bosses and asked if Stine could stay overnight. Stine told him of his plans to have Thanksgiving dinner with his boss, Theodore Grish, the head of Riverside's Washington office.

"We can meet again six weeks," Pavlov said. "Wait for this phone to ring at seven-thirty P.M. on January eighth," he said, pointing to an arrow on a map next to a Giant supermarket at Heritage Mall in Annandale, Virginia. Instead of giving Stine a copy of the map, he told him to draw his own copy.

Pavlov took out an envelope and opened it. Inside was $500 in twenty-dollar bills. Stine pulled the money out.

"Follow me, please," Pavlov commanded. He escorted Stine through a hallway into a garage, where a Plymouth Volaré with diplomatic plates was waiting. He opened the trunk and motioned for Stine to get in.

As if in a kaleidoscope, Stine saw his life pass before his eyes. O'Keefe had told him that if anything were to happen, it would be at SMO rather than on U.S. territory. Stine figured he had come this far, and he might as well go all the way.

He got in.

FBI surveillance teams in the area noticed an unusual amount of activity around SMO just then. Soviet cars were pulling in and out of the driveways and cruising around the block. It was a ploy to divert attention from Pavlov's car.

For fifteen minutes, Pavlov drove around the area, slowing down, speeding up, and making turns. Finally, he dropped Stine off beside an empty lot on Connecticut Avenue NW.

"Thank you," Pavlov said. Stine jumped out of the trunk. "See you in six weeks."

Stine stopped at a store to buy cigarettes. His hands were still shaking. He hailed a cab that took him back to the Marriott in Virginia. By the time he got there, it was 5:00 P.M.

Before getting into his car, he took off his Irish walking hat and placed it on the roof, then took off his jacket and put it inside. That was a signal to O'Keefe, who was watching from his suite: everything had gone well. If there had been a problem, he would have simply gotten in the car.

Stine was expected for Thanksgiving dinner at 3:00 P.M. but he got there at six. He told Grish, his boss, that he was stuck in traffic on the way back to Washington from Baltimore. Grish later would recall that he noticed Stine seemed a little drunk, but he gave no thought to the fact that Stine was late. He was often late for social occasions, showing up with some beautiful young woman on his arm, making every man jealous. During dinner, Stine tried to concentrate on the conversation, but his mind kept wandering back over the events of the day. He couldn't discuss them with Grish, because he, like the rest of Stine's immediate superiors, thought the idea of cooperating with the FBI had been vetoed.

The next morning, Stine drove to work, cruising side streets and checking in the rearview mirror to see if anyone was following him. Then he drove into the underground garage in his office building and waited for fifteen minutes. When no one showed up, he drove to a higher level and parked. He walked to the Marriott, where he met O'Keefe in an eighth-floor suite. Stine gave the agent the money and reviewed the events of the previous day.

O'Keefe was pleased. Operation Jagwire—a play on the word "jaguar"—was working.

Six weeks later, at 7:30 P.M., Stine walked up to the pay phone at Heritage Mall in Annandale. He stood there for forty-five minutes. The phone never rang. O'Keefe had told him the six-week delay was so the Soviets could check him out. Had they uncovered the ruse?

As he drove into the parking garage at his condominium that night, Stine was startled by a horn honking behind him. He immediately connected it with the Soviets. Were they going to kidnap him? But as he looked in his rearview mirror, he saw his boss, Grish, waving at him. Grish lived in the same building and was parking his car, too.

The next morning, Stine's phone rang.

Introducing himself again as "Nick," Pavlov said, "I'm sorry I couldn't meet you last night. Could you do it next Saturday, same time, same place?"

O'Keefe told Stine that the Soviets probably watched him the first night to see if he was under surveillance by the FBI. The next meeting would be for real. O'Keefe told him to take a pencil along. Pavlov would probably be giving him instructions, and the icy winds could make a ballpoint pen freeze up.

On Saturday night, Stine parked his car and walked to the phone. Almost immediately, it started ringing. Stine decided Pavlov must have somehow watched him walk to the phone. Pavlov gave him his instructions, which included driving to suburban Maryland. Known within the FBI as a "kidnap route," it was a way for the Soviets to find out if Stine was being followed. In fact, there was no need for the FBI to follow Stine. It was tapping the phone.

Stine had rarely been to Maryland, and now a light snow was falling. He gripped the phone and tried to follow Pavlov's poor English.

"Go on Route 495 and 270," Pavlov said, without explaining how Route 270 branches off the Beltway, 495. Stine quickly got lost. Pavlov had told him to go to another public phone next to Rian Cleaners in Germantown, Maryland. The trip was supposed to take half an hour, but almost an hour had elapsed by the time he got there. As he walked up to the phone, it started ringing.

"Put your back to the wall," Pavlov said. "Look straight ahead to the right. You'll see another road that crosses the shopping center. It comes to a dead end at the fence posts," he said. "At the fourth post from the right, you'll find a crushed pack of Marlboro Green cigarettes with further instructions."

"Okay," Stine said wearily. "If I don't understand the instructions, I'll come back to the phone booth."

The snow was starting to accumulate. Stine wondered why he had gotten himself into this. On a Saturday night he was picking up cigarette packs in the snow. He found the instructions, which told him where to leave his drop of documents and where to go for more directions. But Stine didn't have any documents. Being a novice, he was not supposed to know that he should bring any.

The instructions told him to drive to the Twinbrook Plaza shopping center in Rockville. He was to park his car, walk across the street, and find a utility shed next to a 7-Eleven on a side street. At the base of the fourth fence post from the left, he would find a crushed Coke can containing more money and instructions for the next meeting. But Stine couldn't find the can. Perhaps Pavlov had decided not to leave it, since Stine had not left any documents at his drop site.

As Stine hunted on his hands and knees for the can, a man on a motor scooter drove by. Stine gave it no thought. Then a jogger came by wearing an Adidas warmup suit. It was Pavlov.

Pavlov motioned with his hand for Stine to follow. They crossed a pedestrian bridge over a brook. It was so dark that Stine could barely make out the houses two hundred feet away.

"What's the matter?" Pavlov asked. "I thought you'd come to the phone booth if you couldn't understand my instructions."

"No, I understand your instructions," Stine said.

Pavlov gave him the crushed can. He asked for the documents.

"What documents?" Stine said. "You didn't tell me to bring any documents."

Just then, a powerful flashlight interrupted the conversation. The motor scooter was parked on the path, and a Rockville policeman was approaching them. Pavlov ran off in a different direction.

"What's your name?" the officer asked.

"John Stine," he replied.

"What are you doing here?" he asked.

"I was visiting a girlfriend nearby, and we had a fight. I was walking around to cool off," Stine said.

"Who was he?" he asked, pointing in the direction Pavlov had taken.

"He asked me for a light. I never saw him before," Stine said.

"The other officer will find him," he said. "Could I see some identification?" the policeman said.

Stine pulled out his driver's license.

"You don't know that fellow?" he asked.

"No," Stine said. He was mad that the officer had screwed things up.

"Do you have any more questions?" Stine said. "If not, I'm leaving."

"Okay," the policeman said. "We know how to get hold of you."

Stine got in his car and drove home. He never learned if the other policeman had apprehended Pavlov. O'Keefe didn't want to call attention to the incident by asking. Inside the Coke can, Stine found $5,400 in fifties, along with a note addressed to "Jim."

"Thank you for your November visit and your parcel," the note said. "All the docs are valuable. I hope you agree the money you received covers your efforts and good start. I think we will continue our mutually beneficial business. I will do my best to ensure your security. Please do the same on your part."

The note told Stine to continue to collect "up-to-date, complete, with highest classification docs" and copy them with a camera. He recommended an Olympus OM-1N with an f/1.4 lens.

"Use black-and-white Kodak films, Panatomic-X 32 ASA," Pavlov wrote. He suggested that Stine buy the film at different stores. For light, he should use a hundred-watt table lamp. The camera should be eighteen to twenty inches away from the light.

"For the sake of security our meetings or exchange of parcels will take place not more than four times a year," the note said. "The more docs you collect in films the higher the reward."

The note contained maps and instructions as to the next meeting. It told Stine to take notes on its contents and then to "destroy this message." It was signed "Your friend Nick."

The next meeting was set for April 9, 1983. O'Keefe decided it would be the last one. He had no patience for endless double-agent operations.

"My thing is beat their ass," he told Stine. "Every day they're in this country, they're screwing us."

Before the next meeting, O'Keefe and Stine met at the Key Bridge Marriott. They toasted the success of the operation as an FBI photographer took pictures of the next batch of documents. He purposely muffed a few frames so it would seem that Stine had taken them.

According to Pavlov's instructions, Stine was to wrap the undeveloped rolls of film in a black plastic garbage bag. Pavlov said to leave it at the base of a large, gnarled tree at the intersection of Schaeffer Road and White Grounds Road in Boyds, Maryland. He also gave him an alternate site if the Boyds location created problems. At 8:00 P.M., Pavlov would meet him at the municipal pool in Rockville, Maryland. If Pavlov did not show up within thirty minutes, he was supposed to pick up Pavlov's parcel at another location near Travilah Road in Potomac, Maryland. Finally, to signal that he had gotten Pavlov's package, Stine was to leave a Colt .45 beer can at the base of a stop sign along Glen Mill Road in Potomac.

Later, during the arrest of longtime Soviet spy John A. Walker Jr., CI-3 agents realized that several of the sites were within two hundred yards of the drop points used by the Soviets to obtain Walker's documents. "Spy country" was what CI-3 agents called it.

At 3:00 P.M. on Saturday, April 9, fourteen CI-3 agents converged near the gnarled tree. A "No Trespassing" sign was nailed to it. Dressed in green ponchos and raincoats, they looked more like campers out for a weekend of warm beer and barbecued hot dogs than FBI agents. Some wore baseball caps, or wool hats pulled down over their eyebrows. Under his poncho, O'Keefe wore a plaid flannel shirt and Levi's.

As a group, they appeared fearless and determined, like a pack of mountain lions looking for their next meal. Yet tonight they would be disappointed.

As they waited for Pavlov to show up, the rain began to pour. There was no way to watch the site except to hide in ditches or behind trees. Several times, Pavlov drove by the area, stopping at the black garbage bag but never leaving his car. Watching another nearby site where Pavlov had previously left money for Stine, Special Agents J. Stephen Ramey, known as the "Red Dog," and Al Zupan, known as "Zooman," lay flat down in the mud.

Powerfully built and redheaded, Ramey was a Tennessee boy. He worked as an accountant and attended law school for two years before he joined the FBI in 1972. In the Chicago office, he chased draft dodgers and tracked obscene material. Then in 1973 he was transferred to the Washington field office, where he worked white-collar crime cases. He was sent to headquarters to work on the FBI's budget, then back to the field office to act as liaison with government inspectors general. He later became the night supervisor for the office.

At his request, he transferred into counterintelligence in 1982 and was assigned to CI-3. Later, after O'Keefe had become squad supervisor, Ramey ran it when O'Keefe was away. He acted briefly as the public information officer for the field office, then was put in charge of the FBI's counterintelligence budget back in headquarters.

His wife, Kathy Burns, is a former newspaper reporter who now teaches journalism at American University. At their wedding, Burns's mother insisted that all FBI agents check their guns at the coatroom. (In fact, most agents leave their guns at home during social occasions.)

For Ramey, as for most others who had been on CI-3, nothing could replace the excitement, camaraderie, and feeling of doing something worthwhile that went with being on the squad. What distinguished CI-3 from some other squads, Ramey felt, was teamwork.

"If there's a job to be done, everyone will turn out and give it 150 percent," he said. "Sometimes you have a case that may or may not be important. You'll ask another agent if he can help with surveillance tonight. The supervisor may or may not know about it. The other agent may have planned to go to a movie with his wife or take the kids to King's Dominion. He may yell at you. But he'll do it anyway."

"Maybe what set CI-3 apart was the work-hard, play-hard ethic," Phillip A. Parker, a former CI-3 squad supervisor who later became deputy assistant FBI director for counterintelligence operations, told me. "You had a group of people who worked together for three days for fifteen to twenty hours a day, culminating in success. There's usually a celebration afterwards. You don't always see that in other squads. I think every office has a squad similar to that. You wind up with a bunch of people who are very compatible. Everybody feels very close to their work, and the new guy gets the same treatment."

"The FBI is like a brotherhood," said Parker. "You certainly can relate to lying out in the bushes all night, in steaming heat or rain or snow. But with a common goal of, 'I'm going to get that SOB. He is not going to do his job while he is in the U.S. I'm just not going to let him get any secrets.' "

Because of the esprit de corps in CI-3, O'Keefe often claimed his job was easy.

"When there's a job to be done, you have agents lining up to volunteer to work without extra pay," he said. "They live and die for the job."

On the lonely road in Boyds, it was around midnight and sheets of water were pounding down, when Ramey saw what he thought was a deer or a large dog coming toward him. As lightning lit up the sky, the form appeared to be a jogger. Ramey remembered that Pavlov had posed as a jogger when he last met Stine. He couldn't fathom why anyone else would be out in this rain. He was sure the man had seen him, and he was scared. Why would two idiots be standing in a ditch in the rain at midnight? Had he blown the entire operation? But apparently he hadn't been noticed as the man jogged past.

At 5:00 A.M., Nicholas J. Walsh, the agent who then headed CI-3, decided to call it quits. A New York native who had been a counterintelligence agent for ten years, Walsh later became assistant special agent in charge of the Washington field office for Soviet counterintelligence.

Perhaps Pavlov was still skittish from the incident with the Rockville policeman. Maybe he had seen the agents. The center—intelligence jargon for headquarters—instructs GRU agents to hold off if they feel anything is not right. They are told to go with their instincts and never take a chance. During the night, the FBI found out that Pavlov was in SMO sending messages by satellite back to the center, a nine-story rectangle surrounded by another, fifteen-story GRU building inside an airport in Moscow.

That same morning, Stine went to the drop site and picked up the package. In the afternoon, a different Soviet called. Stine had no idea who he was and became apprehensive.

"There's been a problem," he said. "Can we meet at the same time, same place, next week?"

"Okay," Stine said.

On the evening of April 16, 1983, the same CI-3 agents waited near the gnarled tree in Boyds. Then, at 7:45 P.M., a blue Chrysler LeBaron pulled up to the drop site. The night was clear. The agents could easily see a heavy-set man creep from the car. O'Keefe noticed that the man was not Pavlov. It was Pavlov's boss, thirty-nine-year-old Soviet Army Lieutenant Colonel Yevgeniy Nikolayevich Barmyantsev, the acting military attaché at SMO.

Most CI-3 agents knew all of the SMO officers by sight. Barmyantsev had arrived in the United States in May 1981 for his third tour. Apparently, he had decided to show Pavlov how it was done.

Walking into the weeds, Barmyantsev picked up the garbage bag. Nine agents rushed him. Meanwhile, other agents were blocking off the road at either end with their cars and flares. Blinded by searchlights, the Soviet flung the bag—and its eight rolls of film—into the air.

"You're under arrest," Walsh said coolly, studying the Soviet officer's face with his steely blue eyes.

The Soviet was wearing a red nylon ski parka, a plaid flannel shirt, jeans, and sneakers. His face was pale, and he had wet his pants from fright. His reddish hair seemed to stand on end. And as the FBI agent spoke to him, the lieutenant made guttural noises in his throat, like the sound a cat might make when it meets up with another animal.

"Turn around," Walsh said. "Now we're just going to search you. When we're finished searching, we'll talk to you," Walsh told him.

Slowly, deliberately, Walsh pulled out his FBI badge and flashed it at the man. Other agents pushed Barmyantsev against his car and searched him. William Warfield, then assistant special agent for counterintelligence in the Washington field office, held his arm firmly.

"Special agents of the FBI," Walsh said. "You're under arrest for violation of the espionage statutes of the United States. Do you understand that?"

Barmyantsev did not reply, but continued to make the noise of a frightened animal.

"You're in no danger," Walsh said, trying to calm the man. "Do you understand? No harm will come to you as long as you cooperate."

More unintelligible noises. Walsh was not surprised by the Soviet's reaction. Even a person who is not engaged in wrongdoing can become scared out of his wits when confronted in the middle of the night by a team of FBI agents.

Walsh took out a notepad and asked the Soviet to spell his name.

"How long have you been in the United States?" he asked.

"Two years," the Soviet answered, finding his voice.

"What are you doing out here now?" the agent asked, raising his voice over the screech of two-way car radios and walkie-talkies.

"I am lost my way and went to the improper road and came over here. I peed," he said, pointing to his wet pants.

"What did you pick up back there?" Walsh asked.

"I peed," Barmyantsev repeated. "I don't know. I don't think, I see it maybe something." His voice trailed off into wounded sounds.

Walsh asked for the name of his superior at the Soviet Embassy. Even though he already knew the answers to many of his questions, he hoped to elicit new information when the Soviet was off guard.

By now, Barmyantsev was beginning to regain his composure.

"I don't know the purpose why you arrest me. Maybe you're looking for somebody else." He laughed thinly.

"We're calling now to verify that you are a diplomat," Walsh said.

"Yes, of course," Barmyantsev said.

"If you're a diplomat, you will leave. We're checking now to see if that's correct. You understand?" Walsh said.

"Yes," he answered.

Walsh knew that Barmyantsev was a diplomat, and there was no need to check with the State Department. Yet the agents were expecting Pavlov, not his boss. It was a good idea to verify Barmyantsev's credentials, In any case, the procedure bought time so Walsh could ask questions. Meanwhile, a second arrest team was deployed at another site in case Pavlov showed up there.

"You were just out for a drive?" he said. "You happened to be out here? You know you're near the twenty-five-mile limit?" Walsh said, referring to the area around Washington where Soviets may go without seeking special permission.

"I know," Barmyantsev said.

"Why did you pick up that package? I saw that," Walsh told him.

Seeking to turn the tables on his inquisitor, Barmyantsev placed his hands on his hips, looking like a preadolescent boy trying to play it cool.

"What's your name?" he asked Walsh.

"You don't need my name," Walsh said.

"You need my name, I need your name," he said, laughing.

Pointing to Barmyantsev, then to himself, Walsh said, "You are under arrest. I'm not under arrest."

"I am not under arrest," the Soviet said, laughing nervously. "I am diplomatic—diplomat," he said.

"If it's verified that you are a diplomat, you are free to go," Walsh told him.

"Please verify," the Soviet said.

"Until that's verified, you will remain here," the agent said.

"Okay."

As they talked, other agents searched Barmyantsev's car. CI-3 agents always find it amusing that they have to obtain a search warrant even to search a Soviet's car. Meanwhile, the Soviets rifle through Americans' belongings in Moscow whenever they feel like it. What's more, the Soviets cannot believe that the FBI really observed all the rules anyway.

"They think it's all a scam," a CI-3 agent said.

Inside Barmyantsev's car, the agents found the Colt .45 beer can that Stine had used as a signal the week before.

Walsh asked who had taken the place of Major General Vasiliy I. Chitov. Chitov was a GRU officer who had headed SMO until the CI-3 squad caught him spying in northern Virginia in February 1982, a year and two months earlier. Chitov had almost run over one agent as he gunned his car and tried to get away.

"The general got caught in the same business last year," Walsh said. "It's a risky business, I guess."

"I don't take any risk," Barmyantsev said, shrugging. "I don't take anything. You can check everything," he said.

"We will," Walsh replied. Turning to another agent, he said, "He claims he was lost and just out for a ride and went to the bathroom. That's a very good story. The story's good. I like that."

Turning back to Barmyantsev, he said, "Why did you pick up the garbage bag? I can't understand that."

"There was water," he said, referring to the rain. "It was to cover my shoes," the Soviet said wanly.

"Were there other officers working with you tonight on this operation?" Walsh asked.

"No," the Soviet said. Then realizing what he had said, Barmyantsev added, "What operation?"

As he talked, Barmyantsev looked around at the agents and their cars. As a trained intelligence officer, he was no doubt trying to pick up details to report back to the center.

Walsh asked another agent if the State Department had verified that Barmyantsev was a diplomat.

"Yes," the agent said.

"Okay, you're free to go. Good luck to you," Walsh said.

"Good luck to you," the Soviet replied.

"Stand back there and let him go out," Walsh said to the agents surrounding Barmyantsev's car.

At 9:00 P.M., Stine called a number at the Crystal City Marriott in Virginia. Whenever possible, the FBI liked to operate out of Virginia. The FBI thought the judges there were tougher than those in Washington, an assumption that sometimes was not true. Hearing the sounds of a party, Stine knew the operation had been a success. He met the FBI agents in their suite, where they clinked glasses.

Two days later, the State Department declared Barmyantsev *persona non grata*. He was gone by the end of the week. A year later, the hydra-headed GRU replaced him with another GRU intelligence officer. Pavlov left when the center recalled him two weeks later.

Was it worth it? O'Keefe felt that besides teaching the Soviets to be more careful about accepting walk-ins, the fact that SMO had to replace Barmyantsev and Pavlov with two new officers from the Soviet Union would disrupt their operations, at least temporarily. It takes a new officer at least six months to get acclimated. Just learning the layout of the streets of Washington takes time.

Of course, banning the GRU outright would only mean the U.S. would have more difficulty spying in Moscow. The agents were engaged in a game that two can play.

Stine became an honorary FBI agent, and then FBI Director William H. Webster presented him with the FBI's Lewis E. Peters Award. Named for a California auto dealer who placed himself in danger of being killed by organized crime figures to help the FBI, the award is given once a year to a citizen who has helped the FBI the most in either criminal or counterintelligence areas.

But Stine's cooperation had become a two-edged sword. After O'Neill, the chairman of Riverside, approved his participation, a Defense Department security officer told Riverside officials that they must not cooperate in any counterintelligence efforts by the FBI.

"We don't want the exposure," he said.

After this comment, O'Neill had to rescind his approval, but secretly he gave Stine the go-ahead anyway, even meeting with Theodore M. Gardner, a former Marine who then headed the FBI's Washington field office, to verify that O'Keefe was who he said he was.

When Stine's cooperation eventually came out, high-ranking Riverside officers were furious that Stine had successfully gone around them. They felt they had been misled. Unable to vent their fury on O'Neill, they made Stine the scapegoat.

In January 1987, Riverside fired Stine. Incredibly, he was not given the opportunity to find another job first.

"People's noses got out of joint," explained Grish, who hired Stine and was his immediate superior until just before he was fired.

A secretary to Lawrence H. O'Neill, chairman and president of Riverside Research, said he would not comment on why Stine was fired.

5

"What's in the Bag?"

Just weeks after the arrest of Barmyantsev, Leonov asked Armand Weiss, the double agent in McLean, Virginia, for the four-volume proceedings of the twentieth annual U.S. Army Operations Research Symposium. When Weiss told Leonov that the third volume was classified "secret," Leonov said, "Well, I'd like to get the whole set." It was as if he were collecting baseball cards.

Several months went by as Weiss tried to get the other three volumes, which were out of stock. Meanwhile, O'Keefe got approval from the Pentagon for Weiss to give the classified volume to Leonov. Weiss had to stall him while the State Department determined if it had any objections to his arrest. Only the Justice Department can approve an arrest of a foreign agent. But the State Department can interpose objections on diplomatic grounds. Usually, it does. But this time, the State Department wanted to retaliate against the Soviets for two recent expulsions that the Soviets had chosen to publicize. In March 1983, Richard Osborne, a first secretary of the U.S. Embassy, was expelled after allegedly having been caught with a portable electronic transmitter and special paper that dissolved in the event he was caught. In June 1983, Louis C. Thomas, a U.S. Embassy attaché, was said by the Soviets to have been caught "red-handed during a spy action in Moscow."

On August 3, 1983, Leonov called Weiss at his home to say he would be coming over to his office the next evening.

Because this meeting might be the last one before Leonov's arrest, it was crucial. Before he was arrested, the FBI wanted to test once more whether he might be persuaded to defect or become a double agent. Toward that end, FBI psychiatrists had prepared a series of questions that Weiss was to ask the Soviet.

Just as it had videotaped Leonov's other meetings with Weiss, the FBI wanted to tape this one. But three days before Leonov called, Weiss moved from his Elm Street office in McLean to a new office at

1449 Laughlin Avenue, seven blocks away. The videotape equipment had not yet been installed in the new office.

After Weiss told O'Keefe that Leonov was coming over, four FBI technicians—called "wires and pliers" people by the squad—worked feverishly to install the equipment at the new office, which was in a small, one-story brick house. To conceal the lens of the video camera, they had to remove wall panels and drill holes. They placed microphones everywhere.

An hour after the technicians left, Weiss's new landlord showed up. She happened to go down to the basement, where she noticed dozens of wires running from the first floor to the taping equipment, which had been placed on her spare dining room table in the furnace room. Storming up the stairs, she confronted Weiss.

"What's that equipment doing on my table?" she fumed. "I want it removed. And the fire marshal says you cannot have any material near the furnace."

Weiss knew Leonov could show up at any time. Weiss ran to the pay phone at McLean Shopping Center and called O'Keefe.

"What should I do?" he asked.

"Stall her," he said.

"I can't," Weiss said. "She wants it out immediately."

Weiss drove to his home two minutes away and picked up a card table. He drove back and moved the equipment to his own table, which he placed farther from the furnace. He rewired the equipment and covered it with a cloth to try to appease the landlord.

Weiss turned on the video machine and hurried upstairs. He always had it going several hours before Leonov was scheduled to arrive, just in case.

Leonov came at 7:30 P.M. As instructed, Weiss asked him how he felt about America.

He complained that he had made only a few friends.

"You're the best friend I have in the U.S.," Leonov told him. "I don't have any other friends. People don't want to talk to me when I say I'm from the embassy."

Then Leonov complained about FBI surveillance. He said he took a vacation in Niagara Falls but was so harassed by agents that he couldn't enjoy himself.

"I am looking at the falls, and there's an agent standing on each side of me, crowding me," he said.

Leonov asked Weiss about the classified document he wanted. Weiss told him he had the document but that it was in the safe of a friend who had gone on vacation. He expected the friend to be back soon.

When Leonov left, Weiss went to the basement to remove the tape from the video machine. He flipped on the light switch at the top of stairs. Suddenly, it wasn't working. He decided to try changing the tape in the dark. In his scouting days, he had excelled at night stalking.

As he reached the foot of the stairs, he sensed that someone was standing there in the dark. Then he noticed the door to the outside was slightly ajar. Moonlight was streaming through the open doorway.

He had asked O'Keefe to be there that night in case something went wrong with the video machine, but O'Keefe said he couldn't make it. Now he felt in real danger. Perhaps a Soviet spy was checking up on him. By looking at the monitor on the taping machine, anyone could see that his office was wired.

Weiss decided to make the odds even. He walked back up the stairs, closed the basement door behind him, went to his office, and turned off the lights. He slammed the front door shut, as if he were leaving for the night.

Then he crept back down the stairs. Now he didn't have the feeling anyone was there. Clearly, though, someone had been in the basement and had partially unscrewed the light bulb, then left when he thought Weiss had gone.

Weiss thought back over his conversation with O'Keefe. Even though this was to be an important meeting, the FBI agent professed no interest in being there. Was he the man in the basement? Had he shown up to check on him? If Weiss were a triple agent for the Soviets, he could have staged the meeting with Leonov for the benefit of the video camera. If O'Keefe had decided to watch from the basement, he could have detected if the two men were conspiring to fool the FBI, Weiss thought.

In fact, O'Keefe had decided not to show up. There was no need to expose himself to the risk of being detected when a video machine was recording the entire meeting.

The next day, Weiss met O'Keefe for lunch at a Chinese restaurant. He told him about his experience in the basement the previous evening.

"You could take fingerprints and find out who was there," Weiss suggested.

But O'Keefe just nodded.

Weiss began to wonder, too, how O'Keefe could meet with him in restaurants when he knew Leonov knew what he looked like. O'Keefe always said that he knew where Leonov was at any given time. But once when they were in Weiss's office, Weiss was telling the agent about a slightly wacky colleague of his when at that very moment, the same man walked up the front walk.

"Oh, my," Weiss said. "Guess who's coming?"

Both O'Keefe and Young dove under desks and chairs, and Weiss realized they thought he had been referring to Leonov. Most of the time, after double agents become operational, meetings are in hotels, apartments, or military bases.

Weiss was upset, too, because early on he had asked for something in writing, saying he was acting for the FBI. O'Keefe would say headquarters had approved the operation but would never give him any document. O'Keefe told Weiss he would have to trust him. This is the way it is: The relationship is founded on trust; a counterintelligence agent does not ask an individual to become a double agent unless he trusts him. He may on occasion trail an asset who is meeting with a Soviet, just to see what the Soviet is doing. But unless something creates suspicion that the asset is a triple agent working for the Soviets, the FBI does not check up on him. In return, the double agent is expected to trust his handler.

"If you ain't got trust, you ain't got nothing," said a CI-3 agent.

At first, O'Keefe told Weiss to give the classified document to Leonov on August 15, 1983. Weiss grimaced. He had promised his wife he would take her out for her birthday that evening. O'Keefe had Weiss postpone the meeting.

At the time, the FBI was occupied with the issue of Andrei Berezhkov, a sixteen-year-old Soviet diplomat's son seeking asylum in the U.S. "Little Andy," as CI-3 agents called him, was visiting his parents in Washington for the summer and had become enamored of American life. In letters to the White House and *The New York Times,* he said, "I hate my country and its rules, and I love your country." He said he was "running away on 11th of August."

On that day, his father reported to the State Department that his son had taken the family car and not returned it. After fourteen hours, the blond, curly-haired young man came home, but for the next week, State Department officials tried to interview him to make sure he was not being held against his will. The Soviets refused to let him be interviewed and were insisting that he should return to Russia.

In case he had been drugged, or harmed in some way, CI-3 and other agents were busy conducting twenty-four-hour surveillance at the eight Soviet establishments in Washington. Besides SMO at 2552 Belmont Road NW, the main Soviet Embassy at 1115 Sixteenth Street NW, and the Mount Alto complex at 2650 Wisconsin Avenue NW, the Soviets have an information office at 1706 Eighteenth Street NW, the Soviet fisheries office at 1609 Decatur Street NW, the Soviet trade representation office at 2001 Connecticut Avenue NW, the Soviet consulate at 1825 Phelps Place NW, and the office of the maritime attaché at 1555 L Street NW.

In addition, the FBI keeps an eye on Tass News Agency at the National Press Building; Pravda at 4601 North Park Avenue in Chevy Chase, Maryland; Izveztia at 4701 Willard Avenue in Chevy Chase; and the Soviets' dacha, or country place, a forty-five-acre estate at Pioneer Point in Centreville, Maryland.

O'Keefe figured Leonov had purposely chosen to pick up the classified document from Weiss just when "Little Andy" was creating havoc. Probably, the GRU thought the entire FBI would be occupied with the sixteen-year-old. But O'Keefe finally told Weiss to tell Leonov that he could make the pickup at seven on the evening of August 18.

Weiss could not believe it when his landlord showed up that morning. Having spotted the video equipment still in the furnace room—albeit not on her dining room table—she again demanded that it be removed.

Weiss called O'Keefe, who said he would handle it. O'Keefe then called the landlord and identified himself as an FBI agent.

"My God! What has my son done now?" she asked.

"I can't tell you why, but please leave the card table where it is," he said. "We'll have it out soon, I promise I'll call the fire marshal."

Later in the day, a dozen FBI agents drifted in, telling Weiss, "Bill sent me." Some wore suits; others, jeans.

Weiss thought he heard them cocking their weapons as they took up positions in the musty basement. In fact, the agents were not expecting any trouble and did not cock their guns. He offered them Cokes and told them they could take chairs. Later he realized Leonov would think something was wrong if too many chairs were missing from the office upstairs. So Weiss took the opportunity to ask about his own safety.

"What if Yuri gets wise and decides to shoot me?" Weiss asked O'Keefe.

"It has never happened before," the agent said. "If it did happen, there's not much we could do about it."

"What if he pulls a gun on you?" Weiss asked.

O'Keefe said Leonov would be apprehended outside the building, and Weiss would be in no danger.

"It doesn't sound like a well-balanced program," Weiss muttered.

To himself, he thought, "These people are asking me to risk my life and they won't even give me a piece of paper saying I'm a double agent."

As 7:00 P.M. approached, Weiss noticed that his office was beginning to smell of cigarette smoke from the agents below. Since neither he nor Leonov smoked, he suggested that the agents snuff out their cigarettes.

O'Keefe knew Leonov was on his way. Over a scrambled radio communication, he had gotten a report that he was doing an excellent job of dry cleaning himself, driving into a cul-de-sac, parking at an apartment complex, taking two buses, and then walking ten blocks.

At 7:20 P.M., Leonov showed up. He was wearing a heavy wool suit. Weiss had been watching the live coverage on TV of the departure of "Little Andy" from the U.S. The diplomat's son had denied sending any letters to the White House and the *Times,* and he was being allowed to go home. At 7:08 P.M., he left for Moscow on a flight from Dulles International Airport, telling reporters, "Say hi to Mick Jagger." After Leonov walked in, Weiss and the Soviet watched TV.

"What an uncertain world. When are you leaving?" Weiss asked, knowing that his expulsion was imminent.

"I don't know. It could be four years; I could be leaving next week," Leonov said.

"Here it is," Weiss said, moving to a corner of his office. On the floor was a cardboard box filled with 4,500 pages of documents Leonov had requested. Among them was the classified volume Leonov had been waiting for. As he was about to lift the box, Weiss noticed that "WFO"—for "Washington field office"—had been written with a thick, black felt-tip pen on one flap of the box. The FBI agents had not noticed it when they brought the box over.

Holding that flap down, Weiss opened the other flaps to show Leonov the documents. Leonov took the secret volume and placed it in his briefcase. Then Weiss went to get an empty grocery bag. He grabbed one labeled "Someplace Special." That was the name of the gourmet supermarket behind his office. While Weiss was gone, the agents viewing the scene on the video monitor saw Leonov looking at the huge pile of documents and helplessly shrugging his shoulders, smiling.

After transferring the documents into the grocery bag, Weiss dropped the box on the floor. It made a loud bang, like a gun going off. He wondered if the agents downstairs would think he was in trouble.

Weiss had never seen Leonov so happy. From two envelopes, the Soviet took out four $100 bills and two fifties. Apparently, both envelopes were to be used only if Weiss delivered the classified document. At 7:38 P.M., the Soviet went charging out the door into the sultry Washington evening.

Meanwhile, the agents had been filing out of the basement through the rear basement door. As Leonov walked to the end of the front walk and turned right on the sidewalk, O'Keefe was rounding the corner to the left of the walk.

"Hello, Yuri," the FBI man said.

Leonov looked around with a quizzical expression, as if he thought he might have heard something but wasn't quite sure.

Leonov took two more steps.

"Stop, Yuri, I want to talk to you," O'Keefe said.

The Soviet stopped, dropped the bag, and began running up the street.

O'Keefe had hoped to try to "turn" the Soviet to the American side just before his arrest. He wanted to "pitch" him when the two were alone, before any other agents were within earshot. But now that Leonov was running away, O'Keefe realized there was no time to suggest becoming a double agent. The military had lent him the classified document only on condition he would not let it out of his sight. The only option now was to apprehend him.

"Close in, guys," O'Keefe said into a walkie-talkie. All along, it had been transmitting his conversation to the other agents.

The agents came at Leonov from all directions and pushed him against a tree.

"Halt, FBI!" O'Keefe said. "You're under arrest."

Leonov's face was white, and his knees were buckling.

As Leonov started to reach in his right pocket, Special Agent Natalie Gore, a six-foot-tall female agent with a build like a football player, blocked him and pinned him against Weiss's parked car.

Protesting and saying he was a diplomat, Leonov shouted, "Let me call to my office."

"What's in the bag?" O'Keefe asked.

"What bag?" Leonov asked.

O'Keefe pointed to a camera held by an agent who had filmed Leonov dropping the bag. When O'Keefe asked for his briefcase, Leonov refused to hand it over. When O'Keefe said he would take it anyway, the Soviet gave it to him.

Meanwhile, O'Keefe asked if Leonov wanted medical assistance. He seemed to have the dry heaves. He declined.

O'Keefe opened the case and displayed the secret volume for the benefit of the camera.

"What's this?" O'Keefe asked, pointing to the classified document.

"I don't know. You gave it to me," Leonov said.

"Arrest that man," O'Keefe said for show, pointing to Weiss standing in the window of his office.

Two agents rushed into his office and told him he was under arrest.

The FBI uses the term "arrest" in a generic sense when dealing with diplomats. Theoretically, the FBI does not always know for sure if an individual has diplomatic immunity. The agents say a diplomat has been "arrested" until his identity and diplomatic status are verified.

While Leonov remained outside, several other agents pretended to notify the State Department that Leonov had claimed he was a diplomat. In fact, State had posed no objections to the arrest. But O'Keefe got final approval from headquarters to free him. Because he had diplomatic immunity, Leonov was not under arrest and O'Keefe told him he was free to go.

Leonov stared at him in disbelief. Then he took off, with several agents following.

Over walkie-talkies monitored by the agents in his office, Weiss could hear the agents panting as they followed him for a mile to the first bus stop. Meanwhile, two agents went to Someplace Special to buy soda, pretzels, and potato chips, bringing them back to Weiss's office.

As the agents celebrated, they continued to check on Leonov's progress by listening to the surveillance team's walkie-talkies. Weiss excused himself to take a swim at his health club before it closed at 9:45 P.M.

When he returned, the office was dark. There was no trace of the evening's events. Even the smashed potato chips on the floor had been cleaned up. He ran to look in his refrigerator. The soda was gone. The only sign that the agents had been there was a note on his desk: "Gone fishing. Will call Monday or Tuesday for lunch—thanks again. Bill."

In fact, O'Keefe had taken a long-delayed vacation to go deep-sea fishing.

The next day, the State Department declared Leonov *persona non grata*. Two days later, he left for Moscow, where he now has a desk job.

There was no publicity until September 12, when the State Department decided to announce Leonov's expulsion in retaliation for the third publicized Soviet expulsion that year of a U.S. diplomat. This time, U.S. Vice Consul Lon David Augustenborg and his wife, Denise, had been expelled from the consulate at Leningrad for "carrying out an act of espionage." Besides that, the Soviets on September 1 had shot down a South Korean airliner, killing all 269 people aboard.

On September 14, FBI Director Webster wrote a letter to Weiss saying his "exemplary performance in this operation was a primary factor in the overall success of the operation." There was a ceremony at the Washington field office, and Weiss got a plaque. In addition to the $1,800 he had gotten from Leonov, Weiss got $2,000 as a present from the FBI.

Over the course of the operation, he figured he lost $50,000 in business attending to Leonov's requests. But what troubled him was not the monetary loss. Weiss felt he had made a friend in O'Keefe, but after the operation was over, the two drifted apart, and Weiss felt the agent had not kept his word.

O'Keefe had promised to try to get him into the 1984 Olympics in Los Angeles but never did. He also promised copies of some of the videotapes. Later, he said they were classified and could not be given out.

Weiss sensed a chill the evening he got his award. He thought it might have to do with the fact he had called a friend who then produced *Nightline* and told him he could go on and talk about the case. At the time, the FBI thought the arrest was about to be announced. When the announcement was delayed, the fact that ABC-TV had learned about it from Weiss got O'Keefe in trouble with headquarters. Whenever the Leonov case came up, higher-ranking FBI officials ribbed O'Keefe about it, and Weiss's attempts to garner publicity had created a distance between them.

The FBI has a schizophrenic attitude toward the press. On the one hand, the bureau recognizes that publicizing its feats creates more respect for its agents. That, in turn, makes it easier for them to get the cooperation of the public. On the other hand, the bureau abhors publicity about individual agents—even if that publicity has been approved by headquarters. Since the press needs to focus on individuals to make stories more interesting, relatively little appears in the press about the FBI beyond announcements of arrests.

Weiss was never told that he had become stuck in the FBI's bureaucratic gears. He is glad he helped his country and would do it again. But he has scars from his triple life. When he opens a door, he swings it open first to see if anyone is on the other side. Driving on George Washington Memorial Parkway along the Potomac River one day, he thought he saw two men videotaping him from another car. Another time, he became convinced that two men were going through his trash after he had disposed of it in a dumpster late at night.

Weiss does not know who is trailing him or why. Maybe he has become paranoid. He finds that while the FBI worked diligently on the Leonov case, it is not interested in pursuing his suspicions. Once so eager to meet with him, O'Keefe now is slow to return his calls. Sometimes he thinks his experience as a double agent was all a dream.

Not long ago, someone broke into Weiss's office. The only thing that was disturbed was a desk set that held a clock and two ballpoint pens. Both the clock and its base had been smashed, he said, leaving only the pens intact. The desk set had been given to him as a present—from Leonov.

Deep Cover

On April 4, 1984, Richard Craig Smith, a lean, blond former Army intelligence officer, got off a plane at Dulles International Airport in Washington and walked into the hands of waiting FBI agents, who arrested him for espionage.

During repeated interviews with the FBI over the past ten months, the forty-one-year-old Smith had admitted giving classified information about Army double-agent operations to a Soviet KGB officer in Tokyo. What's more, he admitted to having received $11,000 from the Soviet in exchange for the information. But he said he did it all on assignment for the CIA, which somehow wasn't owning up to the fact.

It was a pretty standard defense, often invoked without success by traitors who have a background in intelligence work. But in Smith's case, there was a difference: Smith was very believable, and there was some evidence to corroborate his story, raising unprecedented and troubling questions about the FBI's and CIA's procedures.

A devout Mormon, Smith grew up in Salt Lake City, where people wear their patriotism on their sleeves. His great-great-grandfather, Hyrum Smith, was the elder brother of Joseph Smith, founder of the Church of Jesus Christ of Latter Day Saints.

When Smith was fifteen, his father moved the family to the Washington area, where he worked for the U.S. Office of Education. After graduating from high school in suburban McLean, Virginia, Smith got a job as a clerk at the CIA not far from his home. He planned to save money to become a missionary, but meanwhile he enjoyed the glamour and prestige of working for the spy agency. Smith had always been thrilled by the television series *I Led Three Lives,* the story of Herb Philbrick, an FBI double agent targeted at the Communist Party U.S.A. With a "top secret" security clearance, he thought he might get a chance to live some of his fantasies.

However, after a year with the CIA, he became a Mormon missionary in France, spending two and a half years proselytizing on behalf of the church. In 1965, he returned to the U.S. and enrolled at Brigham Young University. After two years of college, he was drafted into the Army. Because he was over twenty-four, the fact that he was going to college did not defer him from the draft. However, unlike most college students of the time, Smith was eager to go. He was enthusiastic about the Vietnam War and happy to serve his country.

Because of his "top secret" clearance, Smith found himself working for the Army's Intelligence and Security Command. After three years of active duty, he transferred into Special Operations, which coordinates the work of double agents with the FBI and the CIA.

By this time, Smith was married and had four children. The family lived in Salt Lake City. Smith's work took him on extended trips overseas, and his wife, Susan, objected both to the long hours and to the fact that he could not talk about his work. In 1980, after thirteen years in intelligence work, Smith quit the government and tried to start his own business in Salt Lake City organizing a trade and investment mission to Japan on behalf of the state of Utah.

As Smith told it to me, it was during one of his trips to Japan that he was visited in his hotel by two men from the CIA—Ken White and Danny Ishida. White was in his thirties and about six feet tall. Ishida was a Japanese-American in his late twenties.

People in the intelligence business don't flash identification to show they're with the CIA or the KGB. Credentials can always be counterfeited, and agents under cover would not want to have anything in their possession identifying themselves as spies anyway. Instead, to establish their *bona fides,* spies either use prearranged code words or go through a ritual of exchanging information to show they are who they say that are.

In this case, White and Ishida knowledgeably discussed the CIA, its sections, and its people. They also seemed to know all about Smith's background as an intelligence officer.

"If they were with the KGB, we're in trouble," Smith recalls thinking at the time.

After going through the required palaver, the two men asked if Smith would assist them by acting as a courier—bringing packages back and forth between the U.S. and Tokyo. Based on his own experience running double agents, Smith knew that their request was probably the prelude to more demanding assignments. Doing courier work would give them a chance to size him up and become comfortable with him.

Smith had promised his wife he would leave intelligence work, but he missed the excitement and the intrigue. As a supervisor, he had never gotten into the action himself. This was an assignment he could do in his spare time while engaged in his own business. He had always been a gung-ho patriot, and he saw this as a chance to do something for his country.

After a year of carrying packages—including a letter to the Soviet consulate in San Francisco hinting that he might have secrets to sell—Smith had proved himself reliable and had developed the proper psychological dependence on his two handlers. During a meeting in Tokyo, they asked him to become a double agent by walking into the Soviets' commercial compound in Tokyo and offering to sell secrets about double-agent operations he had run in the Army.

Smith readily agreed, and to make sure it came off, he primed the pump by calling Tass first. Smith knew that the Soviets were extremely suspicious of walk-ins. Very frequently they were double agents. He also knew, from his experience running double-agent operations in Tokyo, that the reporter who answers the phone at Tass is usually a KGB agent. If he talked with Tass first, the KGB agent there could smooth the way with the embassy.

Calling from a pay phone, Smith told the Tass representative on November 5, 1982, that he had some information to discuss, according to what Smith later said.

"Does this have to do with a news story?" the Tass man said.

"No. This is much more important," Smith said. "I'm not really interested in any publicity. This is a matter that requires delicate handling."

"Perhaps then you should call our embassy," the man said. "We are only a news organization. Here's the number. Good luck, and good-bye."

Smith waited thirty minutes, giving the Tass man enough time to call the embassy and let officials there know that he would be calling. When he finally called, the phone rang for seven minutes. Finally, the operator connected him to a man who seemed to Smith to be waiting for his call.

As prearranged with the two CIA men, Smith told the Soviet he had contracted a terminal illness.

"I used to work in the military in Japan," he said. "We should do business."

Smith gave the Russian the number of a nearby coffee shop. If the Soviets were interested, they should call the number in a few minutes. Smith was drinking coffee when the phone rang. The Soviet said he was still waiting for approval. If they wanted to meet with him, they should page a "Mr. David" in the lobby of a local hotel at 7:00 P.M.

Smith felt his initial rush subside as he waited in the lobby for the call. Finally, at 7:30 P.M., the operator paged "Mr. David."

"Come right over," said the man on the line.

Smith took a taxi to the commercial compound, located in an aging neighborhood of small businesses. A security guard introduced him to Victor I. Okunev, a KGB agent. Smith immediately showed he had good information by describing several double-agent operations he had run. So that the Soviets could check up on him, he named double agents who had been compromised but not publicized in old cases. Then he hinted that he had fresh intelligence information from friends in the business. After thirty minutes, Okunev set up another meeting the next day.

White and Ishida were delighted, or so Smith now says. So that Smith could get in touch with them, they gave him a number in Hawaii. Known as a "hello" number, it was answered by a secretary at a CIA proprietary or "cover" company. When Smith left a code word, White or Ishida would call him back. If for some reason another CIA agent had to talk with him, he would identify himself as Richard Cavannagh of Consolidated Mutual Investments (CMI).

By February 1983, the Soviets were talking about having Smith fly to Vienna. Smith thought they wanted to give him instructions for slipping behind the Iron Curtain for training as a spy. In March, Smith flew to Honolulu to meet with White and Ishida to give them the good news. By this time, he had collected $11,000 from the Soviets and given it all to the CIA men, who returned it to him to cover his expenses.

White and Ishida did not show up for their scheduled meeting. Instead, another man flashed a business card that said "Richard Cavannagh" and told him the two CIA men would get in touch with him later.

"Go back to Salt Lake City and wait," the man said, according to Smith's story.

Ever the military man, Smith did as he was told, but by April he was becoming frantic. If he met with the Soviets in Vienna, he was sure he could pull off a major intelligence coup for the U.S. by learning how the Soviets train agents. He told his secretary to interrupt him even if he were meeting with the governor of Utah if a call came in from Ken White. But a call never came. His messages at the "hello" number went unanswered.

How does one get in touch with the CIA if the CIA doesn't want to get in touch with you?

Very carefully.

Smith knew Paul Shields, who is in charge of the FBI's counterintelligence operations in San Francisco. Shields was Smith's former bishop in the Mormon church and a family friend. Although they had never worked together on an intelligence project, Shields knew that Smith had been in the business.

Smith called Shields from a pay phone in San Francisco and explained that he had given some information to the Soviets at the request of the CIA. He said he needed to get back in touch with his handler. Because Shields knew him and dealt with CIA people all the time, Smith figured he could make the right connection without creating too many waves.

Fifteen minutes later, Smith told me, a CIA man called him back at the pay phone. He seemed to know who he was, but his manner was anything but friendly.

"You're into something you don't understand and don't know anything about," the man said.

"I want to meet with you face-to-face," Smith said. "It's important I understand what's going on."

" 'Keep your fucking mouth shut,' " Smith quoted him as saying. " 'Don't say anything to anyone, especially your friends in the FBI. Go home, keep quiet, and I'll be in touch.' "

Smith never did hear from the man again, nor from White or Ishida. But six weeks later, at 7:30 A.M. on a Saturday, two FBI agents knocked on his door in Salt Lake City.

Smith knew both agents. Rick Smith was an old friend from the FBI's San Francisco office, and Peter Chase was assigned to the Salt Lake City field office. But when the agents flashed their badges, Smith realized they were not on a social call. Shields had reported Smith's call to his superiors, who wanted to know why Smith had been giving classified information to the Russians. The CIA, meanwhile, claimed to know nothing about Smith.

For two days, Smith submitted to interviews by the agents. At first, he claimed he had given no information to the Soviets, and he passed a lie-detector test on the question. Several weeks later, William Smits, who was in charge of Soviet counterintelligence in the San Francisco area, interviewed him again in Seattle, where Smith was then living. This time, Smith claimed he fooled the Soviets into giving him some money but never gave away any information. Smith failed a lie-detector test, and the polygraph operator questioned the first test because Smith had not been asked for a urine sample to make sure he was not taking any drugs. Slowly, Smith made more admissions, including that he had given away the details of some old Army double-agent operations.

Smith claims that because of the warning the CIA man had given him, he refused to divulge further details or even say flatly that he had been on assignment for the agency. Instead, he implied that he had been working for the agency.

"If you'll get back to the right people in Washington, they'll back me up," he now claims he told them.

If he did, the agents never picked up on it. They began a ten-month investigation that culminated in Smith's arrest in 1984. During the course of it, the FBI questioned him nineteen times, usually at the field office in Alexandria, Virginia. He signed eleven waiver-of-rights forms declining a lawyer. He took seven lie-detector tests.

Call it naïveté, call it stupidity; Smith claims he was sure the CIA would come to his rescue.

"I had blind faith," Smith told me. "I always have been sort of a red, white, and blue guy. I felt the CIA would eventually acknowledge what was going on and tell the FBI what was going on. I didn't want to get in a legal hassle."

Desperate to show that he had nothing to hide, Smith told the FBI he would tell the whole story and even take truth serum and submit to hypnosis under one condition: he wanted a friend who was a psychiatrist with the government and a representative of the CIA to be present as witnesses. Somehow, Smith thought that having the CIA present would mitigate the fact that he was disobeying agency orders to keep the double-agent operation secret.

If it was convoluted reasoning, it was also not the kind of offer the FBI would accept. The FBI decides how it will interview suspects, not the suspects being interviewed.

As Smith was about to submit voluntarily to another FBI interview in Alexandria, Virginia, the FBI arrested him as he stepped off the plane.

After interviewing Smith in jail, William B. Cummings, his court-appointed attorney, decided his best bet was to plead insanity. How else explain the fact that Smith was insisting he was a double agent but refused to offer any evidence to corroborate his story? A second lawyer, A. Brent Carruth, a former newspaperman who got in touch with Smith through Mormon friends, hired a psychologist to test his client. Her conclusion: the lawyers should believe their client. He was telling the truth and was straight. Too straight.

As his lawyers became more insistent that he come clean, Smith says he realized the CIA was never going to call and he could be sentenced to life in prison. After six weeks in jail, his Mormon friends raised the money to release him on bond. As FBI agents, including several from CI-3, trailed him to make sure he didn't make a run for the Soviet Embassy, Smith took his lawyers to a Mormon chapel in northern Virginia where he knew no one could listen in.

"You've got less than a one-in-a-thousand chance of winning," Cummings told him in May 1984.

"No way," Smith said. "If the jury won't believe the truth, then baloney. And if you won't find the evidence I know is there, then you're not representing me."

"Where can we look?" the two lawyers pleaded.

Smith finally began unraveling the story of White and Ishida. His lawyers wondered if it would have been better if he had kept quiet. The story was too fantastic for anyone to believe. But they found they could corroborate several of the points independently.

"Call my wife in Seattle," Smith told his lawyers. "Ask her to bring my box of business cards."

When Susan Smith arrived in Washington, Peter B. Silvain, a Washington psychologist and investigator who worked for Smith's lawyers, met her at the airport and took the box of business cards to Cummings's law offices in Alexandria.

Without touching the cards himself, Smith told Silvain how to read numbers he had written on the back of the cards and reconstruct them into a telephone number in Hawaii—the "hello" number he used to call White and Ishida. Then he told Silvain how to look up the number in reverse directories at the Library of Congress. Silvain reported the number was one of many belonging to an investment firm called Bishop Baldwin Rewald Dillingham & Wong in Honolulu.

Smith told me he had remembered the name as one of several on packages he delivered for White and Ishida. He said the press had not yet reported that Bishop Baldwin might be a front for the CIA.

Ronald Rewald, its forty-one-year-old chairman and founder, was said to have bilked investors out of millions of dollars through a pyramid scheme. Offering insured returns of 20 percent a year, he squandered the money on a $950,000 waterfront mansion for himself, a fleet of classic cars, a string of polo ponies, two Hawaiian ranches, chauffeured limousines, and bodyguards. If anyone had looked into his background, they would have found Rewald's degrees in law and business, his professional football career, and his claimed business expertise were all a sham. He was a high school graduate with a penchant for lying. In 1975, he had declared bankruptcy. Not only were the investments he offered not insured, they didn't exist.

Rewald's defense was that he had been acting as a covert agent for the CIA. While the CIA denied that, the agency admitted that it had used the firm as a "drop" for mail and phone calls.

As Smith's lawyers probed deeper, they found the CIA had, in fact, paid for the monthly phone bill for the "hello" phone used by Smith. In response to requests made prior to the trial, the CIA disclosed records showing that the CIA agent who called Smith back after Smith called the FBI in San Francisco was Charles Richardson, who was the CIA man with responsibility for Bishop Baldwin. Moreover, one of Richardson's CIA aliases was "Richard Cavannagh," and CMI was a CIA "cover" that was supposed to be a Bishop Baldwin subsidiary based in Sherman Oaks, California.

As it turned out, about the same time White and Ishida were disengaging from Smith, Richardson was being investigated by the CIA for having exceeded his authority and investing in Bishop Baldwin in violation of CIA conflict-of-interest rules. Presumably, if Smith had not called the FBI, the CIA men might eventually have resumed their relationship.

Smith's lawyers decided they wanted to talk to Richardson. But in papers filed in court, the CIA claimed he was no longer with the agency, and the CIA did not know where he was. Later, the week before the trial, U.S. District Court Judge Richard L. Williams, troubled that no CIA officials were scheduled to testify, ordered the CIA to produce Richardson in response to a motion by Smith's lawyers.

"The defendant has reason to believe Richardson was sent into deep cover, perhaps demoted, but certainly reassigned," the motion said. "Further, the defendant has reason to believe the government still has control over [Richardson] and his activities."

After claiming for two years it did not know where he was, the

CIA produced Richardson's address and telephone number the day before the trial was to begin. The CIA had known where he was all along. When the CIA said it didn't know where he was, he had been getting a government pension.

But was the CIA trying to cover up its relationship with Smith, or its relationship with Bishop Baldwin?

On April 7, 1986, Smith's trial began in Alexandria. Assistant U.S. Attorney Joseph J. Aronica, who had successfully prosecuted Larry Wu-Tai Chin two months earlier, portrayed Smith as a traitor who had sold out his country for $11,000.

"It was a straight trade: money for information," he said.

Aronica said Smith had called the FBI originally because he was afraid he would be caught and wanted to fabricate a cover story involving the CIA. During his initial meetings in the Soviet commercial compound, he speculated, Smith realized the Japanese police had spotted him.

But Smith called the FBI a year and a half after the initial meetings. As an experienced intelligence officer, he knew that embassies are watched by the local police anyway.

During the five-day trial, a former receptionist for Bishop Baldwin testified that she occasionally answered the "hello" phone and that she had taken several messages from Ken White.

"That name was very familiar to me because I had an old friend by that name. So it always stuck in my mind," she said.

Smith's own secretary testified that Smith had instructed her to interrupt him in meetings if "Ken White" called.

With much fanfare, Aronica played tapes of an FBI agent posing as Smith and talking with a Soviet consulate official in San Francisco. The Soviet seemed to be aware of who Smith was—he knew the hotel where Smith had stayed while in Tokyo—and he agreed to pay his way to Tokyo so the Soviets could meet with him again.

What the tapes proved was far from clear. Aronica, who dismissed Smith's story as pure nonsense, felt the fact that the Russians were so eager to meet with Smith again showed how corrupt Smith was. But the tapes only corroborated Smith's story.

Nor did Aronica try to refute the points that seemed to corroborate Smith's story. Could Smith have woven an alibi using names and details that he got from the press or other sources? Contrary to what Smith told me, the press had already reported that Bishop Baldwin might be a CIA cover long before Smith first mentioned the firm to his lawyers.

The most damaging testimony from the government's point of view came from Richardson, not because of what he said but because of the way he said it. Stylishly dressed and sporting a glowing tan, he first denied under oath that he had lied to CIA investigators about his investment in Bishop Baldwin and had been forced out of the CIA. After Smith's lawyers cited CIA documents showing otherwise, he belatedly admitted that he had been forced out for "exercising bad judgment."

By then, Richardson's credibility had been shot, and when he denied knowing anything about Smith except that they had talked once on the phone in San Francisco, no one was impressed. Smith, on the other hand, came across as very believable.

"Mr. Smith, are you a spy?" Carruth asked him.

"I have been, yes," Smith said.

"For whom?"

"For the United States of America," Smith answered. "I have never been a spy for the Soviet Union, but I sold secrets to the Soviets as part of another mission."

Carruth portrayed Smith as the innocent victim of a renegade CIA operation.

"This was a double-agent operation all the way," Carruth said. "Somebody is lying. It's either Smith or Richardson. Which one is it?"

Aronica said Smith was "desperate financially and decided to meet with the Soviets and sell what he had—his honor, his oath, and classified information." He said Smith gave the Soviets the names of six of the twenty-one double agents he had run.

Saying the idea that one branch of government would prosecute someone for helping another branch of government was "preposterous," the forty-two-year-old Aronica asked the jury, "Do you really think your government would do something like that?"

It was the wrong question to ask. The jury included a pension consultant, a computer programmer, a school-bus driver, a physical therapist, a secretary, a librarian, and a steam fitter's helper. They lived in the Washington area, and most of them had seen the government lie repeatedly during revelations of illegal activities by the CIA and FBI in the early 1970s.

Aronica's question underscored the fact that the trial was as much about the CIA's integrity as Smith's. For another spy's trial held two months earlier in the same courthouse, Aronica had been able to persuade John H. Stein, the CIA's deputy director for operations, to testify, along with Cy Braegelmann, Chin's boss at the CIA. Yet somehow, beyond Richardson and officials who testified about agency records, no one from the CIA seemed willing to take the stand against Smith.

The reason: the CIA was trying to hide the full extent of its covert activities carried out through Bishop Baldwin, government officials who have seen sensitive documents about the case have told me. It is a problem the Justice Department faces whenever the CIA is involved in prosecutions. Even if the CIA is willing to be forthcoming, prosecutors find witnesses from the agency often do not come across as being credible.

Smith had been told by his lawyers that it was a good sign if the jurors deliberated for a long time. When they came back after five and half hours, Smith told me he prepared himself for the worst.

But as the jurors took their seats, one of the female jurors winked at Smith's wife. Smith didn't see the wink but soon heard the foreman read the verdict: not guilty on all counts.

Susan Smith began sobbing uncontrollably, while Aronica stormed out of the courtroom. Michael J. Waguespack, the FBI agent then in charge of the case, walked over and shook Smith's hand.

"It was unanimous from the start," Joan Shoemaker, a juror who is a Fairfax County public school teacher, said. "I didn't think Richardson was particularly heartwarming. Why should he be walking around free? Clearly, he had been involved in shady dealings."

In effect, the CIA was on trial, she said.

"The CIA didn't come across as being very credible. Smith seemed to be the more believable. A lot of it [comes down to] people's feelings about the FBI and CIA, certainly for Washington people."

While the CIA's representatives were not convincing, "Smith's lifestyle was exemplary," she said. "There was no sleaziness there. The fact he called the FBI was convincing. It seemed to me the only thing the government had against him was what he had told them. It didn't make a very effective case," she said.

"Richardson said he didn't know a thing about Smith," she added. "I didn't believe him. They went to great lengths to play a recording of an FBI agent going and calling the Soviets [to show Smith had been in touch with the Soviets]. What it amounted to was exactly what he had told them. So what? All you did was confirm he was telling the truth. I don't know what they were trying to prove. I still don't."

Smith and his family are now living in Los Angeles, where he is helping Carruth appeal Rewald's conviction on fraud charges. In that case, the judge ruled that any evidence of CIA involvement was not relevant to the fact that Rewald defrauded investors.

If Smith is no longer involved in intelligence work, he has left his mark. Among the forty-nine defendants charged by the Justice Department with espionage since 1975, he is the only one to have been acquitted.

Did the FBI err in seeking Smith's indictment? Or did Aronica—with his arms tied behind his back by the CIA's refusal to cooperate—simply fail to prove his case beyond a reasonable doubt?

Given the fact that Smith would not disclose the details of his recruitment by the CIA until he was put in jail, Carruth, his lawyer, says the FBI performed properly.

"They certainly had probable cause to indict him," he said.

7
A Worthy Opponent

If CI-3 agents involved in trailing Smith cared that he was acquitted, they concealed it well.

"That's the way our system works," one told me. "A judge or a jury decides guilt or innocence."

But it's one thing to lose a case and another to find a traitor within the ranks. On October 3, 1984, FBI counterintelligence agents from Los Angeles arrested Richard W. Miller, an FBI counterintelligence agent based there. After becoming sexually involved with Svetlana N. Ogorodnikova, a Russian émigrée who was a KGB agent, Miller had given her and her husband a classified document outlining the types of intelligence information the U.S. seeks. In return, he demanded $50,000 in gold and $15,000 in cash.

The FBI found out about Miller when agents began investigating Ogorodnikova, who visited the Soviet consulate in San Francisco on a Saturday even though she was ostensibly not connected with the Soviet government.

CI-3 agents took Miller's treason personally. It was the first time in the history of the FBI that an agent had been arrested for espionage. To function in the FBI, one must be able to rely on one's fellow agents. An agent who runs away when breaking down the door of an armed fugitive, or who leaks sensitive information to the other side, is a liability not only to the bureau but to his partner and the other agents in the office. Then, too, the specter of having a spy within the bureau tarnished the image of the FBI and of each of its agents.

When Thomas Patrick Cavanagh read the news of Miller's arrest in the *Los Angeles Times,* he saw something else in it entirely. Cavanagh was an engineering specialist at Northrop Corp.'s Advanced Systems Division in Pico Rivera, California, where he worked on the Stealth bomber. Although he was making $40,000 a year, he was at least $25,000 in debt. Two years earlier, he had divorced his first wife and remarried. He was paying $200 a week to support his two sons. His sister in Arizona had just divorced as well. To help her out, he had agreed to pay her $200 every three months. On top of that, his mother was going blind. Her pitiful calls were driving him crazy. He dreamed of being able to buy a home, where she could come live with him.

Cavanagh picked up the paper in his apartment at 10700 Downey Avenue, a two-story stucco building in Downey, California. He read the Miller story with fascination. At work, there were always jokes about selling classified material to the Russians. As he read the story, Cavanagh thought, "Things must be getting bad. Even the FBI is doing it."

An idea began germinating, an idea that would culminate in a case that the Senate Select Committee on Intelligence has called one of the six potentially most damaging in recent U.S. spy history.

In the opinion of many top FBI counterintelligence officials, all spies are slightly wacko. Cavanagh fit the description, although not in appearance. Cavanagh looks like the all-American hero. Six feet, four inches tall, he has blue eyes, a clear complexion, and lustrous black hair parted in the middle. At forty-one, he walked with the easy grace of the athlete he once was. Attending school in Brooklyn, New York, and then Uniondale, Long Island, Cavanagh played basketball and later tried out for the New York Nets.

Yet Cavanagh always had a chip on his shoulder, going back to when his father, a newspaper photoengraver, favored his younger sister over him. When it came time for her to go to college in 1962, his father found it was no trouble to finance his sister's education. But to his son, he said he didn't have the money even to send him to a state school.

Cavanagh came to accept the idea that life is unfair and that there was a stigma attached to being male. But his resentment against authority manifested itself in other ways.

Cavanagh began working at low-level jobs at Long Island electronics companies. When he got his draft notice in 1963, he enlisted in the Navy, where he learned electronics. But he often railed against the mindless regimentation of military life.

"You had to fold your clothes a certain way, and if they found a hair on your shirt, they'd mark you down," he later complained.

Yet Cavanagh was gung-ho on the Vietnam War and signed up for three tours, from 1963 to 1967. It was only later, after he saw the south overtaken by the north, that he came to feel that the entire war had been pointless—that the real heroes had been those demonstrating against the war.

Cavanagh reached the rank of petty officer third class. During his last tour, he was stationed in Long Beach, and when he left the Navy, he decided to stay in California. By this time, he had gotten married, and he enrolled at Cerritos Junior College in hopes of eventually getting a bachelor's degree. Instead of finishing school, he began working in the aerospace industry: first at North American Rockwell Corp. on the Apollo program and then at Hughes Aircraft Co. on the F-14 and F-15 fighter planes.

At the Hughes plant in El Segundo, California, Cavanagh resented having to punch a time clock and got into trouble over being late for work. He would complain that the parking lot was too far from the plant, but then acknowledge that he was purposely late because he felt hostility toward his boss.

One supervisor found him high-strung and temperamental but manageable. Another recalled a heated argument that almost ended in physical violence. He seemed to want to test the system to see how far he could go.

In 1981, a headhunter called Cavanagh and told him of a job at Northrop paying $100 more than he was getting. The company was impressed not only by his thirteen years in the business but also by his self-confidence and ability to sell himself. He was given the title of senior engineer.

Cavanagh's "secret" clearance was transferred from Hughes to Northrop, and he began working on the MX missile. In January 1984, he was transferred on loan to Northrop's Advanced Systems Division in Pico Rivera. His supervisors were glad to get rid of him. They had decided he was more trouble personally than he was worth technically.

In his new job, he worked on the Stealth bomber, a combat aircraft so secret that the military to this day doesn't admit that there is such a thing—even though by now it has been well-publicized. When a Stealth plane crashed near Bakersfield, California, on a night training mission, the Air Force told civilian controllers that it was a different plane. The Stealth is designed to fly undetected by radar, a trick partly produced by the plastic and other materials used to make the plane and partly by its shape. The plane's wings are rounded, and in place of a normal tail it has two small fins canted toward each other.

Cavanagh complained constantly that others were being promoted while he was unfairly kept back. One supervisor thought he had an inflated view of his own capabilities, but decided he might respond to additional responsibility. Cavanagh was promoted to lead engineer, which meant he was in charge of developing tests of all equipment on the ATF.

Other workers who bowled and played softball on company teams with Cavanagh were only vaguely aware that he was going through a divorce and having financial problems. In fact, his money situation was getting out of hand. He could barely pay the interest on his loans, which included balances on two MasterCard accounts and five Visa accounts. He had just been hit with a $500 bill for federal taxes he should have paid the year before. His checks were beginning to bounce, and Lucky Stores, where he shopped, was refusing to take his checks.

Cavanagh was devoted to his two sons. When they were smaller, he had coached their Little League baseball team. Now he saw them once on weekends and three more times on week nights. His second wife resented the amount of time he spent with them; this exacerbated the frictions they had over money. They continued to keep separate checking accounts, and they argued over which bills should be paid from whose account. Meanwhile, his first wife tried to make him feel guilty if he missed a visit with his two sons. And his mother, faced with the prospect of going totally blind, was calling and talking irrationally.

Cavanagh's greatest fear was that Northrop would find out about his financial problems and fire him as a security risk. He had been amazed that the company had not uncovered the problems during a routine check in 1982. He now had "secret, special access" clearance, which meant he could work with "top secret" material on a limited basis. Now Northrop was checking on him to see if he should be given "top secret" clearance.

Cavanagh knew he was in deep trouble.

Meanwhile, Ismaylov had returned for another tour in the U.S., and FBI Special Agent Michael Grogan decided to take a look at his new assignment. The GRU had arranged for Ismaylov to live in a two-bedroom, $600-a-month apartment on the fourth floor of Wildwood Towers, a bleak brick building on a hill at 1075 South Jefferson Street in Arlington. GRU officers live in northern Virginia so they can be closer to the military. They are usually clustered in one of three or four different apartment houses so they can socialize among themselves.

Three other Soviets lived in Wildwood Towers, a ten-story building populated by government employees and retired people. The Soviets are model tenants, always pleasant, never noisy, yet aloof from other residents.

The day after Ismaylov arrived on October 11, 1984, Grogan and his partner, Al Zupan, drove up in front of his building at 6:30 A.M. A native of Yugoslavia, Zupan is as gregarious as Grogan is quiet. The two are inseparable. Because they both like to eat crusty bread, their colleagues complain that they leave FBI cars full of crumbs.

Members of the GRU squad like to tell about the time "Zooman" greeted a GRU man who had been assigned to him on his first tour. Returning for his second tour, the Russian arrived at his apartment house from the airport at four in the morning. Outside, Zupan was sitting on the hood of his FBI car, munching on freshly baked Vienna bread. Recognizing him from several years before when Zupan had been assigned to him, the GRU agent scurried off in a different direction. Undoubtedly, he was thinking, "Oh, no, not you again."

Besides getting a feel for Ismaylov, Grogan hoped to convey the message that he was no threat to him, like the policeman who teaches fourth-graders about Officer Friendly. Grogan was convinced the GRU feared their own KGB—which polices other Soviets and infiltrates the GRU—more than they feared the FBI.

If there were a need to tail Ismaylov surreptitiously, other agents or lower-paid members of the FBI's Special Support Group would do the job. They might pose as joggers, derelicts, skaters, priests, or secretaries. And instead of using FBI cars, they would employ anything from skateboards or bicycles-built-for-two to moving vans, bulldozers, or helicopters.

At 7:30 A.M., Ismaylov strode out of his apartment house. Grogan was impressed. He seemed trim and confident. Grogan liked to have a worthy opponent. Some of the Soviets assigned to him in the past had been heavy smokers or alcoholics. Grogan himself is so down on smoking that when he picks up a matchbook at a restaurant, he explains to the hostess that he doesn't smoke but likes to collect matchbooks.

Ismaylov climbed into the 1983 blue Chrysler LeBaron that the military office had assigned to him. Parked in the lot on the left side of the building, it bore State Department diplomat tag number DFC-195.

Ismaylov waited for his wife and son to leave the building and climb into the car.

From reading FBI files, Grogan already knew a lot about Ismaylov and his family. The FBI's files are, in fact, many files. The ones at headquarters—6.5 million in all—summarize the ones at the field office. At the Washington field office, the main files spill over most of the tenth floor. Arranged by tens of thousands of individual names, they are stored in vertical blue, beige, and pink file cabinets. Separate rooms on the tenth and eleventh floors house indexes to the files, listings of sensitive sources, and "top secret" files.

From reading the files, Grogan knew that Ismaylov had been a squadron navigator and staff officer in the Soviet Air Force. He played squash with other Russians at an embassy court, and he and his blond, attractive wife, Nina, had two children, Dimitri, eighteen, and Igor, thirteen.

Only the younger son had been allowed to come to the U.S. To discourage defections, the Soviets require children over fourteen to stay in Russia. So they'll have a large bank account to come back to in Moscow, the Soviets also withhold half their diplomats' salaries.

Grogan followed Ismaylov from two or three cars behind. Ismaylov crossed into Washington on Memorial Bridge. He dropped his son at the new Soviet Embassy complex known as Mount Alto at 2601 Tunlaw Road NW, which is protected by two-story-high electronically operated gates with signs that say "No Trespassing." Then Ismaylov let Nina out near the Soviet consulate at 1825 Phelps Place NW, where she did clerical work. Finally, Ismaylov parked the car on Belmont Road near Tracy Place and entered SMO.

Many times, Grogan's surveillance of GRU agents ended as they entered the new Mount Alto embassy, and each time the U.S. government's sellout to the Soviets galled him, as it did the other members of CI-3. At night, the new Soviet Embassy complex at Mount Alto looks like an abandoned spaceport, with its white buildings and its towering mercury vapor lights that give off an unearthly glow. A self-enclosed minicity of restaurants, hotels, offices, apartments, health clubs, and a car wash, the embassy is scanned constantly by infrared cameras operated by the Soviets.

But what makes Grogan and other CI-3 agents see red is not the embassy's forbidding appearance. The embassy sits on Mount Alto,

349 feet above sea level. After the Washington Cathedral, this is the second highest point in the city. The location—about a five-minute drive from SMO—gives the Soviets a panorama of Washington.

From their perch, they have an unobstructed view of the Pentagon, the State Department, the White House, and the CIA. Theoretically, laser beams trained on the windowpanes of those agencies could pick up vibrations from within and transmit back more than chatter from office parties.

High above Washington's electronic clutter, the Soviets can tune in on secret communications between Air Force One and the White House, or between the Pentagon and the National Security Agency.

The Soviets can—and do—listen in from their nest on most microwave communications, which include most long-distance calls and facsimile and data transmission circuits as well as many local calls. The site offers an unobstructed view of several key microwave relay towers that transmit most telephone and data transmission communications between Washington and other major cities. In fact, placing the embassy at Mount Alto was like handing the Soviets a leased line to each telephone exchange in Washington so they could tap telephones.

Using computers, they can hone in on calls of interest—ones placed between particular telephone numbers, for example, or those mentioning "Trident" or "CIA." By briefly listening in on a sampling of calls, they can choose which ones to transcribe in Moscow.

Besides gleaning information on U.S. defense capabilities, the Soviets monitor calls to find out which U.S. officials with access to sensitive information might be having financial difficulties that they can exploit.

Conversations about marital breakups, child support payments, or overdue debts are clues that the Soviets use quite extensively to target Americans for possible recruitment, according to FBI sources. At other times, the Soviets use a more direct approach, checking bankruptcy court records for names of employees of sensitive government agencies, then targeting their phones so they can zero in on their problems and lifestyles. When the stranger sitting next to the targeted employee at a bar turns out to be a friendly KGB officer, it is no accident. The KGB man comes fully prepared to help the man out of his financial imbroglio, perhaps offering $10,000 for the first set of classified documents and additional sums thereafter.

In the long run, the U.S. government's decision to give the Soviets the Mount Alto site may be almost as damaging to U.S. security interests as the possibility that the KGB temporarily overran the U.S. Embassy in Moscow in 1986, according to some intelligence sources.

"It's a very desirable location," a former National Security Agency official told me. "The higher the antenna is, the more you can pick up. The benefit [of the Russians' location] is access to any microwave link. You can record it and listen later."

Discussing Mount Alto on the phone, one former member of the President's Intelligence Oversight Committee from the Carter administration said, "I daresay they can hear our conversation if they want to."

And James Geer, the FBI's assistant director for intelligence, said, "We have long recognized the significant implications of their occupying that particular piece of ground as far as their ability to make technical collections."

"It's the most serious, single institutional Soviet threat in the U.S.," said a former high-ranking CIA official, referring to Mount Alto.

Because of that, FBI counterintelligence agents do not give out their direct dial numbers. They would rather inconvenience people by having them go through a switchboard than take a chance that their number might leak to the Soviets at Mount Alto.

Meanwhile, in Moscow, the Soviets have placed the new U.S. Embassy in a lower section of the city and so riddled it with electronic bugs that it is thought to be a giant antenna. While the Soviets were doing everything right, it seems, the U.S. was doing everything wrong.

When a spy makes off with sensitive information, all the forces of government are brought to bear to apprehend and convict him. Yet when it is the government that is at fault, nothing happens. The fact that the Soviets have been blessed with the quintessential listening post in the nation's capital has provoked no outpourings of concern from the administration and only a few murmurs of dissent from Congress. Nor is it a simple matter to pinpoint how or why the U.S. government engaged in the biggest giveaway since the Indians sold Manhattan Island to Peter Minuit for twenty-four dollars.

The story involves a member of Congress who did not care to have the Russians as neighbors, Presidents from both parties who preferred not to upset the Soviets, and the same bureaucratic lassitude that impels the government to pay $640 for toilet seats and $9,606 for Allen wrenches.

Almost since the U.S. and Soviet Union established diplomatic relations in 1933, each has wanted to build a larger embassy in the other's country. The Soviets occupied an ornate home at 1125 Sixteenth Street NW, built just after World War I for Hattie Sanger Pullman, widow of the designer of the first practical sleeping car. The Americans occupied an old apartment house on Ulitsa Chaykovskovo in central Moscow.

By 1963, the Soviets thought they had a suitable site in Washington—the Bonnie Brae estate owned by Nathaniel H. Luttrell Jr., heir to the Woodward & Lothrop department store fortune, at 6036 Oregon Avenue NW off Rock Creek Park in Chevy Chase, Maryland. But the property was zoned for residential use, and the idea of a Soviet embassy enraged the neighbors. When the District government granted the Soviets a zoning change, the neighbors went to court. In 1964, a U.S. District Court judge overturned the decision.

The Americans, meanwhile, were eager to move out of the embassy on Ulitsa Chaykovskovo in central Moscow. The Soviets proposed that each country lease government-owned land for their respective embassies. That way, neighbors in the U.S. could not object.

When the Veterans Administration moved its hospital from Mount Alto to larger quarters on 50 Irving Street NW in 1965, the General Services Administration notified the State Department that the 12.8-acre plot was available. In 1966, the State Department broached the idea to the Russians. They were not overjoyed. They had wanted a quieter, more residential neighborhood.

Enter Richard W. Shear, a former Marine who describes his tastes as running to "young women and old whiskey." At fifty, Shear, a real estate broker, retains his soldier's crewcut and rock-hard muscles. At the time, he was working for Weaver Bros. and looking for a buyer for Tregaron, a magnificent, red-brick mansion at 3100 Macomb Street NW in Cleveland Park. Joseph E. Davies, a former U.S. ambassador to Moscow and a former husband of Marjorie Merriweather Post, had died, and Davies's three daughters wanted to sell it.

When he read about the State Department's plan to lease the Mount Alto site to the Soviets, Shear met with the Soviets at their embassy on Sixteenth Street NW and proposed that they buy Tregaron instead. During the negotiations, Shear met with the Soviets thirty times. A former intelligence chief of an artillery battalion in the Marines, he became convinced that the FBI or CIA was following him because of his frequent meetings with the Soviets.

One night, Shear got home from duck hunting and noticed a light shining from a small attic window in his apartment house on Q Street in Georgetown. When he unlocked his door, he heard a shuffling noise in the attic.

Shear later recalled, "I said, 'I'm sick and tired of the sons of bitches,' and got out my twelve-gauge shotgun and slammed the action—whoomp! whoomp! All of a sudden there was a stampede up there. I tried to head them off but they got away," apparently through a rear entrance to the apartment building.

After a year of negotiations, the Soviets agreed in principle to buy Tregaron. The State Department was willing to approve it, but only if key members of Congress went along. The most important member was Representative John J. Rooney, a Brooklyn Democrat who lived at 3228 Woodley Road, just two blocks up the road from Tregaron's rear entrance at 3029 Klingle Road.

Pink-cheeked and balding, Rooney was the crusty head of the House appropriations subcommittee with jurisdiction over the State Department and Justice Department budgets. With his tirades against "striped-pants entertaining," Rooney struck terror in the hearts of State Department officials.

Shear met with Rooney off the floor of the House. The meeting was brief.

"I'd rather have a nigger living next to me than a Russian," Rooney told the broker.

That was the end of Shear's efforts.

In October 1967, the Soviets accepted Mount Alto as their second choice. At the time, 80 percent of all long-distance calls traveled by microwave rather than wire. Because of the curvature of the earth, microwaves require repeaters every twenty-eight miles. The fact that the Soviets could easily intercept long-distance calls was well known.

By then, the search for new space in Moscow had taken on new urgency. Offices were spilling into other buildings. The State Department wanted to get the locations for both embassies approved—and fast.

"What I was terribly interested in was getting a new embassy for us. We were living in a rabbit warren," said Malcolm Toon, who had just returned as ambassador to Moscow and was then director of Soviet affairs in the State Department.

In a recent official briefing paper, the State Department maintained that U.S. intelligence agencies were asked for their comments on the proposed Mount Alto site. No objections were raised, according to the State Department.

"My recollection is we vetted this to the intelligence community," Toon said. "While some said we would prefer another site, they said we could live with it."

But officials who were with the FBI, NSA, and CIA at the time tell a different story.

"The NSA wasn't even given the privilege of commenting on it," a former high-ranking NSA official said. "Hell, we've known about the interception of microwaves for thirty years."

To this day, neither Toon nor Dean Rusk, who was then Secretary of State, see the Mount Alto site as a problem.

"All this Mickey Mouse stuff was not considered a central problem because the technology is such that it doesn't make that much difference," Rusk said.

"There are other ways of doing it, and I'm not going to go into it," he said, apparently referring to the fact that the Soviets listen in from their seven other establishments in the city.

FBI sources say that while the Soviets listen in from other locations, none gives them the range and access of Mount Alto.

As techniques for sorting massive data from electronic communications became even better, the foolhardiness of giving the Soviets Mount Alto became even clearer. Subsequent administrations could have reversed the decision. But it was a time of détente, and no one wanted to upset the Soviets. More to the point, the State Department wanted a new embassy in Moscow without delay. Traditionally, the State Department has never been terribly interested in security. People apply to work at State because they are outgoing and like making friends, not because they want to conduct investigations.

In 1969, just after President Nixon took office, the U.S. signed the Embassy Sites Agreement, giving each country an eighty-five-year lease on its respective site. The Americans got a site next to the Moscow River, one of the lower points in the city. In 1972, the Nixon administration and the Soviets signed a second agreement governing how the Mount Alto construction was to proceed.

The new embassy was designed by John Carl Warnecke and a

Soviet architect. The complex was built of white marble in two phases. The first section, to the right of the complex as one looks at it from Wisconsin Avenue, is the living component with a school, a clinic, a social club, and a pool. The second phase, to the left of the complex, consists of a two-story reception hall, an eight-story administration building, and a three-story consulate.

The reception building includes the ambassador's residence, six reception rooms, banquet facilities, an auditorium, a greenhouse, two halls, and a banquet hall. The administration building houses the offices of embassy personnel. The underground level has parking for sixty-two cars and a car-repair and car-wash facility. The consulate has a projection room, conference library, offices, and visitor parking.

The apartments have 160 units, from studios to two-bedroom units, plus twenty suites for visitors. There is parking for eighty-five cars. The adjoining building of two stories contains the club, a school with eight classrooms, medical facilities, a gym, and a pool.

The way the embassy was finally constructed tells a lot about spying and counterspying in Washington.

When Sharon Credit heard that Whiting-Turner Construction Co. was going to build the second phase of the Soviet Embassy, she asked if the Towson, Maryland, company needed an interpreter. Then twenty-two, she had majored in Russian studies at the University of Pennsylvania and spent five months in Moscow as an exchange student. The daughter of an architect, she had worked as a clerk at the construction company the previous four summers.

Whiting-Turner hadn't given much thought to the need for an interpreter, but when she applied, the company hired her.

For the next two and a half years, Credit wore a hard hat as she ran interference between the Soviets and the Americans. Five feet, two inches tall and weighing ninety-eight pounds, she stood out on the site not only because she was the only female in a sea of two hundred to three hundred men, but because of her eating habits. While the construction crew brought lunch pails filled with hefty meat sandwiches, Credit ate yogurt or an apple. But appearances can be deceiving. Credit has a handshake like a trash compactor.

Credit was often the fulcrum of disputes between the Soviets and the Americans. Ever since the Soviets had found electronic bugs in the first phase of the project—including one in a toilet partition—

they insisted on inspecting every inch of material that went onto the site. At any given time, eight people were assigned to observe the construction, and nothing moved on the site without their approval.

So that listening devices couldn't be mixed in before it hardened, the Soviets refused to allow precast concrete to be used unless it was formed at the site. Windows and door frames were taken apart and put back together at a cost of $180,000. Instead of using the usual thin marble slabs glued onto backing, the Soviets wanted two-inch thick marble with no backing. That way, bugs could not be hidden in the epoxy glue holding the two pieces together.

Normally, structural steel is installed as soon as it arrives on a construction site, but the Soviets wanted to X-ray it overnight. So they paid $40,000 to $50,000 extra to have it delivered a day early and stacked up on the ground.

Even after these precautions had been taken, the Soviets spent three months moving X-ray equipment over the skin of the consulate, looking for bugs, which they found in abundance.

Nothing could enter the site unless the Soviets had been told at least a day in advance that it was coming. This led to endless frustration when deliveries came early, or when the markings on the materials didn't quite match what the Russians had been told to expect.

It was Credit's job to explain to the Soviets that "mortar" marked on bags was really the same as the "cement" that they had been told to expect. Brand names had to be translated into generic names. And Credit had to explain slight deviations in procedures because of weather conditions or changed schedules before the Soviets would give their approval.

"Sometimes the Soviets wanted to chew someone out, and they would drag me along," Credit said. "They got irritated if it wasn't done their way, even if it was done by the drawings," she said.

"The biggest problem was getting their okay. They took a two-hour lunch break every day. They wouldn't be seen for two hours. I kept trying to push them to come back, or we'd have to work around it," she said.

For the most part, the Soviets and Americans worked smoothly together. At the end of a particularly heated meeting, the Soviets broke out vodka. And they gave the workers bottles of Stolichnaya at holidays. The American workers were surprised that the Soviets were like everyone else. The Soviets asked the Americans where to find stereos or girls.

One day, a painter cleaning his brush painted a hammer and

sickle on a wall, then painted over it. Within an hour, the Americans had escorted him off the site, and he was never allowed back in.

"You could have gotten away with it anywhere else," Robert Dunn, project manager for Howard P. Foley Co., the electrical contractor on the job, said of the incident. "On a sensitive job, it was a stupid thing to do. Every crew was schooled: 'This job is different. We're not here to antagonize these people. We'll show them we're a class act.'"

The construction people didn't have to worry about security. When a young man broke into a Whiting-Turner trailer one night looking for calculators, the Soviet security guards apprehended him and called the police, reportedly after beating him up.

To many of the Americans, conditions on the site seemed to mirror U.S.-Soviet relations. When some incident caused strain between the two countries internationally, the workers would find that they were subjected to more security checks. On several mornings, they arrived to find the gates to the site locked.

"It was a microcosm of the cold war," said H. Russell Hanna Jr., a principal of EDAW Inc., which did the landscape design for the project. "The relationship would go from friendly to cool, from cool to friendly."

Sometimes, he said, "It would take a half hour to get a photo for an ID on each visit. It was tit for tat."

Meanwhile, from apartments all around the site, one of the FBI's squads that focuses on the KGB took video film of the site as construction progressed. Every month, Warnecke, the architect, viewed the tapes at the FBI's Washington field office to help pinpoint changes in design or new Soviet inspectors.

It was not hard to tell who the KGB agents were. They were the ones who hovered around in hard hats but knew nothing about construction terminology.

Every few weeks, a U.S. Army helicopter flew over the site taking pictures. When that happened, everyone naturally looked up. The result was that U.S. intelligence agencies got good shots of them.

When the Mount Alto embassy was finished in May 1985, it had cost $65 million, or $119 a square foot. It was built on time and within a half of one percent of the original budget. In contrast, the American Embassy on Ulitsa Konyushkovskaya so far has cost $190 million, or $271 a square foot. The cost overrun has been $100 million, or 111 percent. The embassy has yet to be completed, and now it appears the U.S. may abandon it.

The Soviets are not supposed to occupy the second phase of the Mount Alto project until the U.S. Embassy is finished. Meanwhile, their embassy remains on Sixteenth Street. But some sources say they are using the buildings in the second phase of the Mount Alto complex anyway. The listening equipment is located on the top floor of the residence, hidden behind windows that are always shuttered.

In contrast to the U.S. Embassy in Moscow, which leaks and is plagued by floods and by falling concrete and plaster, the Soviets got an embassy that is so well built its roofs are warranted against leakage for ten years.

To this day, the U.S. could call it quits, withdraw from the agreement, and start both embassies from scratch. Indeed, that is exactly what intelligence advisory boards composed of citizens have advised several Presidents.

"There were objections from the early 1970s by NSA, the CIA, and the FBI," said James E. Nolan Jr., a former FBI counterintelligence official who is director of the State Department's Office of Foreign Missions. The office was established by Congress in 1982 to better coordinate the construction of foreign embassies here.

"The Nixon administration and others made political judgments to go ahead. They could have abrogated. Even the fact you signed an agreement doesn't mean you can't impose other restrictions—even revoke the agreement and take whatever consequences there are. You're always free to break it and pay the penalty. The intelligence [oversight] boards have opposed it under Nixon, Carter, Reagan, and probably Ford, too. But it's equally true that they have never made a case convincing enough to have the President change it," Nolan said.

Instead of moving the Mount Alto embassy, first the Carter and then the Reagan administration elected to spend billions of dollars to install scrambler phones at federal agencies and lay underground cable.

Yet that does not solve the problem, either for the government or for private citizens. Inevitably, said a report in September 1986 of the Senate Select Intelligence Committee, government employees and contractors working on secret projects will discuss sensitive information on unsecured phones because it is easier.

"We just got snookered," said Senator Daniel P. Moynihan, the New York Democrat who is a member of the intelligence committee.

To which point a Soviet Embassy spokesman responds, "We

were given this land by mutual agreement with the U.S. government."

Meanwhile, the Soviets have already installed deep-dish antennae in several of the buildings they occupy at Mount Alto and are listening at this moment, according to U.S. intelligence sources.

While the Soviets are good neighbors ("The children are so well-behaved," said a woman who lives next door to the complex), some 40 percent of the embassy's personnel are said to be engaged in snooping.

Like $640 toilet seats, the government considers the Soviets' superior position to be a fact of life.

"Of course, if I could pick it up and move it, I would," said the State Department's James Nolan. "But given the options, no one has felt we should start again."

To CI-3 agents, the location of the new embassy is a persistent sore spot and symbolic of the tensions that arise between the FBI and the State Department.

"The State Department thinks we're cowboys, and we think they're stuffed shirts," said a CI-3 agent.

Occasionally, the disputes threaten to surface in the press, as when O'Keefe tipped the U.S. Customs Bureau that an Aeroflot flight originating at Dulles International Airport might be carrying high-technology, defense-related electronic equipment out of the country.

O'Keefe and six other members of CI-3, along with fourteen Customs agents, boarded Aeroflot Flight 316 at 5:00 P.M. on May 12, 1981, and seized some equipment. But just before they boarded the plane, a Soviet unloaded some items into a van. O'Keefe believed those were the goods he had been told to look for. Still, the Customs agents found three high-technology items that were not supposed to be taken out of the country. In an action that was never publicized, Customs cited the Soviets for illegal exporting practices. Yet the State Department sent two furious officials out to the airport to chew out O'Keefe and the agent in charge of the Customs Bureau search team. The State Department had not been notified of the planned action, and it created an international incident after the Soviet government accused the agents of using brute force and filed an official protest with the U.S. government.

As O'Keefe's job dangled, White House spokesman Larry Speakes assured reporters, "This has no connection with our foreign policy. It was not directed by the Department of State." Meanwhile,

State and the Customs Bureau each referred reporters' inquiries to the other, while an FBI spokesman said the investigation was being handled by the Customs Bureau.

After President Reagan praised the Customs' agents actions in a letter, the heat on O'Keefe subsided.

As fall turned to winter, Grogan tried to develop as much information on Ismaylov as he could. He pored over transcripts of wiretaps and reports from other agents and agencies. But the best sources were people—known as assets—who knew Ismaylov or had contact with him.

To develop them, Grogan played a little game. If he knew Ismaylov had talked with a woman at his pool, the barber down the street, or the waitress at a pizza parlor, he introduced himself and asked if they had seen any Soviets.

"Come to think of it, I have," they would say.

With their baggy clothes, accents, and tax-exemption cards, Russians were easy to spot.

Grogan would ask them to call him if they saw the Soviet again. From photographs, he could get them to identify the individual.

Grogan had left his card in bars, restaurants, filling stations, and stores all over Washington, and employees routinely called him to report sightings.

He also got reports from secretaries who answer a special FBI number that citizens can call to report the locations of cars with "DFC" tags. The FBI discreetly distributes cards listing the number. While this program produces a lot of junk information, it sometimes pinpoints patterns.

As Grogan learned more about Ismaylov, he sensed that he would not be a potential recruit. He seemed hard and ambitious, interested mainly in rising within the GRU and not at all interested in America or Americans. Even when taking his family to the country for picnics, Ismaylov checked out the area to determine where he could locate drop sites. If there was a sensitive side to this man, Grogan never found it.

Ismaylov had attended military officers' school and received three years of training at the GRU Academy in Moscow. That compared with Grogan's fifteen weeks of training at the FBI Academy plus counterintelligence training while on the job.

FBI agents never had to be lawyers or accountants, and today only a quarter of them are. New applicants must be U.S. citizens between twenty-three and thirty-five years of age. They no longer have to meet a height requirement but must fall within certain weight limits. Applicants are chosen in order of their combined scores on an interview and aptitude and judgment tests. Consideration is also given to useful experience in previous jobs. Even a previous career in the diamond business, for example, could turn out to be useful in an investigation of diamond thefts.

Once accepted, they are sent to the FBI Academy and sworn in as agents. Upon graduation, they receive a badge, gun, and credentials.

The FBI receives more than 8,000 agent applications a year. In the most recent fiscal year, 431 were accepted. Of the FBI's 9,220 agents, 4 percent are black and another 4.5 percent are from other minority groups. Nearly 8 percent are women. Because of a recent increase in the number of agents needed, the training program has been compressed to thirteen weeks.

Visitors to the academy at Quantico, Virginia, find FBI agents can assume any number of disguises. In the past, some of the window washers and janitors have been trainees conducting discreet surveillance. One day, Vincent P. Doherty, then the academy's feisty comptroller, was showing the facilities to official guests. He happened to match a description of the perpetrator of a bank fraud given to a training class. A trainee spotted Doherty and gave the usual warning: "Freeze, FBI!"

Saying he was giving a tour, Doherty told the agent to "get lost."

Whereupon she flipped Doherty, who found himself lying on the carpet.

Even though the FBI's training was relatively short, Grogan felt that what counted in the end was smarts. He knew that if Ismaylov beat him, it would only be because Grogan had not been imaginative enough to outwit him.

Toward that end, Grogan was willing to use any tool that presented itself. In evaluating Ismaylov, he asked for help from a psychiatrist, who read background material about him and agreed he was not likely to come over to the American side. Routinely, Grogan used powerful photographic and sound surveillance devices that Ian Fleming never dreamed of for James Bond.

Grogan even kept an eye on the biorhythm charts that Zupan loved to generate on his Apple computer.

Zupan pointed out that Ismaylov had several minor car accidents on days when he was listed in his charts as "critical." These are the times, based on birth dates, when emotional and intellectual strengths are supposed to be at an ebb. Maybe biorhythms are sheer nonsense, but Grogan insisted on examining every clue he could find to gain insight into this man.

8 "We Know Who You Are"

A month after Ismaylov's arrival in the U.S., in the fall of 1984, Barbara Walker, the former wife of now retired Navy warrant officer John A. Walker Jr., called the Boston field office of the FBI. Scorned by her former husband and trying to support herself and one of her daughters on a job at a gift shop, she had wanted to turn him in for years. Ever since 1968, when she inadvertently discovered his activities, she had known about Walker's spying. She had even accompanied him on two trips to northern Virginia to leave documents at "dead drops."

For Walker it had begun in January 1968. He was depressed over his unhappy marriage, his boring job as a Navy communications watch officer, and his mounting debts from a restaurant he had opened in North Carolina. Making his fateful decision, he drove north from Norfolk, Virginia, to Washington, D.C., parked his car near the Soviet Embassy at Sixteenth and L streets NW, and sauntered in, he later told the FBI.

By his own account, he took with him a "top secret" list of key settings. It would enable the Soviets over a period of thirty days to decode messages sent by the Navy's KL-47 cipher machine. Impressed, the Soviets gave him $2,000. He asked for $1,000 a week for more information, and they agreed. His first drop would be the next month in a locker at National Airport. An hour later, he was bundled between several Russians in the backseat of a car that sped away from the rear of the embassy.

Each day, dozens, even hundreds, of people enter the embassy. Many are staff members, while others are delivery and repair people and official guests from the U.S. and other governments. While the FBI has a surveillance post across the street, keeping track of each of them would be an impossible task. In the past, U.S. citizens who have been questioned by FBI agents after leaving the embassy have complained to members of Congress that their constitutional rights were infringed upon. To begin an investigation, the FBI needs some reason for suspecting that an individual is up to no good—what FBI people like to call a "predicate."

It would be seventeen years before the bureau got what it needed, and then it took three months before it realized what it had.

Several times, Barbara Walker had started to call authorities, then hesitated, always afraid of him and of what his exposure might do to their children. Yet just recently, Laura Walker, one of their daughters, had urged her to do it.

Now, sipping vodka, she told the FBI clerk who answered the phone on November 17, 1984, that her former husband had been supplying the Soviets with classified material since 1968. The clerk referred the call to an agent in the FBI's Hyannis office. He interviewed her and was unimpressed. As she rambled on, she downed one glass of vodka after another, and her words were slurred. Her story seemed dated. She had not lived with Walker for ten years. And she made no secret of her hatred for her former husband, who was living with a pretty blonde young enough to be her daughter. Probably the FBI's greatest slipup was to send an agent with no experience in counterintelligence work. He therefore failed to recognize that the details she cited were genuine signs of a Soviet spy operation.

The agent could have obtained more corroboration by interviewing Laura Walker, who was also aware of her father's activities. Instead, he wrote up the report and recommended that it not be pursued. As a result, the FBI almost missed catching Walker.

In New York, after trying for two years to develop evidence that could be used to charge the Koechers with espionage, the FBI had found out a lot about the spy team's personal lives but very little about their spying activities.

From bugs and surveillance, the FBI knew, for example, that on Sunday, June 3, 1984, Hana Koecher ran in Central Park, went to a sauna, took in a museum, made quiche for dinner, watched *60 Minutes*, and read. On Tuesday, June 5, she and Karl Koecher went to the Whitney Museum. On Wednesday, June 6, she baked bread. The following week, on June 15, they visited another swinging couple in Westchester County and lounged around their pool in New Paltz, New York. The next day, they went to Rock Lodge, a nudist colony in New Jersey. At other times, they went to Pine Tree Associates, a nudist camp on 108 densely wooded acres near Annapolis, Maryland.

The transcripts of their activities show that when other swingers came to visit them, Hana would go into the bedroom with their male guest, while Karl went into another room with their female guest.

The transcripts account for what happened next with the terse description: "Sounds of sexual intercourse."

In June 1984, the FBI learned that the couple was planning to leave the U.S. and live in Austria. As Koecher later admitted, he was entitled to a generous pension as an officer in the Czech Intelligence Service, along with a promotion and other honors for his successful work as a mole.

To friends, Koecher explained his decision by saying he could get a good price for his apartment and live comfortably in Austria.

". . . We are seriously preparing ourselves to move to Austria," he wrote on June 26, 1984, to a relative there. "The time is right: we can now sell our property in America very favorably. . . . It is hard to believe that we have finally decided, isn't it? At times, it is hard for us to believe it ourselves. But it is true."

By now, the FBI was convinced that Koecher was responsible for compromising Ogorodnik, leading to his death. Reviewing the material Koecher had access to at the CIA, CI-3 agents who interviewed CIA officials realized he had probably given up hundreds of sensitive items.

Yet so far, the FBI had no proof. The fact that Koecher had been seen engaging in "brush contacts" with Czech intelligence agents as recently as a month earlier, and that his wife, Hana, had been seen engaging in "brush contacts" and filling "dead drops," was circumstantial evidence. Presumably, people do not go to the trouble of spending hours "dry cleaning" themselves and passing messages in the woods unless they are passing secret information. Yet presumption is not fact. Until the FBI could catch Koecher passing classified information to the Czechs, it had no case against him.

For the bureau, it was a classic dilemma, one that it faces all the time, particularly in the counterintelligence field. Bank robbers do not normally try to escape to foreign countries. Even if they do, the countries where they go normally have extradition treaties with the U.S. The Communist countries where spies go not only have no extradition treaties with the U.S., they are also accessories to the crime.

This leaves the bureau with two choices: it can let the suspect flee, opening itself to criticism in Congress and the press that it did not do enough to catch the spy before he left. Or it can arrest him without having sufficient probable cause, knowing the case in all likelihood will be thrown out of court, tarnishing the bureau's reputation for bringing spy charges that stick.

The FBI had patiently watched the Koechers for two years. Now the FBI's Czech squad decided to move in on Koecher and his wife. From electronic intercepts, the agents knew the Koechers had already sold their co-op. They were planning to leave for Zurich on an 8:00 P.M. flight from John F. Kennedy International Airport on November 27. Still lacking any evidence to arrest him, they decided to make a desperate attempt to buffalo him into confessing before he was gone for good.

From watching Koecher's activities, Kenneth M. Geide, who had until recently been the agent in charge of the Koecher case, knew that the only way to get Koecher to talk would be to catch him when he had no other plans for the day. Koecher hated to have his schedule interrupted. Given the size of Koecher's ego, Geide knew the other crucial requirement was that he be treated deferentially.

For several weeks, he and Jerry G. Brown, chief of the CIA's security analysis group, had been planning what approach to take—where they would confront him, what time of day, where they would try to interview him, and what they would say. Since there is usually no physical evidence, espionage is one of the most difficult crimes to prove. Often, the interview is the only way to get a conviction. Frequently, psychiatrists and psychologists are brought in to give advice on what approach to take. In addition, Justice Department and FBI attorneys normally review the approach to make sure it does not violate the suspect's rights.

If there is probable cause to believe the suspect committed a crime, the agents will arrest him, and he must be warned right away of his right to have an attorney and to remain silent. If there is no probable cause—as in Koecher's case—and the suspect winds up confessing, the confession will be ruled involuntary and therefore inadmissible as evidence if it was obtained through promises or threats.

In the Koecher case, no Justice or FBI attorneys reviewed the approach, nor were Justice Department attorneys told about it until after the fact. If they had been informed, the problems that later arose could have been avoided.

Geide decided that the morning of Thursday, November 15,

1984, would be the ideal time to approach Koecher. Karl and Hana had made a profit of $218,000 from the closing of their co-op, and they had a 10:00 A.M. appointment at the bank that day to wire the money to a bank in Zurich. Just two days earlier, Koecher had written to one of their swinging friends laying out in meticulous detail his plans to build a home in St. Valentin, Austria. He assured them that he and Hana would continue to see them in Austria and in the U.S.

". . . in all probability we will now be coming to the U.S. the same way we used to go to Europe, which was, more or less, once a year," he wrote. "I believe that it would be a damn shame to let so old a friendship fade out. It happens faster than one would expect, and for that reason, it is, in my opinion, good to write a few lines now and then, even if there is not much to write about. It is not the actual information that matters that much . . . as the continuity of the contact and affirmation that you care to stay in touch," he wrote.

After the appointment at the bank, Hana would probably walk to work, the agents figured. Karl had no other plans for the day.

At 10:45 A.M., Geide and nine other agents watched as Karl and Hana walked out of the bank building at 9 West Fifty-seventh Street. Karl was carrying a black Samsonite attaché case. Karl and Hana chatted as they walked east to Fifth Avenue and turned south toward the diamond district.

As other agents followed in cars, Geide and two other agents followed the Koechers on foot a block or two away. On Forty-seventh Street, they saw them enter the Diamond Club Building, where Hana's office was. Two agents waited in an Impala parked up the street near Fifth Avenue. Another agent sat right behind them in a Bonneville. Other agents pretended to window shop across the street.

When Karl came out of the building alone at 11:15 A.M., Special Agent Joseph Downs was standing on the sidewalk outside. Downs had been chosen to make the first approach because he and Koecher knew each other from working out together at the Ninety-second Street YMHA. First impressions are important, and if the first contact with Koecher was by someone he knew, he would immediately let his guard down.

"Hello, Karl. I'd like to introduce someone to you," Downs said.

"Hello, Karl. I am Ken Geide, a special agent of the FBI," Geide said.

"Karl," he continued, "I am aware of your plans for the future, and in view of your past communication with the FBI, and in view of your past employment with the CIA, I think that perhaps we should talk."

"I think we should, all right," Koecher said.

Koecher was calm, as if being approached by the FBI were an everyday occurrence.

"Well, I have a place, Karl, where we could go and talk that is convenient and where we won't be disturbed, and where we could go right now if you have time," Geide said.

"Yes, sure, I am not doing anything right now," Koecher said.

"Good. I have a car that can take us there," Geide said.

Geide signaled to Special Agent David Craddock, who was in a third car, to drive to the curb where they were standing. Mistaking his signal for a summons, a cabdriver drove up and stopped. Geide waved the cab away.

Geide opened the rear door of the FBI car, and Koecher climbed in.

Craddock took the microphone of the car's two-way radio and transmitted a coded message to Special Agent Susan A. Chynoweth: "The male package has been picked up."

Geide had been promoted to a job at headquarters, and Chynoweth had recently become the agent in charge of the case. She was at the Barbizon Plaza Hotel at Fifty-eighth Street and Sixth Avenue, where the FBI car was headed.

As they weaved through New York traffic, Downs asked Koecher if he was still jogging, and they discussed the YMHA. So there wouldn't be any problems at the hotel, the agents had arranged to use the hotel's service entrance and the service elevator, which would be operated by the hotel's manager.

They got out at the twenty-sixth floor and walked to room 2640—one of a series of rooms the FBI had rented under a phony name.

"I'll see you, Karl," Downs said as Koecher and Geide entered the room together.

Geide had made sure the room was up to Koecher's exacting standards. It was a two-bedroom suite with a dining area and a balcony that looked out on Sixth Avenue and Central Park.

Already in the room was the CIA's Jerry Brown, sitting on one of two overstuffed love seats. He asked Koecher if his pipe bothered him. Koecher said it did not.

As Koecher sat on the other love seat and a video camera secretly recorded the interview, Geide began in a friendly, confiding tone. But what he had to say was anything but friendly.

"I think we should establish one thing," he said. "We know who you are and what you've done since you arrived in this country. Um, in other words, your association with the, as we would term it, the opposition, hostile intelligence services, and we don't really wanna sit and discuss that. We, we just wanna establish right away that we do know who you and who your wife are, and your activities on behalf of those folks over the years.

"With that established," Geide continued, "what we wanna do is talk about a proposition for you, and talk about your future—your future and your wife's future—and that future I think is gonna depend on what we accomplish today in our conversation with you. Umm, we think we have some things that will be interesting to consider as time goes on."

"Yes, yes," Koecher said.

Geide continued: "We appreciate who you are, and your abilities, and we would like to look at this as where we will mutually help one another and, uh, hopefully, as they say, as we go on, we will be able to make certain proposals to you that I think you'll find very, very attractive."

What he had in mind would cause no disruption to the Koechers' lives, Geide promised.

"But, uh, on the contrary, and in your, you know how things can happen? Certainly we don't want anything like that to happen to you and Hana," Geide said.

Geide did not specify what could happen to Karl and Hana. But he said that it would not happen if Koecher helped them fill in some "blanks."

"Okay," Koecher said.

Reiterating that what they had in mind would not disrupt their travel plans, Brown interjected, "Now what can you gain out of this? Ah, you can gain just, right at the present time—which would be very much in your favor—would be just a continuation of your life as it is."

"Uh-hum," Koecher said.

"Now, and I think under the circumstances, I think you would probably be elated with just that."

"Correct," Koecher said.

"And, I think you can look forward to a harmonious relationship, and we are not going to try to do anything which will harm you or Hana in any way or any of your relatives."

"I'll certainly go along," Koecher said, "certainly if you will."

"Well, we chose to do it this way. Certainly, there were a lot of other choices," Geide said.

"Because you know," Brown said, "if you leave, it could be a major thing and my God, the flaw. And you know something could happen, terrible could happen."

"Yes," Koecher said.

By now in the elliptical conversation, the agents had established that they were talking about using Koecher as a double agent. Apparently referring to what the Czechs would do if they discovered he was a double agent, Brown said he was giving him their assurance that Koecher would not be "out of one fire into another."

"I give you my absolute, guaranteed assurance right now," Brown said. "We can't run this that long; very short time, we will be through with it."

Brown asked if Koecher would still want to go to Austria, since it would be close to Czechoslovakia.

"I think I would," he said.

"Then let's do that," Brown said.

"It's a new beginning for you," Geide said.

"It's the way I also feel," Koecher said.

On that happy note, Koecher began giving the agents a detailed confession. He said he had been recruited by the Czechoslovak Intelligence Service in 1962 to get a job with the U.S. government, preferably the CIA. One of his first case agents was Kralik, the same man he later reported was trying to recruit him. He would meet with Kralik occasionally at Columbus Circle. Later, either he or Hana used "dead drops" or "brush contacts" to pass documents in Washington, Queens, Paris, and Prague. There were meetings as well at safe houses in Vienna and Czechoslovakia. During her trips overseas to buy diamonds, Hana often picked up money for Koecher from the Czech Intelligence Service.

When going to Prague, Koecher said, he had either slipped across the border or used phony passports. During his spy career, he gave the Czechs hundreds of classified documents, including a classified evaluation of Ogorodnik, as well as lists of CIA assets and employees and their photographs. He told the Czechs which CIA employees might be good targets for recruitment.

Koecher said he had a disagreement with his Czech handlers in the late 1970s but resumed being an active agent in late 1981. He said he used a one-way pad, a way of sending secret messages by code. As recently as 1983 and 1984, he said, the Czechs had communicated with him through documents hidden in a Listerine lozenge box. During the Christmas season in 1983, he said, he met with his case supervisor in Austria. In July 1984, he flew to Zurich to meet with his handler. Another meeting had been planned for March 1985. He boasted to the agents that in 1976, after ten years of service with the Czechs, he received decorations in Prague.

Over the years, he estimated, he had received $50,000 to $70,000 from the Czechs, in addition to the $20,000 bonus so he could buy his co-op. (Koecher told me he made up the figure, which was, in fact, much higher. "Money creates speculation about buying people," he said. "You don't have to pay people off. If you can take them to very expensive places and give expensive gifts—I didn't say I did or didn't. I'm not commenting on it. That's why the amount of money is important to know.")

At 2:30 P.M., the agents had lunch delivered to the room. Geide mentioned that Hana had been picked up by another agent and was being interviewed in an adjoining room. In fact, she was demanding to see a lawyer, and the agents with her were stalling her.

Brown suggested that Koecher write her a note saying he was cooperating and urging her to talk. Koecher wrote the note and gave it to Brown.

Late in the afternoon, Koecher agreed to take the first in a series of polygraph tests administered by FBI agents. While the tests indicated he was telling the truth when he said he was an agent of the Czechoslovak Intelligence Service, they showed he was not telling the entire truth about how much he gave away to the Czechs. This is quite common in spy cases; suspects invariably seek to minimize the extent of their activities and to confine their admissions to material they think their interrogators already know about. When an agent is sent by a foreign power to get a job in a sensitive agency, it is assumed that he will provide his handlers with virtually any classified material he can get his hands on.

On the phone, and then later that evening over dinner, Karl and Hana talked with each other with the agents present. Calmly, Karl urged her to help the agents. But she was distraught and tried to tell him to shut up.

"I understand your shock," Koecher told her. "You're worried, and you don't want to get into trouble."

"Well, I think you are in trouble," she said. "I don't think you see it even."

"What you have to understand is that we're gonna work together for the future," Geide said.

Hana said that if she didn't end up in prison now, she would surely have to carry something for Karl again.

"I delivered things," she said in tears. "That's all I can offer because I don't want to, to really be, I'm not a spy, I'm not by nature a spy. I don't ever want to be in my whole life."

"Hana, I promise you," Karl said. "If you don't want to be involved in anything, you will not be."

Hana insisted she would be sitting in prison for delivering Karl's messages. Perhaps, she said, Karl is really a "CIA man."

"This is it, this is true," she said. "I'd rather be in prison. If I have to go, I will go."

Brown insisted Hana would be free to go to Austria in two weeks.

"And I promise," Brown said.

"I don't think so! No! I don't think that I will be free. I don't think so. I will not be free," she said.

At Karl's suggestion, he and Hana slept in the hotel that night in separate rooms. Over the next two weeks, the interviews continued in the hotel and over meals at the Parker Meridien Hotel and the Essex House while the FBI kept the Koechers under surveillance. Koecher took the agents to his apartment and showed them a blue Mephisto pencil given to him by the Czech service for secret writing. The videotapes of his confession go on for fifty hours. Hana's last twenty hours.

Based on what Koecher had said, Geide drew up an eight-page confession, which Koecher corrected and signed.

In the first four minutes of the interview, Koecher had said enough to warrant his arrest. Yet it was not until November 21—six days later—that he was finally warned of his rights by Special Agent James K. Murphy, then a supervisor of polygraph examiners. At the time, Koecher signed a form stating that no promises were made to him, he was not threatened, he knew he had the right to remain silent, and he did not want a lawyer. But later, at lunch, Koecher told Geide that he thought Brown had promised that nothing would happen to him if he posed as a double agent for the FBI.

"I would hate to find I was double-crossed," he said.

In fact, Koecher told me later, he made up some of the admissions. The Mephisto pencil, he claimed, was simply an ordinary colored pencil made by Mephisto. He and Hana laughed when relating how Geide had believed that a book sent to him by the editor of a Prague publishing house might be used for secret codes.

"You see, I knew a certain writer when I went to the film institute," he said. "We had a conflict because he married a woman I was dating, and he just took her over from me. Then he wrote some novels. Somebody who knew about the whole thing sent me the book with his picture. I got part of it. The FBI made it disappear. The woman who sent it to us—the senior editor of a publishing house—sent me another copy and another copy. She wrote me letters: 'What's happening?' I never got a copy of it. I asked the Post Office, and that made them [the FBI] even more suspicious. Later, I asked Geide about it, and he admitted he made it disappear."

Koecher dismissed book codes as outmoded. As far back as the American Revolution, spies have used copies of the same book for communicating in code. Certain letters stand for other letters; certain figures represent specific words or names of individuals.

"I've never used it in my life," he said, offended that anyone would think he was so stupid. "At one time, it was the normal way. It is a one-time pad in a way. But the book can be found. What if it's disposed of? Why use a code at all when people go places? There are so many ways to communicate in the U.S. A book code is clumsy. That's the way any intelligence agency would operate. Simply take advantage of the lifestyle. People have two-way radios in their cars, people use wireless phones. You could even use a cellular phone, a cordless phone."

What's more, he said, he was free to travel to other countries to exchange information.

"It's perfectly normal for Americans to travel. That would be the easiest way to communicate in my opinion. You can do it fast. You don't even have to go to that country. You can meet, you can have a brush contact somewhere. Switch attaché cases. By God. This is so easy. A book? You have to be really dumb to think of that."

The Koechers had made previous plans to drive to Hewitt, New Jersey, for a last Thanksgiving dinner in America with Czech émigrés on November 22. Geide and Chynoweth offered to drive them. On the way, they discussed how the agents' presence would be explained when they dropped them off. Koecher decided he would say they were friends who were going to another dinner in the area.

Koecher commented that the Czechoslovak Intelligence Service has no female agents.

"They only have a female chemist," he said.

The host, Dr. Miro Paroulek, a veterinarian from Czechoslovakia, and Dr. George Kukla, a Czech geologist who was a friend of Koecher's, noticed that Karl drank a little more than usual at the dinner. Feeling expansive, Koecher referred to Hana several times as his "guardian angel."

The next evening, Koecher decided to jog one last time in Central Park.

"Of course, the FBI had to run with me," he said. "It was what we call an open tail. But I did want to run. I wondered how fast they would change into shorts and running shoes, and if they would have it ready."

According to Koecher, the FBI tail—a man and a woman—were jogging along behind him within five minutes after he left his apartment.

"When you really follow someone you have to have all kinds of clothes, for good and bad weather. You have to bring running shoes and shorts," he said.

"But the young lady wasn't much of a runner. About halfway into the run around the reservoir, she had a hard time breathing. So I heard her say, 'I can't run any more. What shall I do?'

" 'Well, I'll pick you up later,' the other agent said.

" 'I'm afraid,' she said."

On Sunday, November 26, 1984, an FBI supervisor from headquarters called John L. Martin, the chief of the Justice Department's internal security section, at home. In his former career as an FBI agent, Martin, who stands six feet, three inches tall and has rugged good looks, helped bring to justice members of the Ku Klux Klan who murdered three young civil rights workers in Mississippi in 1964. After transferring to counterintelligence and becoming a supervisor at FBI headquarters, Martin entered private practice as a lawyer.

In 1971, he rejoined the government as an attorney in the internal security section of the Justice Department. In 1980, he took over as chief. As such, he has been a vigorous advocate of prosecuting spies legally, without violating their constitutional rights and without engaging in cover-ups.

Over the years, he has successfully fought off government officials who tried to suppress prosecutions on the grounds that too many secrets would be exposed and those who have advocated arresting spies when there is not sufficient evidence to bring a conviction.

In part, the apparent increase in spy activity in recent years reflects a conscious decision during the Carter administration by the Justice Department, under Attorney General Griffin B. Bell and Martin, to prosecute cases rather than keep them secret for fear of revealing sensitive information.

In 1978, for example, the CIA and the Pentagon strenuously objected to prosecuting William P. Kampiles, a former CIA watch officer. Kampiles sold portions of a "top secret" technical manual on how to use the product of the KH-11 "Big Bird" surveillance satellite to a Soviet agent in Athens for $3,000. The satellite is capable of photographing billboards from hundreds of miles in space and tricking the Soviets by transmitting its data up—to another satellite—instead of down to earth as expected. The Soviets therefore thought it was a "dead" satellite.

"If there were two secrets in the country, that was one of them," a former intelligence officer says of the KH-11's workings.

Bell took the issue of prosecuting Kampiles to President Carter, who decided in favor of prosecution.

In 1980, the CIA again argued against prosecuting David H. Barnett, a former CIA officer who had been in charge of CIA operations in Jakarta. While another squad was in charge of the case, CI-3 agents happened to be the ones who finally arrested Barnett. He got $92,600 for giving the Soviets the identities of a group of CIA informants and letting them know that the CIA—through Operation HA/BRINK—had found out how to control the guidance systems for their SAM missiles. As a result, HA/BRINK was compromised.

The fact that the Soviets already knew that Barnett had given them the information did not deter CIA officials from insisting that Barnett should be let go. Somehow the CIA felt any public discussion of the case would damage the agency and its operations.

Very often, said a former Justice Department official involved in the case, the CIA simply wants to avoid the embarrassment that comes with publicity about its penetrations. Other CIA officials sincerely believe that *any* information about their operations can only help the other side, a throwback to the days when the CIA's headquarters in Langley, Virginia, were marked by a sign saying "Federal Highway Administration."

"The intelligence community had come to believe that every time you prosecuted a spy, you would lose the secret, and that it was better public policy—the best of two evils—to let the spy go and keep the secret," Bell said. "But I had the idea that you could prosecute these cases without losing the secret."

"The old school was you don't tell anyone anything," said an FBI supervisor. Before 1975, according to FBI sources, the FBI uncovered a number of highly damaging spy cases that never came out because of the secrecy policy.

Those that did come out were often mishandled. Between 1950 and 1975, 39 people were arrested for espionage. Nineteen were acquitted, had their convictions overturned on appeal, or were sent back to the Soviet Union without a reciprocal trade.

Frequently, the CIA's insistence on secrecy is to hide its own lax security, according to several high-ranking FBI and Justice Department officials. For example, during the prosecution of Kampiles, the CIA could not account for an additional thirteen copies of the manual he gave to the Soviets. Either the individuals who had signed them out did not know where they were, copies had been destroyed without keeping proper records, or no one had signed for them.

The CIA found that one of the copies had been signed out to George Bush. Bush had left as director of the CIA a year earlier, in March 1977.

George Hart, Bush's deputy press secretary, recently quoted Bush as saying that he never received the manual.

"The Vice President had no involvement in it," he said.

Whether someone on his staff might have signed it out and failed to return it, or whether the manual was sent to Bush but never received, is not known. What is clear from the incident is that the CIA kept about as good control of the "top secret" manuals as a public library keeps of its romance novels.

Even after the policy change initiated under the Carter administration, the government still occasionally declines to prosecute some spies rather than reveal anything about the operations they were reporting on. Beyond the fact that spies are now being prosecuted, the FBI has become more effective at detecting spying, helped by an increased number of defections, a larger counterintelligence budget, and a sharper focus.

"I believe, and the people with whom I have consulted believe, that there is both more espionage going on now, number one, and number two, we've gotten a lot better at detecting it," said Associate Attorney General Stephen S. Trott.

In 1982, Congress approved an increase in the FBI's counterintelligence budget of more than 20 percent spread over five years.

"We have a hell of a lot more resources than before," said Donald Stukey, chief of the FBI's Soviet section and a former supervisor of CI-3. "Also, the training has improved. We've gotten more professional than before."

The fact that the public is more aware of espionage as a problem because of the prosecutions has helped uncover more espionage, he said.

Normally, Martin and his staff of sixteen attorneys (including some who handle registrations of foreign agents) are kept informed on major spy cases as they progress so they can offer legal advice. Unless an agent witnesses the commission of a felony, the FBI cannot make an arrest without the approval of the local U.S. Attorney. In espionage cases, no arrest can be made without the approval of the internal security section. Yet the call from the FBI supervisor was the first time Martin had heard anything about Koecher.

Martin later said that he was shocked by what the supervisor told him. Apparently the FBI and CIA had no clear idea of what they were trying to do with Koecher. They didn't seem to know whether they wanted to turn him or obtain a confession so they could prosecute him.

When Martin later viewed the videotapes of the interviews with Koecher and his wife, he was even more appalled. Geide and Brown appeared to be offering Koecher immunity from prosecution—something they had no right to do. Hana Koecher had asked if she was entitled to a lawyer and had been told there was no need for one.

To Martin and his staff, it was clear that Hana could not be prosecuted for espionage. The case against Koecher also seemed weak, but Martin thought his confession after Murphy warned him of his rights could still be used against him in court.

Martin later said that the fact the FBI and CIA had not notified him earlier and had handled the case improperly was another example of the confused thinking that sometimes pervades the intelligence community.

"It's a product of the hermetically sealed atmosphere of secrecy which unfortunately propels them into action without an appreciation of the legal consequences," he said.

In lectures to new agents at the FBI Academy in Quantico, Virginia, Martin often cites what the FBI styled the "Cruise Missile Case" of 1977. Working themselves into a frenzy, FBI counterintelligence officials at headquarters had decided Carl Lutz Wieschenberg and Carl John Heiser III had been trying to steal the secrets of the Cruise missile and sell them to Cuba or East Germany.

"We have arrested two enemy agents," the FBI announced after their arrest on July 20, 1977.

But after sifting through the results of the FBI's fifteen-month investigation, Martin and his staff saw no hint of espionage. While he was out of town, Justice finally approved indictments charging the two businessmen with conspiring to export navigation systems without an export license.

Even that charge was eventually thrown out by the Fifth U.S. Circuit Court of Appeals, which complained that the 3,500-page trial record and more than six hundred exhibits "have very little to do with the alleged conspiratorial agreement. . . . Our task is to seek a kernel of wheat from this veritable mountain of chaff."

The court concluded that the evidence in the case "is as consistent with a plan to export with a license, a legal act, as it is with exportation without a license, an illegal act."

"In order for us to meet the challenge of espionage, all we have to do is do our jobs right," Martin has told government investigators.

On November 26, 1984, the Koechers had a last swing with their favorite couple. The couple—call them Tom and Marjorie—live in New Paltz, New York. With white hair and a tanned face, Tom looks like Cary Grant. Marjorie has blond hair cropped short, with skin like something from an Ivory Soap commercial.

Tom and Marjorie told me they met the Koechers at a swinging party in New Jersey in 1981. Hana, fully clothed, was sitting on a sofa. Tom sat down beside her. After introducing himself, they went up to a bedroom and engaged in sex.

Marjorie, meanwhile, talked with Koecher but did not have sex with him. However, they exchanged telephone numbers. Tom and Marjorie subsequently invited them to a "straight" Christmas party. After half an hour at the party, however, the Koechers left. Apparently, Koecher was dissatisfied with the people.

"Maybe people weren't paying attention to him," Marjorie thought. "He wanted to control."

Despite his behavior, Tom and Marjorie found Koecher fascinating, while Hana was warm and engaging. They accepted the Koechers' invitation to dinner at their apartment, which was furnished in contemporary style. The living room had a blond, built-in bookshelf and liquor cabinet, beige carpeting, and dark brown modern sofas. Koecher's den had a sofa bed and 2,000 books arranged alphabetically.

That night the two couples began a swinging relationship. As a rule, Karl and Marjorie went to Karl's den and had sex, while Tom and Hana stayed in the master bedroom. After having sex, they each rejoined their own spouses for the night. They saw each other at least once every other month.

When the Koechers visited Tom and Marjorie in New Paltz, they usually stayed for the weekend. The home has no number in front and no mailbox like the other houses on the street. Tom and Marjorie give directions by telling visitors to turn into the sixth driveway on the right after a stop sign. The house itself is set back behind an apple orchard and flanked by a pond and a swimming pool.

The Koechers introduced Tom and Marjorie to nudist camps, and now they run around without clothes most of the time, as does their eighteen-year-old daughter.

Koecher told Tom and Marjorie about orgies he and Hana had attended in Washington and about Plato's Retreat in New York. He called Washington the "best sex city in the world." He also took Tom and Marjorie to the Hellfire, a New York club where members mainly watch deviant sex acts—men dripping hot wax on women's breasts, for example.

"It was total degradation," Tom recalled. "They put on a show with a great deal of homosexual activity. There were little rooms where homosexuals would have sex. You could observe them and walk around. There were women there in subservient positions, kissing guys' feet. There were a lot of men dressed as women. They looked like women but were actually men."

While Tom and Marjorie were not as impressed by the Hellfire as Koecher appeared to be, they found swinging with the Koechers to be satisfying.

"Sex was very important to him, and he performed very well," Marjorie said of Koecher. "He was warm, he was considerate, he was all those things." Tom thought Hana was "very loving. Of the women I was involved with, she was the best."

Neither felt any jealousy and claimed swinging improved their own relationship by introducing change and excitement.

Koecher was interested in having affairs outside of swinging and had asked Marjorie to see him alone at his apartment. She did it once. For that reason, Tom thought Koecher was more interested in swinging than Hana.

"His theory was he could persuade anyone to swing," Marjorie said. "He didn't think it would be any problem. I think he had a nerve to say that."

When Koecher was alone with Marjorie, he sometimes expressed dissatisfaction with Hana. She thought the comments were consistent with his negative outlook.

"He was like a spoiled child. Hana would just go out of her way to calm him down and cater to him and take care of his every wish," she said.

"Sometimes he was such an obnoxious bastard, you didn't want to see him again," Tom said. "He never wanted to go out anywhere. He wanted to eat here. We'd see a Mexican restaurant or a church barbecue. He wouldn't do anything like that. It had to be certain things. He was very conscious of what he put in his body. He was a real health nut. He took vitamins."

"It always impressed us as a mother-child relationship, with Karl being the twelve-year-old and Hana the doting mother," Tom said. "I never saw any woman so giving to a man."

Koecher told Tom and Marjorie that he was moving to Austria because he was disenchanted with the U.S. He claimed he was having trouble finding jobs, that Americans don't have the same respect for a Ph.D. as Europeans. Hana told them she didn't want to leave the U.S. but had to go with her husband.

A year before they left, Koecher had pointed to what he called a "peeping Tom" looking at them through binoculars from an apartment across the street from theirs.

"He laughed about it," Tom said. "Then we got binoculars and watched him. We thought he was just a guy in New York City. Then the apartment was empty, and we never saw anything more there."

"He said, 'Can you imagine? We've got a peeping Tom,' " Marjorie recalled.

Tom and Marjorie had a date to see the Koechers the same day the FBI confronted him. Koecher told them they were being followed but gave them very few details. They rescheduled their meeting to the night before they were to leave the U.S.

"On the last night, they were frightened to death," Tom said. "They didn't know if they were going to make it or not—if the FBI was going to double-cross them."

"They had already sent all their things from their apartment, so we went out to dinner," Marjorie said. "We walked from their Madison Avenue apartment to a restaurant. We were followed, so Karl told us. We sat down, and when another table opened up nearby, two people sat down immediately. I had the worst feeling. I felt I was being watched," Marjorie said.

"We walked back to their apartment. I was walking with Karl, and Tom was with Hana," Marjorie said. "Karl said, 'I wish I could tell you about it but I'm afraid to get you involved.' We went back to the apartment. Tom and Hana got together, and I was with Karl. Then we separated."

"He told me when he was with me that Hana was mad at him for talking to them [the FBI], but 'I think I read them right,'" Marjorie said. "Then he would be quiet and say, 'I hope I read them right. Yes, I think I read them right.'"

In the other room, Hana and Tom undressed but, Tom said, "I didn't do anything with her that night. I was trying to get some information from her. I still didn't know what was going on. She just giggled and laughed and changed the subject. I couldn't get two cents out of her. I said, 'Hana, what the hell is going on?' She said, 'It's a lot of baloney; the things they say are not true. It's better that you shouldn't know.'"

"It was nicely done," he said in retrospect. "She had street smarts. She could handle herself anywhere under any circumstances."

Indeed, Koecher's act was so good that Tom and Marjorie are convinced, in retrospect, that only Hana could have been a spy.

"He was just not clever enough," Marjorie said. "He was a very brilliant guy but he didn't seem to be capable of fooling anybody. She was."

"If anybody was tough enough, it was she," he said.

"I've seen him do everyday things and not be able to do them correctly. Hana was very capable. She could think a thing out immediately and do it immediately," Marjorie said.

During their last night together, the FBI faithfully noted on transcripts from electronic bugs that Karl had sexual intercourse with Marjorie. They noted that the couple left at 8:18 A.M. As the Koechers walked them to their car, Hana said, "We don't know if we're going to make it."

Tom and Marjorie made them promise to call collect from the airport to let them know they had made it.

They never called.

As promised by agents Geide from the FBI and Brown from the CIA, the Koechers' plans to leave the country had not been interfered with—not yet. Ostensibly, as a last goodwill gesture, Geide had offered to take the Koechers to the airport. In fact, it would be much easier to arrest them that way. Geide had told them to meet him at the Barbizon Plaza Hotel.

After getting out of a taxi, the Koechers walked into the lobby of the hotel with their suitcases. Their furniture and other personal possessions were to be shipped to Austria later. As they walked into the lobby, another agent asked them to go back outside to his car. There, Special Agent Paul Dembnicki told Koecher he was under arrest for espionage. Hana was arrested as a material witness.

Handcuffed, the Koechers were taken to the FBI office and then incarcerated at the Metropolitan Correctional Institution.

Saying Koecher had worked for the CIA from 1973 to 1975, the FBI announced the arrests to the press that day. The FBI said nothing about the fact that Koecher had continued as a CIA contract employee until his arrest. Frequently, the bureau summarizes the case against suspects for the press. In this instance, the FBI said Koecher had been recruited by the Czechoslovak Intelligence Service but gave no details about his activities. Similarly, the indictment prepared by the Justice Department cited acts Koecher committed in 1975, creating the impression the Koecher case was history. Most of the material in the case was sealed from public view.

The CIA had wanted it that way. Disclosing that the agency had been fooled by a mole who was still a contract employee was simply too embarrassing.

The story ran 448 words on page four of *The Washington Post* and 969 words on page one of *The New York Times*. In the next two months, the *Times* ran two longer, page-one stories on Koecher.

"It's hard to believe," Irving Peck, one of the Koechers' friends, was quoted as saying in a *Times* story just after the arrest. "He always talked about how he hated the Communists and what they were doing to his country."

Said Michael Reinitz, an executive for a Long Island printing company and a friend, "They said they wanted to escape Communism. Hana said her father was a Communist Party member, and I got the impression that she was rebelling. I never heard Karl say anything good about Russia."

"Spies, absolutely not," said Reinitz's wife. "They sounded like their allegiance was very much to America."

To this day, Dr. George Kline, who first met Koecher when he visited Prague in 1956, becomes agitated when he thinks about him.

"What was his motivation? Why did he do it?" he asked me over a beer in Washington. "I can't bring myself to believe that he was a devoted, fanatical Communist."

After seeing Koecher in handcuffs on the evening news, Tom and Marjorie asked the FBI if they should continue to be in touch with Koecher. The agents said it was up to them. They never really believed the Koechers were spies and continued to write to them. Koecher had asked if Tom and Marjorie would send him American shirts, and they were considering visiting the Koechers in Czechoslovakia. But during a recent interview that brought out more details of their spy activity, Tom and Marjorie realized that Karl really was a spy.

"I think we'll stay right here," Tom said of their plans to visit the Koechers in Czechoslovakia.

9

Stealth for Sale

The financial pressures on Thomas Cavanagh were now reaching crisis proportions. He began getting calls at work from credit card companies demanding payment. An attempt to get financial counseling in early December 1984 had not worked out; he was impatient with the forms he was supposed to fill out.

When the dunning calls came in, he tried to lower his voice, but he knew it would just be a matter of time before the other workers overheard and told his boss. After the third call, he decided he would sell Stealth secrets to the Soviets. He had always been impatient with classification restrictions anyway. Why did Northrop have the right to know where he was going on vacation trips, he had often wondered. In his years in the aerospace industry, he had seen spectacular squandering of taxpayers' money. In Vietnam, he had decided, the country sold out the 55,000 Americans who died there, all for nothing. The government was corrupt. Why shouldn't he sell out, too, he rationalized.

That evening, when his wife was away, Cavanagh wrote a letter to the Soviet consulate in San Francisco.

"I have Stealth information for sale," he wrote. The price: $25,000. (It cost the U.S. an estimated $7 billion to develop and build fifty-six of the planes.)

Cavanagh's handwriting normally slanted to the left, so in his letter he tried to slant it to the right. So he wouldn't leave any fingerprints, he carefully cradled the letter in a cloth as he folded it. He sent it by Express Mail.

In his letter, Cavanagh told the Soviets to drive up in a red car to the Skylark Motel in El Segundo. Several days later, he waited at the hotel for half an hour, but nobody showed up at the appointed time.

In a second letter, Cavanagh listed the names of forty subcontractors that had been approved to work on Stealth, along with their code numbers. He altered the list so the codes did not accurately match the names of the subcontractors. That way, he thought, the Soviets would have to pay him before they got an accurate list.

Cavanagh asked the Soviets to meet him at a hotel in Belfiore. Again, no one showed up.

Cavanagh did not know that Soviet diplomats are forbidden to travel outside of San Francisco or Washington without permission. Because of FBI surveillance of Soviet diplomats, the Soviets would have had to send an illegal, who would have no overt connection with the Soviets, or a diplomat from a Warsaw Pact country. Because Warsaw Pact countries place no restrictions on travel by U.S. diplomats, the U.S. does not restrict their travel in this country.

Persisting, Cavanagh called the consulate two days later, saying he wished to speak with a diplomat.

"Relating to what?" asked the woman who answered the phone.

"Some information I have," Cavanagh said.

"We don't need any information," she said, and hung up.

A week later, Cavanagh and his wife had a violent argument over money. Christmas was coming, and he felt guilty that he would not be able to give his two sons and his wife the kinds of presents he wanted to give them. To pay the bills, he was getting his paychecks two days early.

Cavanagh decided he would call the Soviet Embassy in Washington. From his Navy experience, he had a vague notion that Soviet establishments might be wiretapped. But like a driver who takes a chance by parking in a no-parking zone, he thought he wouldn't be caught.

Calling information in Washington from a pay phone, he was given the number of the embassy on Sixteenth Street. As the operator asked him to deposit his money, he asked to speak with a diplomat. There was a long delay, and Cavanagh got nervous and hung up.

The next day, he tried again. This time, the information operator gave him the number of SMO.

When Cavanagh explained that he wanted to sell information, the Soviet on the other end said, "We don't get involved in that."

Cavanagh quickly hung up.

On Thursday, December 6, Cavanagh decided he would call SMO after hours. Perhaps the possibility that the call would be monitored would be diminished then, and the Soviets less reticent.

Shaking with anticipation, he left work at two-thirty so he could call by three, before SMO closed at six, Washington time. As he picked up the phone at home, he looked at his watch. It said three fifty-five. Cavanagh asked for a diplomat and was immediately connected to a man with a thick Russian accent.

Referring to himself as "Peters," Cavanagh said he had information about the ATF and the MX missile. He said he would meet the Soviets at the bar at the Cockatoo Inn on Hawthorne Boulevard in Hawthorne, California, on December 10 around noon. He described himself as six feet, four inches tall with blue eyes. He said he would be wearing a striped blue shirt.

"Okay," the Soviet said.

That night, Special Agent Dixie Keith got a call at home. An FBI agent for seven years, Keith was one of the three female agents assigned to CI-3. In her early thirties, she is a knockout, willowy blonde. Close up, Keith is not fragile, but wiry. When she enters a room, she fixes her eyes on the people in it with an alertness that is more than curiosity, a spillover from the job. She grins the easy smile of southern hospitality, but offers a steel-grip handshake. With the male agents, she is cocky, swaggering. Asked at a party if the man with her is her boyfriend, she replied, "When I want him to be." She laughs easily and doesn't seem threatened by much of anything.

Although a woman in a male-dominated profession, she's not so feminist that she objected to being referred to in a magazine article as one of "two female agents."

"That's the only way our mothers would know it was us," she explained.

FBI agents are supposed to let their office know if they will be away from home for more than two hours, even on days off. They are to leave word on where they can be reached. Whether fishing in the Chesapeake or taking a transatlantic flight, they must notify the office that they will not be available so supervisors can call other agents in the event a major case breaks and more agents are needed.

Keith happened to be the agent assigned to any matter that might arise at SMO, duty that rotates every six months. O'Keefe reached her at her Washington apartment overlooking the Potomac River, where she was cooking dinner for her boyfriend, an Air Force officer.

"We've got a hot one," he said. "You'd better come on in."

As the case agent, Keith was responsible for making sure all leads were followed and doing the reports and paperwork from the Washington end, as well as coordinating with other offices.

Other agents working the next morning noticed the unusual activity. Keith was dictating reports, listening to a cassette of the call, and meeting behind closed doors with O'Keefe and others. But sensitive information is supposed to be compartmented as much as possible. If Keith brought up the case at lunch, other agents were all ears. But for security reasons, it was considered bad form to ask another agent what he or she was working on.

Keith notified the Los Angeles field office over a scrambled teletype circuit of the details of the call. Her message was sent "immediate," meaning that the message should be given priority over other messages and hand-carried to the special agent in charge of the office.

"You've got to make contact with the caller," she said in her message to the Los Angeles field office.

The Los Angeles office assigned Special Agents David A. Silva and Daniel P. McLaughlin to pose as Soviets and meet with "Peters." Both spoke the language, but neither looked Russian. Silva was distinctly Hispanic looking, while McLaughlin looked like an Irish wrestler. But lately, Soviets had taken to dressing like Americans, with Brooks Brothers suits, striped shirts, and short American haircuts. Very often, they could not be distinguished from the average U.S. citizen.

The day after his call to SMO, Cavanagh walked to the black, four-door filing cabinet next to his walnut-grain desk in area U300 of the Northrop plant. He twirled the combination and opened the cabinet, removing a document stamped "secret." It showed the silhouette of the ATF plane. He stuffed it under his leather jacket and walked out of the building, his heart thumping. Northrop security officers searched employees, but only sporadically. He thought he could tell when there would be a search.

Over the weekend, Cavanagh saw his sons as usual. He was nervous and having second thoughts. But on Monday, December 10, he showed up at the Cockatoo bar at 11:30 A.M. A heavy-set, blond woman was drinking at the bar, and they struck up a conversation. Twice, she got up and made calls on the motel's house phone in the bar. That seemed strange to Cavanagh. Was it just paranoia that made him think she was an FBI agent? He noticed, too, that the bartender didn't seem to know how to mix drinks very well. Of all things, there was a walkie-talkie next to the cash register.

Several times, he thought of bolting. But he needed the money.

After twenty minutes, no one had showed up, and he left and walked to his 1984 white-and-brown Chevrolet Blazer. As he was about to get in, a man walked up to him.

"Are you Mr. Peters?" he asked.

The man—who was agent Silva—suggested they go up to his room, where another agent was waiting.

Lacing his conversation with Russian words, Silva said, "You mentioned on the phone you had some information. Was it about the B-1 bomber?"

"It's the ATF," Cavanagh corrected him, then mentioned the two letters and two numbers that represent the code for the secret program. He said he had already sent something to "the western office."

"I also have access to the MX and the SR-71 Blackbird," Cavanagh lied, referring to a proposed missile that was supposed to move around the country on tracks and a sleek, manta-shaped plane that can fly four times faster than the speed of sound and photograph up to 100,000 square miles in an hour.

Cavanagh explained that he was up for receiving a "top secret" security clearance and would not get it if he didn't pay off his debts and "get the creditors off my back."

"So somehow we have to have an agreement, uh, on money," he said. "I need $25,000 cash for information, and it's that simple," he told them. "You get the cash, I give you the information.

"I'm after big money," he said grandly. "Before our relationship ends, I want to be independently wealthy."

But he said getting documents would be difficult. He mentioned the cases of William Holden Bell, who had been caught for selling documents to Polish intelligence officers; Christopher J. Boyce, the TRW employee who was caught for selling material to the Soviets in Mexico City (the falcon of *The Falcon and the Snowman*); and "the two people in Sunnyvale"—referring to James Durward Harper, a free-lance engineer, and his wife, Ruby Schuler, who sold documents on the Minuteman ICBM and ballistic missile research to Polish intelligence officers.

He said the only way to get information was to take out originals.

"You can't run your own copies in the plant," he said. "They got that regulated, too.

"One of you should come to my car and let me show you what I got," he continued, "and then we'll set up another meeting, okay?"

Silva walked with Cavanagh to his car, where Cavanagh showed him the document marked "secret." He suggested they meet again on Wednesday, December 12, at the Lucky Lodge in Bellflower, California. This time, he said, they should bring cameras to photograph the documents—and cash.

That afternoon, Cavanagh returned the document to his filing cabinet. Periodically, Northrop checked to make sure documents signed out to employees were in their cabinets. No one had come looking for his material. But later in the day there was a surprise audit, and Cavanagh seemed to other workers to be visibly upset.

"What are you messing around with me for?" he asked the security officer. "I served my time in Vietnam."

On Wednesday, he drove around the motel a few times before meeting the two agents in front. He noticed men sitting in trucks parked in the area, but decided he was becoming paranoid.

"So, how are you today?" Silva asked.

"Good. But a little nervous because, ah, getting the documents out is getting tougher and tougher and tougher," he said.

"Why tougher?" Silva asked.

"They're real security-conscious, and all that crap," he said. "Okay?"

"So you were scared," Silva said.

"Well, not scared," Cavanagh answered. "Just very careful and apprehensive. Is it possible to see money by Friday?"

"By Friday, I don't know. By Christmas," Silva said.

"Oh, God," Cavanagh said, thinking about the presents he wanted to buy.

"Oh," Silva said, "you have very, how you say, Merry Christmas. If documents are good."

"To be honest with you gentlemen," Cavanagh said, "I need it before the twenty-fifth for security reasons. I need that money. You have to understand my position," he said. "I feel like I can bring more documents out. I gotta have money, okay? And then I bring more documents out. I'll even bring more documents with me the day you give me the money. But I need that 'top secret' level, or I ain't gonna get nothing, you know. I'll stay at this access level. What I got, what I got now is 'top secret access,' not 'top secret' clearance, just access to what's going on."

"Okay, we do our best," McLaughlin promised.

Cavanagh gave them a document marked "confidential, special access required" and technical manuals, blueprints, and drawings marked "secret, special access required."

As the agents photographed the documents, Cavanagh said they would save the Soviets billions of dollars.

"I'm after big money, $25,000 is a drop in the bucket, believe me," he said. "We might lay low for two weeks and then do it again, you know," he said.

The agents said they would have to show the documents to their bosses before they paid Cavanagh. They set up a third meeting for December 18 at the Hyatt Hotel at 6300 Telegraph Road in City of Commerce, California.

Later that day, as he passed another worker's office at Northrop, he overheard someone say, "Are the federal agents still here?"

Cavanagh's heart stopped. Then he continued walking. Perhaps he had misheard, he told himself.

It was raining heavily on December 18. At their last meeting, the agents ran out of film. This time, they brought along a portable copying machine.

"So, ah, how do you do today," Silva asked. "Good to see you."

"Okay, okay. Any word on the cash?" Cavanagh asked.

"Oh, we got good surprise for you today," the agent said.

"Okay, okay. Am I gonna get it today?" Cavanagh asked.

"Da, da, yes," Silva said.

As the agents struggled with the portable copier, Cavanagh railed against Vietnamese who could get loans for fishing operations while he could not obtain a loan to expand his Amway distributorship.

He handed them several documents, including an entire twenty-page chapter from the ATF technical manual. The chapter listed both the composition of the plane and its specifications. Cavanagh knew that from the document, the Soviets could replicate the plane—a plane that had cost U.S. taxpayers $1 million an hour to develop and build.

At their first meeting, Cavanagh had noticed that the agents carried small guns tucked in their pants.

"No guns, no guns, all right, no guns," he had said to them.

When they showed up the second time with guns, he had said nothing. But this time he brought along a .45 caliber pistol in his briefcase. As he shuffled in the briefcase for documents, he purposely let them see the weapon.

He complained that bill collectors were calling him at work.

"It's demeaning, degrading, 'cause everybody knows your business, you know?" he said.

"Of course, must be problem," McLaughlin said.

"I'm bitter because I worked hard for the company, and sometimes politics plays a big role in getting ahead," Cavanagh said.

As the agents finished copying, they handed Cavanagh $25,000 in small bills. Eagerly, he counted it. He said he wanted to have monthly meetings, with substantial payments each time.

Just then, Cavanagh heard what sounded like loud banging from the room next door.

"It must be the maid, or perhaps the pipes," McLaughlin said.

Cavanagh opened the door to see what was going on. No one was there. He closed the door. But then he heard a knock on the door. As McLaughlin picked up his briefcase with the gun inside, Cavanagh opened the door again.

Three agents confronted him with guns drawn.

"FBI! Freeze, don't move!" one of them said.

Cavanagh saw his life pass before his eyes. He later told me he had wished he were back in Vietnam.

Koecher had been in prison slightly more than a month when he told his lawyer, Robert G. Fierer, that he thought the Soviets would agree to swap him for some major spies.

Fierer could not believe his ears. An Atlanta criminal lawyer, Fierer had had no experience with spies. He was from Pittsburgh, a Notre Dame graduate. He had represented such people as Larry Flynt of *Hustler* magazine when he was charged with selling pornography; Daniel Minchew, Senator Herman Talmadge's administrative assistant, when the Georgia lawmaker faced a Senate Ethics Committee investigation; and Tree Rollins, the Atlanta Hawk who hit Boston Celtic Danny Ainge during a heated game.

Just over six feet tall, with long blond hair and gold-rimmed glasses, Fierer drove a white Mercedes convertible and made his office in a restored townhouse that was once used as a museum for memorabilia from the movie *Gone with the Wind*. He often came to work in jogging shorts and dictated letters from his first-floor office, which was outfitted as a mock courtroom. Done in pastels, it was complete with a witness stand, juror's box, and judge's bench. Here, clients could rehearse their testimony in the appropriate environment and later watch their performance on videotape.

Divorced from his first wife and separated from his second, the forty-four-year-old lawyer had three children. On business trips, he traveled with Lisa D. Dillman, his attractive blonde legal assistant, and her mongrel dog.

Fierer had met Karl and Hana Koecher in the mid-1970s at a bar mitzvah given by a mutual friend in New Jersey. Beyond the fact that they had foreign accents, he noticed nothing unusual about them. After the party, the Koechers gave Fierer and his then-wife a lift back to New York.

Fierer had never met a CIA officer before, much less an agent of a foreign intelligence service. He pictured spies as reasonable, stable individuals. After all, he reasoned, wouldn't a foreign spy agency want to send its country's best people overseas? Koecher jarred that image. When Fierer began interviewing Koecher at the Metropolitan Correctional Institution under the Brooklyn Bridge, he found that Koecher was just the opposite of what he had imagined spies to be. He was testy and threw temper tantrums. He constantly berated Fierer and his then-partner, Steven A. Westby, for imagined failings. Indeed, he seemed unwilling to help his lawyers prepare his own defense. When Fierer learned through interviews with Koecher's friends about his sexual proclivities, he was even more appalled.

Some spy.

Several times Koecher and his lawyer almost came to blows after Koecher—unable to berate his wife, who was in another cell—began lashing out at Fierer, his strategies, and even his taste in clothes.

"Well, let me tell you something," Fierer shot back when Koecher pronounced that his taste in clothes was rotten. "You're the guy sitting here with an orange uniform. I'm not. I'm going home."

By spending three days with a former CIA official in Atlanta, Fierer had tried to bone up on the spy world. But it was not long enough for him to absorb the spy's byzantine thought processes.

Koecher himself never openly admitted to being a spy, but he made allusions to it.

"The KGB thinks highly of me," he once allowed. But he also claimed that, in the later stages of his career, he was not giving the Czechs secret documents but merely analyses. They insisted on receiving the papers through dead drops in the woods because they like intrigue, he had said, later making the same claim to the FBI.

Based on his claims and his lifestyle, Fierer decided Koecher must be a second-rate spy. Surely, he thought, the Czechs must have better people than Koecher. The fact that the CIA had hired him thoroughly confounded Fierer.

Sometimes Fierer wondered if Hana was the real spy and Karl was her cover. For all his degrees, he didn't have as much "walking-around sense" as Hana did. But when he told Koecher he planned to defend him by calling him a "second-rate spy," his client became nearly apoplectic.

What Fierer did not realize is that one has to be at least partly crazy to be a spy in the first place—to spend half one's life undercover in a foreign country, afraid of being caught and possibly executed. It was for love of country, and something more, a highly hazardous ego trip, perhaps. Spies may be just as dashing, erudite, and witty as the fanciful ones in spy novels—but they also frequently come with a few loose screws.

As for Koecher's claim that he was giving the Czechs unclassified analyses by using "dead drops," Fierer had no way of knowing that in the intelligence business agents do not spend hours running around in the woods unless they are dealing in classified documents. Contrary to Koecher's claims, the Czechoslovak Intelligence Service is considered one of the best in the world. To set up a system of "dead drops" takes weeks of effort. If the material were truly unclassified, it could have been passed along over hamburgers at McDonald's. The Czech Intelligence Service did not achieve its preeminent reputation by wasting its agents' time.

When I asked Koecher about his claims that he was merely doing analysis, he agreed that if the material he was providing were not classified, he could have mailed it.

Fierer realized there was much about the case he did not know and probably never would know. When dealing with Justice Department officials assigned to the case, he sensed an undercurrent that they were not telling him the whole story. He decided all the people involved—the FBI counterintelligence people, the CIA, the KGB, and the Czech Intelligence Service—lie for a living.

They just lie.

Yet for all his doubts about Koecher and his sanity, Fierer thought a spy swap was worth exploring. At the Metropolitan Correctional Institution, Koecher told Fierer in early January 1985 that the Czech government could not openly intervene on his behalf. After all, he was a naturalized U.S. citizen. Ostensibly, he had no tie to the Czech government. To intervene openly would be to admit he was a Czech spy. Instead, Koecher told Fierer he should broach the idea to the Czech government as a "humanitarian" gesture on behalf of his and Hana's parents, who were still in Czechoslovakia.

Koecher gave his lawyer detailed instructions. He told him to get in touch with Josef Nowadsczec in Prague, a lawyer in private practice. Fierer later realized that Nowadsczec represented the government.

"Point out that you're making the trip at Hana's request and in secret," Koecher said. "The chances of acquittal are, unfortunately, small. . . . Do not assure him that Karl and Hana are taking it well or that prison conditions are acceptable; point out that Hana's physical condition is very weak and that she suffers."

"The bottom line," Koecher told Fierer to say to the Czechs, "is that unless you get Karl off the hook before the trial, we will be forced to defend him in a manner which will be embarrassing to you both at home and abroad."

Koecher gave Fierer a letter for Hana's father, who was a member of the Communist Party. The rhetoric was in sharp contrast to the anti-Communist tirades Koecher had delivered during his twenty years in the U.S.:

"I agree that the action against us is a provocation, even if this is not quite the right expression: a provocation tries also to invite some response which would eventually be detrimental to the party which is being provoked," he wrote. "The action against us is, however, based on the assumption that there will be no response and that the U.S. government will get away with a gross violation of law and abuse of power with impunity."

Koecher was nothing if not inconsistent. Normally hostile toward his lawyer, he now wrote to Josef Pardamec, Hana's father, that Fierer was trustworthy.

He "belongs to those forces in the U.S. who are determined to oppose creeping fascism in public life and the misuse of political power to generate pro-war hysteria," Koecher wrote.

Fierer arrived in Prague with Westby, his then-partner, on January 30. The Pardamecs and Karl's eighty-eight-year-old mother met them at the airport. They took the lawyers to the Pardamecs' apartment, where they served them sandwiches, beer, and slivovitz at 11:00 A.M. Fierer thought they were trying to get him drunk so he would talk. In fact, they were just being hospitable.

At the lawyer's office in downtown Prague, Fierer and Westby met with Nowadsczec, a tall, heavy-set man whose hair was flecked gray about his temples. He agreed to help out by forwarding to the government a request from the Koechers' parents that the government intercede.

On March 21, 1985, the Czech minister of interior sent Fierer a letter saying the government recognized him as a "legitimate representative" in negotiating the release of the Koechers.

When Fierer told Koecher about the letter, the spy smirked. From the start, he had been confident that he would be sprung. Jail was not what he had expected it to be. He had struck up an acquaintance with Carmine "Junior" Persico, a member of the Colombo Mafia family who was about to be tried for racketeering, extortion, and bribery. He had nearly been killed by a Black Muslim leader and been saved by Sandy F. Alexander, a member of the Hells Angels motorcycle gang who was in jail on narcotics charges. Apparently, Alexander liked Koecher because he taught him to exercise in his cell. Several times, the Black Muslim had gone after Koecher with a pair of scissors.

"Suddenly they had a maniac running loose and threatening me," Koecher told me. "He says, 'Let's hang this mother.' It became very hairy."

But Koecher was nothing if not tough. When he heard from Hana that Fierer was talking with the U.S. Attorney's office in New York about a possible plea bargain in case the swap did not come through, Koecher sent Fierer a certified letter ordering him never to raise the subject again.

"I do not intend to, and never will agree, to any plea bargain which would require that I serve any time whatever in prison," he wrote from prison.

Hana, meanwhile, was released on bail after spending five months in prison. Citing the marital privilege, she had refused to testify against her husband and had been jailed for contempt of court. The Justice Department claimed the marital privilege did not exist when the spouse is also engaged in crime. Eventually, she won her point in the U.S. Court of Appeals. But meanwhile two of the Koechers' swinging friends had raised $1.2 million in bail money for her, pledging all their assets. The entire $218,000 profit from the sale of their co-op was being used to pay legal fees. After her release, Hana stayed with the swinging couples who had raised bail money for her.

One of their swinging friends said they never would have done the same favor for Karl.

"When Hana needed bail money, everybody ran to her defense," she told me. "But the people we spoke to said none would have done it for him. He was a very difficult man."

On May 1 5, 198 5, several weeks after she got out of jail, Hana wrote to President Reagan to protest what she called the "betrayal of my husband's trust" by the FBI.

"U.S. government officials asked Karl to demonstrate his commitment to the American cause by cooperating with them, and promised him safety and security. Whereupon they used his cooperation to arrest and indict him!" she wrote. In a sterling example of chutzpah, she added, "I am writing, of course, out of my love for Karl. And I am praying, Mr. President, that you would understand that I am writing also out of my love for America."

Fierer, meanwhile, was getting the runaround from the U.S. government. The Justice Department told him it would not consider a spy swap until Koecher was convicted. Fierer tried to go around the Justice Department by talking to people at State, but he later learned that Justice had told them not to talk with him.

For the first time, Koecher became glum about his prospects when he learned that twenty-five other spies had been swapped on June 1 2, 198 5. Among them were Marian W. Zacharski, a Polish businessman convicted in California on November 2 1, 198 1, for buying secret information about antitank missile and radar technology; Alice Michelson, a sixty-seven-year-old East German woman who pleaded guilty May 2 1, 198 5, to acting as a courier for the KGB; and Alfred Zehe, an East German physicist who pleaded guilty February 2 1, 198 5, to obtaining classified documents from a Navy employee who turned out to be a double agent.

It seemed to Koecher and Fierer that everyone who could be swapped for Koecher had already been exchanged. The latest spy swap had taken three years to negotiate. How much longer would it take to free Koecher?

When speculation began appearing in the press that the Soviets might agree to the release of Sharansky, who was serving a thirteen-year prison sentence for spying for the U.S., Koecher suggested to Fierer that the Soviets would swap him for Sharansky.

"I was hesitant [to suggest it] at first," Koecher said. "I was hesitant to pass a message about it when Chernenko was in office [as Soviet leader]. The man was a conservative. He was a caretaker. They were hardly inclined to establish precedents.

"The other reason why I was reluctant was despite what you hear about relations between Soviet Union and socialist countries, the

Soviets don't impose their ways on those countries, and vice versa. To confuse the Russian and Czech services is wrong."

Now Fierer was sure Koecher was crazy—a Machiavellian megalomaniac who thought he could be traded for the most famous Soviet dissident of all time. Nevertheless, on July 18, 1985, Fierer flew back to Prague and broached the idea to Nowadsczec. To Fierer's surprise, he said he would take it up with Gustav Husak, the then president of Czechoslovakia, after government officials returned from holiday in early September.

On September 10, Nowadsczec called Fierer to tell him Husak had agreed to propose the idea to the Soviets. Clearly, Koecher had friends in high places. Nowadsczec told Fierer to go to the Czechoslovak Embassy in Washington, a bleak fortress on a hillside just off Rock Creek Park, to receive further instructions. There, Czech officials gave the lawyer a list of others who might be included in the exchange.

Still stymied by the U.S. government, Fierer called the State Department's Czech desk in October. Expecting to get another brush-off, he was surprised when an official told him that Czech officials had met with State Department representatives, and the answer they got "should not have been discouraging to the Czechs." It was a diplomat's way of saying things looked good, and the first time Fierer had detected any interest in a swap from his own government.

Now the pieces were starting to come together. Wolfgang Vogel, an East German lawyer who had arranged spy swaps in the past, was taking up Sharansky's cause, along with Harvard Law School professor Alan Dershowitz. Unknown to Fierer, John L. Martin, chief of the Justice Department's internal security section, had been negotiating for three years to win the release of the dissident and others.

But it would be months before anything happened.

10 *"I've Got Him!"*

After moldering in the files of the FBI's Boston field office for three months, the report of the interview with Barbara Walker by a Hyannis FBI agent had been routinely reviewed. The agent who read it thought it was worth pursuing and sent a copy to the FBI's Norfolk field office, where John A. Walker Jr. lived, and to FBI headquarters.

Joseph Wolfinger, who was in charge of operations at the Norfolk office, jumped on the case and notified FBI officials at headquarters who are in charge of GRU counterintelligence that he would be pursuing it. Because Walker was a military man, the FBI initially assumed that the GRU would be handling him.

When Phillip Parker, deputy assistant FBI director in the intelligence division, read the report, he also recognized it as real. Barbara Walker's description of the drops made by her former husband in northern Virginia contained details of spy operations that she could not have picked up by reading spy novels.

Parker assumed that Walker, if still active, would continue to make his dead drops in the Washington area. He called William Warfield, then assistant special agent in charge of the Washington field office for counterintelligence, and told him to support the Norfolk office.

"We've got a hot one," he told Warfield. "Whatever you want, you've got it."

Wolfinger assigned Robert W. Hunter of the Norfolk office to handle the case. Besides re-interviewing Barbara Walker, the agents ordered an interview with Laura Walker on March 7, 1985. She corroborated many of Barbara Walker's allegations. After both women passed lie-detector tests, FBI counterintelligence officials were convinced the case was for real. But what the FBI still needed was proof. To trap Walker, they drew up a plan called Wind Flyer, one of the many code names that are made up randomly by headquarters, kept in stock, and used as the need arises.

Walker had retired from the Navy in 1976 and now, at age forty-eight, ran his own private detective agency, Confidential Reports Inc., in Virginia Beach. He had grown up in Scranton, Pennsylvania. His family was torn by his father's drinking. When he was eighteen, he was arrested for burglarizing a filling station and a men's clothing store. He dropped out of a Catholic high school and joined the Navy, where he proved to be a quick study at radio communications.

Because of his new occupation as detective, Walker was likely to be on the lookout for surveillance. Above all, the agents assigned to Wind Flyer did not want to tip their hand. So instead of watching him constantly, they obtained approval from the Foreign Intelligence Surveillance Court to wiretap his home phones at 8524 Old Ocean View Road in Norfolk and his business phones at 405 South Parliament Drive in Virginia Beach.

After six weeks, they had turned up no hint of his spying activities. But during the week of May 13, 1985, the agents heard Walker chatting about a business trip planned for Sunday, May 19. To some, he said he was going to Charlotte. To others, he said he was going elsewhere. When his favorite aunt died that week in Pennsylvania, Walker insisted he could not attend the funeral. His business trip could not be postponed, nor could his partner in the detective agency handle the assignment.

To the agents assigned to the case, it meant Walker might be planning a drop. On Saturday, they placed him under constant surveillance. The next day, they watched as Walker, wearing blue jeans, a dark blue pullover shirt, and a black nylon windbreaker, got in his blue-and-silver 1985 Chevrolet Astro Van and began driving into driveways and dead ends. Clearly, he was about to go operational. Overhead, a single-engine FBI plane radioed scrambled reports back to the command car manned by Wolfinger. At 2:00 P.M., the plane radioed that Walker was driving north, not south, along Interstate 95 toward Washington.

Some twenty FBI cars followed him. Never looking directly at him, the agents would pass him, turn off the road, then come back and pass him again. In case they were observed during that time, individual agents changed disguises en route.

Because the FBI was betting that Walker would continue dealing with the Soviets in Washington, a special surveillance plan was devised in case he should head toward the capital. Now Wolfinger called the Washington field office to activate the command center—a cluster of secure phones, television screens, radio transmitters, and blackboards on the tenth floor of the Washington field office over-looking the Anacostia River. The command center was there for just such a purpose, to orchestrate a major arrest in the Washington area. The command center, in turn, notified another forty agents and "Gs," the lower-paid surveillance people used in counterintelligence cases, that the plan was in effect. In addition, John Dion of the Justice Department's internal security section manned the command center.

By now, the Walker case was considered a "special," meaning it took precedence over any other cases. The Norfolk office was the "OO"—office of origin—while the Washington field office was the auxiliary office. A case may require investigations by many auxiliary offices, and each one places a case agent in charge of it for the office.

CI-3's sister squad, CI-6, which targets nonuniformed GRU officers, had been put in charge of the Walker case in Washington. However, because it was thought to be a GRU case, nearly all the CI-3 agents worked on it as well. Each of them carried beepers so they would be found wherever they were. Investigative aides at the command center began calling CI-3 and other counterintelligence agents at their homes, clubs, and their friends' homes. The secret operational plan had been put into effect, one that would soon snare Walker. As they rushed to pick up Walker on I-95 in northern Virginia, some of them changed into camouflage.

At 4:00 P.M., Walker crossed the Potomac River on Route 495 into the Maryland suburbs outside of Washington. To blend in, many of the agents changed their license plates from Virginia to Maryland tags. Walker began traversing the countryside in Potomac, Maryland, just off River Road, slowing down at certain intersections and peering at utility poles.

The lush area has long steep hills and million-dollar homes equipped with lighted tennis courts and swimming pools. Ponds dot the front yards, and golden retrievers romp near the swing sets. It is hunt country, and the residents groom horses on the lawn.

The site was not only beautiful, it was perfect for the Soviets' purposes. Because it was so deserted, Walker could easily detect anyone following him.

Apparently, Walker was spotting the areas where the Soviets had told him to leave documents and signals and to pick up cash. The agents noted the locations in case he returned.

At 4:45 P.M., the agents lost him. To avoid being detected, they had to stay two to three blocks behind him. The FBI reconnaissance plane overhead was having trouble getting clearance to fly in the area because of airport traffic. The agents later learned Walker had gone to check in at a Ramada Inn in nearby Rockville. He registered as "Joe Johnson." Crestfallen, the agents regrouped behind the Safeway at the shopping center at River and Falls roads. There, more than fifty agents and "G's" wrung their hands until O'Keefe and A. Jackson Lowe, the supervisor of CI-6, came up with a plan.

Figuring he would return, the two ordered the agents to conduct "picket surveillance" at choke points—a fence of stationary surveillance at every key intersection leading to the area. At 7:48 P.M., their hunch was proven right. Over the radio, the agents heard the voice of a female "G":

"Hey, I've got him!" she exclaimed.

Walker was driving up River Road again near the shopping center. Now that Walker had turned on his headlights, Special Agent Frank McKenzie could easily spot him from his plane 4,000 feet above.

Walker began following a set of instructions written by his Soviet handlers. Later, when they read them, CI-3 agents were full of admiration.

"Whoever wrote them, I wish they were working for us," one agent told me. "They are legible, concise. . . . We have a well-trained, disciplined adversary."

The instructions described an intricate dance that Walker would follow for the next four hours. While the drop points were all within an area of twenty square miles, it would take two hours of driving to hit all of them.

To avoid getting caught, a good intelligence agent under no circumstances meets with his asset after the first encounter. So the instructions included a way of communicating by placing 7-Up cans in particular locations. If for any reason Walker could not leave his documents where he was supposed to leave them, or the Soviet could not leave his cash, the instructions included alternate sites.

The instructions began by telling Walker to look for "my usual can"—a 7-Up can—at 8:00 P.M. This would show Walker that the Soviet was ready to make an exchange of cash for documents. Pinpointing a 7-Up can at night in rolling, wooded terrain is not easy, and the Soviet gave overlapping instructions to make sure Walker understood.

"For our next exchange we'll use the following sites in Montgomery County, Maryland," the Soviet wrote in printing that appeared to be done by machine. "To signal that I am ready to exchange, I'll drop my initial can of the usual kind at a utility poll on Watts Branch Drive near its intersection with Circle Drive and Ridge Drive," he wrote. "The utility pole in question is the second one to the east of the intersection (the first utility pole is located right at the intersection of Watts Branch Drive and Circle Drive). My signal site will be on your right when you drive on Watts Branch Drive from Circle Drive toward Valley Drive. I'll drop my signal on the road shoulder a foot or two from the surface of the road. Check my signal after 8:00 P.M."

And as if that weren't precise and redundant enough, the Soviet enclosed photos of each drop site taken from different angles, plus a map of the overall area with drop points marked and an enlarged map of each drop site.

Walker was to place the next signal—another 7-Up can—at 8:30 P.M. at the bottom of a utility pole on Quince Orchard Road at Dufief Mill Road. This would show that he was ready for the exchange. Next, Walker was to leave his "delivery"—secret documents—behind a utility pole next to a large tree on Partnership Road at Whites Ferry Road.

At 10:15 P.M., the Soviet would drop his "delivery"—cash—behind two forked trees at Old Bucklodge Lane at White Ground Road. Walker was to signal that he had gotten the cash by leaving a 7-Up can on Esworthy Terrace. At 11:15 P.M., the Soviet would signal that he had gotten the documents by leaving a 7-Up can at a large tree near a bridge on Piney Meetinghouse Road.

Based on Walker's afternoon scouting efforts, the agents had staked out each drop point. Each time he left a drop point, they swooped in to see if he had left anything.

At 8:20 P.M., the agents noticed a 1983 blue Malibu with diplomatic plates in the area. It was driven by a man accompanied by a woman and a child. Running the tag number through an FBI computer, the agents immediately learned that the car belonged to Aleksey Gavrilovich Tkachenko, the third secretary of the Soviet Embassy and a KGB officer. Agents assigned to the squad that focuses on the KGB at the embassy recognized Tkachenko as well.

A few minutes later, the agents again spotted Tkachenko a mile and a half from the place where Walker was about to leave a 7-Up can. The Soviet's presence meant that the KGB instead of the GRU was probably handling Walker. Quite often, Soviet intelligence officers bring their families along when picking up documents at dead drops. They try to give the impression they are on a family outing. Sometimes the family has a picnic.

At 8:30 P.M., Walker dropped the 7-Up can at the bottom of a utility pole on Quince Orchard Road at Dufief Mill Road, signaling that he was ready for the exchange.

Over the scrambled radio, Lowe told the agents to make sure to get the can as evidence. They misinterpreted what he had said and scooped up the 7-Up can immediately after Walker drove away. In retrospect, this was a mistake, since the can signaled that the coast was clear and Tkachenko could pick up the secret documents. If he had gone to the place where Walker had hidden them, and the FBI had left the documents in place, the agents could have arrested him. Instead, the Soviet took off without retrieving any documents or leaving any cash for Walker.

After every counterintelligence operation, the research unit at headquarters analyzes the case and comes up with recommendations for handling similar cases in the future. In the Walker case, the unit decided the FBI could have nailed the Soviet if the documents had been left where they were. But to the agents, nabbing Walker was far more important than grabbing the Soviet.

Walker sped off toward Partnership Road and got out of his car. After he left, Special Agent Bruce K. Brahe II, a member of CI-6, found a brown paper bag near a large tree. The bag was filled with what looked like trash—empty Coke bottles and cereal boxes. Except the material was clean. The bottles had been carefully rinsed out, and there was no food inside the discarded boxes.

The "garbage" concealed another bag inside the bag—a white plastic bag sealed with tape. Inside the agents found 129 classified documents and a note to Walker's handlers. By letter code, it referred to the others who were supplying him with documents now that he had left the military.

Agents rushed the bag to FBI headquarters, where the FBI laboratory—with a new technique that uses lasers to detect fingerprints on paper—found a print of Walker's son, Michael, a sailor aboard the aircraft carrier *Nimitz*.

In case the Soviet returned to the area looking for his drop, the agents left a dummy bag of documents for him.

Still not realizing anything was amiss, Walker drove to the forked tree where he was to get his cash at 10:30 P.M. Special Agent J. Stephen Ramey, a member of the CI-3 squad, and a "G" were stationed in the area. When he heard on his walkie-talkie that Walker

Armand B. Weiss, center, receives an FBI plaque. Left to right, Special Agents William P. O'Keefe, Theodore M. Gardner, William Warfield, Nicholas J. Walsh, and Don Young. *FBI photo*

James H. Geer, assistant FBI director for intelligence. *FBI photo*

Natan Sharansky, wearing a fur hat at center, crosses the Glienicker Bridge into West Berlin with Richard K. Burt, U.S. ambassador to West Germany. John L. Martin, chief of the Justice Department's internal security section, is immediately behind the Soviet dissident. *Courtesy of the Justice Department*

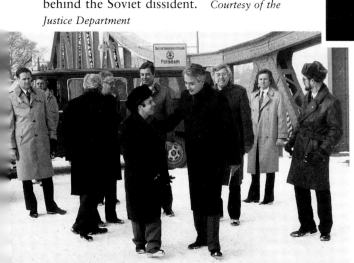

Karl F. Koecher, wearing a hat and handcuffs, is escorted by U.S. marshals from a C-130 transport plane at Temphelhof Central Airport in West Berlin prior to being exchanged for Natan Sharansky. Hana Koecher's white mink hat can be seen just behind her husband. *Courtesy of the Justice Department*

Karl and Hana Koecher, at left, with the author and his wife, Pamela Kessler, in front of the Inter-Continental Hotel in Prague. The sign says, "We Welcome the Glorious May Days"; it was put up when the Soviets liberated Czechoslovakia from Nazi occupation in 1945.

Hana Koecher at the Inter-Continental Hotel in Prague.

Karl and Hana Koecher, at left, with the author in the Old Jewish Cemetery in Prague.

Karl and Hana Koecher in front of the castle in Prague where the president of Czechoslovakia lives.

FBI agents leading Karl and Hana Koecher in handcuffs from the FBI office in New York after their arrest.

AP photo

Karl Koecher, left, with the author.

The game over, Soviet spy Vladimir M. Ismaylov leaves the U.S. on an Aeroflot flight after being declared persona non grata by the State Department. *FBI photo*

"There's no fishing hole where you were digging," Special Agent William P. O'Keefe, center, tells GRU officer Vladimir M. Ismaylov, who was picking up classified documents.   *FBI photo*

Soviet military attaché Vladimir M. Ismaylov is arrested by the FBI. *FBI photo*

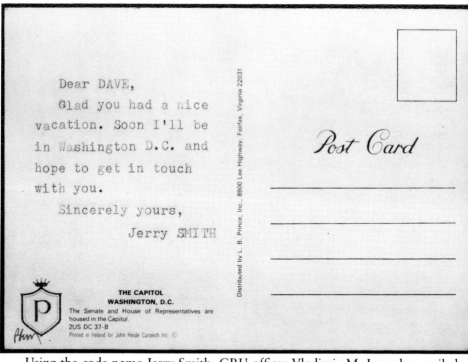

Using the code name Jerry Smith, GRU officer Vladimir M. Ismaylov mailed this postcard to Yogi, an American military officer posing as a traitor, signaling that he was ready to begin play. *FBI photo*

The FBI confiscated Soviet spy Vladimir M. Ismaylov's film, coded messages, cash, and the innocent-looking containers he hid them in. *FBI photo*

John A. Walker, Jr., on the night of his arrest. *FBI photo*

Instructions from Nick Pavlov for John L. Stine. *FBI photo*

The Soviet Military Office at 2552 Belmont Road, N.W., in Washington, where many CI-3 agents spend more time than at home.

DEAR JIM (MAY I CALL YOU SO).
THANK YOU FOR YOUR NOVEMBER VISIT AND YOUR PARCEL. ALL THE DOCS ARE VALUABLE. I HOPE YOU AGREE THE MONEY YOU RECEIVED COVERS YOUR AFFORTS. AND GOOD START. I THINK WE WILL CONTINUE OUR MUTUALLY BENEFICIAL BUSINESS. I WILL DO MY BEST TO INSURE YOUR SECURITY. PLEASE DO THE SAME ON YOUR PART.
ALL NEXT REWARDS - ACCORDING TO THE VALUE OF THE DOCS.
SORRY FOR COMPLICATED WAY OF OUR FIRST TRANSECTION. YOU UNDERSTAND IT WAS DONE ONLY FOR SAFETY REASON.
    IN OUR FURTHER COOPERATION I RECOMMEND YOU THE FOLLOWING:
- KEEP TRYING TO COLLECT UP TO DATE, COMPLETE ,WITH HIGHEST CLASSIFICATION DOCS AND KEEP THEM AT HOME OR IN ANY OTHER SAFE PLACE YOU CHOOSE.
- THE BEST WAY TO COPY THEM IS BY CAMERA. I ENCLOSE ADDITIONAL $ 400.00 FOR THAT PURPOSE AND RECOMMEND YOU TO BUY AT THE W.BELL & CO AN "OLYMPUS OM-1N" WITH f/1.4 LENS. USE WHITE &BLACK CODAK FILMS "PANATOMIC -X, 32 ASA". TO MAKE A COPY OF GOOD QUALITY BE SURE TO FIX FOCUS AT A DISTANCE NOT MORE THAN 18-20 INCHES. LIGHT - 1 TABLE LAMP X 100 WATTS. BEFORE SHOOTING A DOCUMENT MAKE SOME CONTROL SHOOTINGS OF ANY OTHER SIMILAR TEXT. DEVELOP YOURSELF AND CHECK IT. IF STILLS ARE O'K, START SHOOTING DOCS. KEEP THE FILMS UNDEVELOPED IN CASSETS IN A SAFE PLACE. BUY FILMS IN DIFFERENT STORES.
- OUR NEXT TRANSECTION WILL BY IN APRIL. PREPARIED STUFF (FILMS OR COPIES) WRAP INTO WATERPROOF PACKAGE PREFERABLY IN A BLACK PLASTIC GARBAGE BAG.
    PUT THE PARCEL IN PLACE #1 (SEE DESCRIPTION). IF BY ANY REASON THE USE OF THIS PLACE IS DIFFICULT USE PLACE # 3 (RESERVED). THAN GO TO THE PLACE OF MEETING # 4 AND BE SURE TO ARRIVE AT 8 P.M. WAIT FOR 10 MINUTES. IF I FAIL TO COME GO TO THE PLACE # 2 AND PICK UP MY PARCEL. IN CASE THERE IS NO PACKAGE IN # 2, CHECK # 3. AFTER PICKING UP MY PARCEL PUT A SIGNAL AT A PLACE # 5. THAT WILL BE THE END OF THE TRANSECTION.
    IN MY PACKAGE YOU WILL FIND FURTHER INSTRUCTIONS. REED THEM AND FOLLOW THEM CAREFULLY.
- FOR THE SAKE OF SECURITY OUR MEETINGS OR EXCHANGE OF PARCELS WILL TAKE PLACE NOT MORE THAN FOUR TIMES   A YEAR. THE MORE DOCS YOU COLLECT IN FILMS THE HIGHER WILL BE REWARD.
- IF BY ANY REASON WE FAILED TO MEET OR MAKE AN EXCHANGE COME AT 8 P.M. ON LAST SATURDAY OF EVERY MONTH COMMENCING MAY TO THE PLACE # 6. IN THIS CASE YOU WILL MEET ME OR ONE OF MY FRIENDS. PLEASE FOLLOW ALL INSTRUCTIONS GIVEN IN DISCRIPTION OF # 6.
- DO NOT TRY TO CONTACT ME BY ANY WAY. IF EVERY MEANS OF COMMUNICATION MANSIONED ABOVE ARE CUT IT WILL BE MY DUTY TO FIND THE SAFIEST WAY OF GETTING IN TOUCH WITH YOU.
    AFTER USING ## 1, 2, 3, 4, 5 DESTROY THEM AND KEEP # 6 ONLY.
- BE CAREFULL AND WISE NOW AND IN THE FUTURE WITH THE SPENDINGS.
- MAKE NECESSARY NOTES TO REMEMBER AND DESTROY THIS MESSAGE.
                WISH YOU THE BEST.
                        YOUR FRIEND NICK.

John L. Stine with false mustache, wig, and aviator glasses supplied by the FBI before his walk-in to the Soviet Military Office.

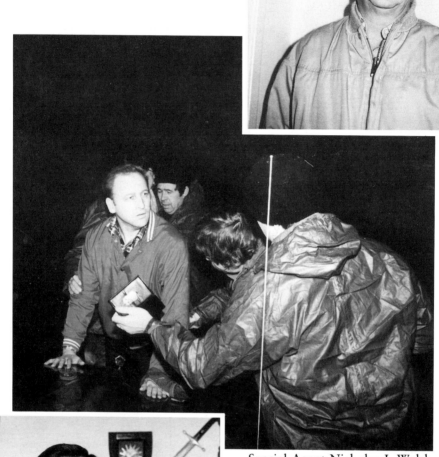

Special Agent Nicholas J. Walsh tells Yevgeniy Barmyanstev he is under arrest.   *FBI photo*

Nick Pavlov as he presents his credentials as a Soviet military attaché at the Pentagon.   *FBI photo*

was driving toward them, Ramey told the "G" to drive away with the car. Meanwhile, he hid behind a tree several yards from the road.

Walker searched for his cash but couldn't find it. Just after 9:00 P.M., his Soviet handler had left the area. Walker got a flashlight from his car and shone it into the woods. Unlike some other agents assigned to the case, Ramey had no camouflage makeup on. In fact, he was wearing a white, short-sleeved shirt. He was sure Walker could see him. He is a big man and was hiding behind a little tree. Petrified, he pointed his .357 Magnum at Walker as Walker shined the light directly on him. But somehow Walker didn't see him and continued to search for the money. Finally, he climbed back into his van. Twice more that night, he returned to the spot, frantically checking and rechecking the directions. Walker could not believe it. In seventeen years of spying, he had never known the Soviets to screw up.

At midnight, Walker gave up and headed back toward the Ramada Inn. He entered the hotel at 12:17 A.M. and went directly to his room on the seventh floor. The only other supervisor on the scene besides Lowe, O'Keefe, as the head of CI-3, was in charge of the arrest which had been approved by Dion. He wanted to take him off guard, away from other guests. Under no circumstances was he to get away.

At 3:30 A.M., after Walker was presumably asleep, O'Keefe had Special Agent William Wang pose as the hotel clerk and call him. Wang is a coordinator of the G's. His name is pronounced "Wong," prompting the joke, "If it's Wang, it's Wong."

Wang apologized to Walker for waking him but said another guest had smashed into his van, causing considerable damage. Would he mind coming down to look and exchange insurance information?

Warily, Walker opened the door. He saw no one. He closed the door again, walked to his window and looked out. He couldn't see his van. Nothing seemed amiss.

Shoving a .38 caliber Smith & Wesson revolver in his belt, he opened the door and walked into the hallway. As he approached the elevators, Hunter, the case agent in Norfolk, and Special Agent James L. Kolouch, the case agent in Washington, accosted him, their guns drawn.

"FBI, freeze," Kolouch said.

Walker drew his gun and pointed it at the agents, who were both wearing bullet-proof vests. There was no way he could have gotten away. Besides the agents outside, agents had blocked off the stairways and elevators. Others waited in one of the rooms.

If Walker shot one of the agents, the other one would kill him. Walker hesitated a moment, then dropped the gun, along with a manila envelope that turned out to contain the instructions from his Soviet handlers. If he had hesitated one more moment, the agents later said, they would have killed him. During their training, they are taught to shoot only to kill.

Throwing him against a wall, the agents searched him and ripped off his toupée. Placing handcuffs on him, Hunter told him, "You are under arrest for violation of the espionage laws of the United States."

Stunned, Walker could think only of the desk-clerk ploy. "An old trick," he called it, grinning.

When O'Keefe saw the drop instructions Walker was clutching when he was arrested, he knew immediately that Walker had been handled by the KGB, not the GRU. The GRU never includes photographs of drop sites in its instructions.

That same morning, the FBI confronted Jerry A. Whitworth, Walker's close friend. Knowing that he would soon be leaving the Navy, Walker had recruited Whitworth, a Navy communications specialist, in 1974 to continue supplying him with secret documents.

In May 1984, Whitworth had written a letter to the FBI's San Francisco field office saying he knew of a major spy operation and was considering blowing the whistle on it. The letter was signed only "RUS." The FBI tried to get in touch with the anonymous writer by placing newspaper ads, but Whitworth had second thoughts and decided against informing on Walker.

The FBI also arrested Walker's son, Michael, and Walker's brother, Arthur, a former submarine officer. After Whitworth retired from the Navy, Walker recruited them to supply him with classified material. If Barbara Walker had known that her son was involved, she later said, she never would have called the FBI.

John and Arthur Walker and Whitworth were sentenced to life in prison, while Michael got twenty-five years. Three days after Walker's arrest, Tkachenko, the elder Walker's apparent case agent, voluntarily left the country and returned to Moscow.

The information Walker had given the Soviets included future naval plans, ship locations, data on weapons, naval tactics, information on covert military and counterintelligence operations, and emergency plans in the event of a nuclear war.

KGB defector Vitaly Yurchenko told the CIA and the FBI that

Walker's information enabled the Soviets to decipher over a million coded messages. In a war between the U.S. and the U.S.S.R., he said, the information could have tipped the balance in favor of the Soviet Union.

CI-3 agents dismissed the later criticisms by the FBI's research unit as "Monday-morning quarterbacking."

"One mistake was made," an agent said. "But what if he had gotten away with the documents? The score speaks for itself. Our team won. The Soviet left anyway. We won 21 to 20. It could have been 21 to nothing."

Yet the fact is the agents should have left the can in place, and FBI director Webster later criticized them for picking it up.

By coincidence, the Walker case affected the fate of Thomas Cavanagh. He agreed to plead guilty to two counts of espionage—technically, delivery of defense information to aid a foreign government. The espionage statute—Section 794 of Title 18—does not distinguish between delivery and attempted delivery. If a bank robber is apprehended before the cashier hands him the money, should he be rewarded for not being as smart as the robber who gets away?

By pleading guilty, Cavanagh thought he would get more lenient treatment. But his sentencing on May 23, 1985, was four days after the arrest of Walker. All of a sudden, espionage was hot news. U.S. District Court Judge Matthew Byrne Jr. sentenced him to two life prison terms.

Ironically, after his initial arraignment, Cavanagh, chained and shackled, was put in the same prisoner van with Miller, the FBI agent arrested for espionage.

"I needed the money," Cavanagh told Miller.

"I have eight kids. I know what you mean," Miller said.

Today, Cavanagh is prisoner number 80922-0123 at the Federal Penitentiary at Lompoc, California, the same prison that Christopher J. Boyce escaped from in 1980. Boyce and his friend Andrew Daulton Lee were arrested in January 1977 for selling classified code material used for the Rhyolite surveillance satellite to KGB agents in Mexico City. Later, Boyce would describe security at TRW as being so lax that he and his co-workers "regularly partied and boozed it up during working hours within the 'black vault,' " the super-secret room housing the CIA satellite project. "Bacardi rum was usually stored behind the crypto machines," he said, while a code-destruction machine similar to a blender "was used for making banana daiquiris and Mai-Tais."

After Boyce was recaptured, he got an additional twenty-eight years at the Federal Correctional Institution in Marion, Illinois, the most secure prison in the federal system.

Since his escape, security at Lompoc—already a maximum-security prison—has been tightened. Razor-sharp wire is draped in the yard to prevent helicopters from landing, and the entire complex is surrounded by twelve-foot-high double and triple chain-link fences laced with more razor wire.

Cavanagh's day begins at 6:00 A.M. when he is awakened by the clanging of the electronically operated gates of his cell block as they open for the day. Wearing a tan prison uniform, he eats breakfast, then works at filling out contracts for a prison shop that makes electrical cables. He is paid $1.10 an hour, which brings him $189 a month. He sends one hundred dollars to his wife and twenty dollars to his two sons.

At 4:00 P.M., he must be in his cell for the prisoner count. Dinner begins at four forty-five. Three nights a week, he takes a prison class in business management. He must be in his cell by 10:00 P.M., with lights out by eleven-thirty.

In theory, he can make collect calls for fifteen minutes every other day. But in practice, because of the demand by other prisoners, he only gets to use the phone every six days. When he finds his wife is not home on a Saturday night, he wonders if she is with someone else. His calls, like his mail, are monitored. If he uses a swear word on the phone, he gets a reprimand.

Visits are limited by a point system. Up to forty hours a month are allowed for social visits. When his wife comes to visit, she must pass through a metal detector and remove any jewelry, belt buckles, or other metal ornaments. Airline tickets, stamps, and tape recorders are confiscated and placed in a locker. She passes through two sets of gates that cannot be opened at the same time, then through a locked glass door into a room the size of a high school cafeteria. There, prisoners sit at low tables across from their visitors. Husbands and wives may kiss at the beginning and end of the visit. A black globe hangs from the ceiling in one corner of the room. Inside, video cameras record every moment while a guard equipped with a body alarm watches. Once, Cavanagh got an official reprimand for touching his wife's left breast.

Because of the restrictions, the scene resembles a high school prom. Husbands and wives joyfully snuggle against each other and hold hands as they walk to vending machines along one wall to get snacks. At the end of the visits, there are long French kisses as the men's pants bulge with lust. After they leave the room, the prisoners are strip-searched. As they pass through the double gates, the wives' glow quickly fades. Many leave crying.

Because of Cavanagh's offense, the other 1,250 prisoners treat him like a pariah. Murder, rape, incest—anything is preferable to selling out one's country. Frequently, they taunt him.

Cavanagh spends every waking moment thinking about his sentence and how unjust it is. By his reckoning, other spies who successfully gave away secrets to the Soviets got lesser sentences. He realizes there is a good chance he will never get out.

"I became desperate over money," he told me. "Family members were making demands on me. I was trying to help my sister financially. My mother was calling me saying crazy things because she was going blind. I was looking for a way out.

"I knew they bugged the embassy. What I didn't know was they couldn't go beyond the twenty-five-mile limit. I knew something wasn't right. I said I'd go one step further. I didn't try to sell us out. I'm not a would-be traitor. I was giving them information because I thought that's what they wanted to hear to get the money. If I went in and said I want $25,000 one time, they're not going to go for it," he said.

After Vietnam, he said, "I realized the government used me like it used everyone else. In the Navy, I saw people in body bags and people getting shot. They lied about the body count. That's appalling. Fighting for our liberty is good. But that wasn't liberty.

"I fought for this country in Vietnam with three tours of duty. I know what a sellout is all about. I understand we have to catch spies. I don't like Russians. I never did. But it's like saying two wrongs make a right: why have the Soviets here while we spy on them in Moscow? We're saying they're terrible, and we're doing the same thing in Moscow.

"I realize that what I did was wrong and stupid," he said. "But I sincerely do not belong around killers, homosexuals, and mentally unstable people. I've never been in prison before. People get kicked, stabbed. I'm going to be here the rest of my life. Other prisoners say, 'I would have done anything except that.' "

Cavanagh knows his family has been humiliated by his offense. "It has such a bad connotation. How can I look at people I knew? They have the perception I sold out. They don't know what the government is all about and what happened in Vietnam. The executive branch is out of control."

Cavanagh is chronically depressed but refuses the pills the prison dispenses. Most of the money he sends his wife goes for the cost of his collect calls. When he finds she is out when he calls, he tries not to ask her the next time where she was, but sometimes he must.

"You're supposed to hold out. But how long can she hold out? My wife says you should have done anything but this," he said.

"I thought life was debits and credits," Cavanagh said. "There isn't a moment in the day when I don't think about my sentence. I never thought that my life would end in front of me."

In a letter to me, he penned this poem:

> And the end of the fight
> is a tombstone white
> with the name of the late deceased,
> and the epitaph drear: "A fool lies here who
> tried to hustle the East."

11
An Incident with a Soviet

Sifting through his messages in late May 1985, agent Grogan came upon one from an asset in a northern Virginia bar. When he called him back, the man said he had seen a Russian the previous evening striking up a conversation with an American Air Force officer.

The asset had copied down the military man's license number. He identified the Russian from photographs.

The same day, OSI agent Michael Scott called Grogan. A nineteen-year veteran of the Air Force, Scott specialized in counterintelligence work for OSI, which investigates crimes against the Air Force or its personnel.

Scott told Grogan that the military man spotted in the bar had himself reported that he had been approached by a Soviet asking him for classified documents in return for money.

The military man was Yogi.

All government employees are supposed to report such contacts. The Air Force alone gets 2,600 reports of contacts with Soviets a year, but OSI believes they represent only a small percentage of the total. Americans want to welcome foreigners. They think they can handle the Soviets. For that reason, military people often don't report contacts with Soviets.

The FBI doesn't want people to think there are spies on every corner. But from defectors, electronic bugs, and other sources, the FBI believes that Soviets in this country are under a great deal of pressure to develop recruits. To find military men, the Soviets attend yard sales, block parties, or computer conferences and strike up conversations. If they see a man in uniform, or notice military books at a yard sale, they try to develop a closer relationship. In doing so, they do not try to hide the fact that they are Russians. Rather, they try to establish rapport by discussing common interests.

Sometimes military personnel warn the Soviets that the contact will have to be reported. This is a no-no. The military personnel are supposed to simply report the contacts so the OSI and FBI can evaluate them. That way, the Americans may be used as counterspies.

Not every military man is interested in such work, nor is suitable for it. It requires a quick mind, an ability to deal with stress, and a desire to help—not to mention some facility at lying.

Zupan and Grogan recalled the sunny morning in June 1983 when they visited the Annandale, Virginia, home of Richard J. D'Aleo, a naval intelligence officer in the active reserves. An intense man who talks so rapidly the agents had trouble keeping up with him, D'Aleo is a computer whiz. He once managed data retrieval for the Naval Intelligence Support Center and later worked for the Labor Department. Several times he had bumped up against the federal bureaucracy, developing a reputation as a "whistle blower" because he complained when he felt his bosses were misleading their superiors.

D'Aleo was trying to make a living working for himself and had just published *Fedfind,* a directory of sources of federal government information.

Two days before the visit from the agents, a man with a foreign accent had called D'Aleo at home and said he was interested in buying a copy of the directory, which had just received a favorable review in the *Wilson Library Bulletin.* D'Aleo told him which bookstores carry it, but the man said he would be in the area that evening shopping at Basics, a discount food chain.

"Do you mind if I drop in then and pick up a copy?" he asked.

At 9:00 P.M., D'Aleo and his wife, Ann, an elementary school teacher, were watching television when the doorbell rang. The visitor had brown hair, twinkling blue eyes, and a clear complexion. Introducing himself as "Val," he sat on D'Aleo's turquoise-flowered sofa and flipped through *Fedfind.*

"I can see you know a great deal about Washington information," the visitor said. "I would like to hire you to do research."

D'Aleo declined, saying he'd had his fill of working for others. But he said he would show the man how to find information on his own.

As they talked, a house guest who was a relative of Ann D'Aleo's was doing her wash in the utility room. A linguist, she had just begun a new job with the CIA. She immediately recognized the visitor's accent as Russian.

"Do you know who Richard is talking to?" she asked Ann D'Aleo. "He's a Soviet!"

D'Aleo's wife snuck out of the house through the garage and wrote down the Soviet's license tag number. D'Aleo had no idea anything was amiss until he walked to his den to find a book he wanted to show the man. His wife was sprawled on the white carpeting of their bedroom taking notes. Their house guest, meanwhile, was cursing her luck. She had only been working at the CIA two weeks and now would have to report this.

D'Aleo is as enthusiastic about information gathering as his two cocker spaniels are about seeing visitors. He gave little thought to his wife's strange behavior and hurried back to the living room to show his visitor the book, a directory of military publications put out by the Institute for Defense Analyses.

Showing the man how to use the volume, D'Aleo said, "You can look up communications and tactical warfare publications, for example, known as COMTAC. Then each listing shows any restrictions on distribution. Here, for example, it says, 'All COMTAC publications are restricted and requests may be sent through channels with certification of need to know.' "

Under his breath, the visitor muttered, "That's what I want."

D'Aleo felt a shiver up his spine. For his naval work, he had "top secret" clearance. Now his training came back to him about what to do if a representative of a Soviet bloc country contacted him. Changing his tack, he said he might consider working for the man. Realizing he had made a mistake, the visitor said several times that he did not want classified information.

D'Aleo presented the man with his card, requiring him to produce one. In flowery script, it said "Major Vyacheslay V. Kopayev, assistant air attaché, Embassy of the Union of Soviet Socialist Republics." To D'Aleo, that meant he was a member of the GRU.

After the man left, D'Aleo called the duty officer in the office of the Chief of Naval Operations.

"I had an incident with a Soviet," he said.

Half an hour later, a duty officer from the Naval Investigative Service called him and took a report on the phone. The next morning, two agents from the service showed up at his door. The following day, Grogan and Zupan came over and asked if he would be a double agent.

Besides trying to make a living by publishing his own books,

D'Aleo was under some pressure at the time because his seventy-eight-year-old mother was dying of heart disease.

"I will under two conditions," D'Aleo told the agents. "I want to be compensated for my time, and I want it to be over in six months," he said, explaining that his mother was terminally ill and would need him then.

The agents agreed to the conditions, but each time he asked for his money, they put him off.

"We're working on it," Grogan said.

Meanwhile, the Soviet dropped by on July 4 to give D'Aleo a bottle of Stolichnaya. In September, he dropped in again, this time with caviar. D'Aleo reported each contact to Grogan. But he had come to realize that at this pace the operation would go far longer than six months. And he had received no money for his time, which he figured already had amounted to a week spent in meetings with the agents.

When Grogan and Zupan showed up later that month as D'Aleo was mowing his lawn, he became incensed.

"What are you doing here?" he demanded to know. "You've been putting me off, and I'm sick of it. It's obvious this is going to go more than six months, and you haven't paid me. You haven't kept your word," he said.

To D'Aleo, the agents were just like his bosses in the Labor Department and the Navy, taking advantage of him and covering up.

Inside the house, Grogan explained that it takes months for a double-agent operation to be approved within the FBI. Even though Grogan's boss felt D'Aleo had provided very little information so far, Grogan told him he had managed to get him $300, which he gave him in cash.

In fact, the FBI had been unable to give D'Aleo money because the Navy had a policy against it. Grogan gave him the money out of his own pocket.

Using "Tonto," the code name he had been assigned, D'Aleo signed a receipt for the money, but Grogan's comments made him even angrier.

"The value of information cannot be quantified," he told him.

It was clear to both sides that they had come to a parting of the ways, and the two agents agreed that the operation would be aborted.

"There are two kinds of citizens who get involved in this type of operation," Zupan told D'Aleo. "Patriots, and people who are after money. You fall in the latter category."

The Soviet dropped in again in October with a list of the material he wanted. But Grogan told D'Aleo to inform the Soviet next time that they should meet at a Pizza Hut restaurant. The two agents would then show up and talk to him, letting him know that the FBI knew what he is up to.

On December 20, Kopayev dropped in again with another jar of caviar. As instructed, D'Aleo told him they could not meet at his home because his wife objected to business meetings at night. Kopayev never showed up again.

In March 1984, D'Aleo was formally told he would not be used as a double agent. The Naval Investigative Service insisted that he submit to a final polygraph test. He had undergone one when he first agreed to participate.

The following year, D'Aleo, by now a lieutenant commander, was notified by the Navy that his "top secret" security clearance had been lifted during a routine, five-year review. He was then in the reserves, working on weekends at Naval Intelligence Command headquarters, and was about to be transferred to the Naval Investigative Service. But even though he still had "secret" clearance, he was booted out of that assignment.

The only explanation D'Aleo received was that he did not meet the standards for "top secret" clearance, which require that an individual be "stable, trustworthy, reliable, with excellent character, judgment, and discretion, and of unquestioned loyalty to the U.S."

Was his clearance lifted because he had demanded to be paid for helping catch a Soviet? Was it because he had told several people in the reserves about his participation when he had been warned not to tell anyone? Was it because he had recently complained to the Navy inspector general that the Navy was funding a pet program by taking the money from the wrong appropriation? Or was it a combination of these?

D'Aleo never found out. He is appealing the Navy's refusal to show him a complete copy of his file. Pulling a rumpled three-by-five-inch index card from his shirt pocket, he reads a pronouncement from the General Accounting Office, the audit arm of Congress: "Auditing is an important part of the accountability process."

"The FBI had a hidden agenda," he believes. "The idea it would take six months, and I would be compensated, was hooey. I was raised a Catholic. I was an altar boy. I have high scruples. If I realize you're lying, I'm livid."

More recently, Leakh Bhoge, a Guyanese computer student who worked with the FBI in New York to trap Gennady Zakharov, a Soviet spy attached to the United Nations, complained that he had not been compensated adequately for his services.

Zakharov's arrest on a subway platform in Queens prompted the Soviets to arrest U.S. journalist Nicholas Daniloff, later leading to a swap of Daniloff for Zakharov.

From the start, according to Bhoge, Zakharov wanted him to obtain classified documents. But first he had him photocopy articles. For three and a half years, Bhoge was a double agent for the FBI. In January 1985, when Bhoge completed his computer studies, Zakharov asked him to look for a job in robotics or artificial intelligence. But at the FBI's request, he took a $250-a-week job as a machinist at H&G Machine and Tool Co., a military subcontractor. When the gray-haired Zakharov took from Bhoge a document marked "secret" on August 23, 1986, a male and a female FBI agent who had been kissing on the subway platform arrested Zakharov.

Over the course of the operation, Bhoge received $10,000 from Zakharov and $20,000 from the FBI. Since he had to turn over the Soviets' money to the FBI, he wound up with a net of $20,000, which he figures came to less than the minimum wage.

After the Daniloff affair became an international incident, Bhoge began to feel used. Daniloff had signed book contracts that would bring him hundreds of thousands of dollars, and Bhoge was now unemployed and living in a basement apartment in the Brooklyn slum of East New York.

Bhoge asked the FBI for an additional $100,000, but the FBI has declined to pay him any more money.

"I worked with them loyally," he said. "I did it for the country. When I asked for the extra money, I was asking them for help. I did some delivery work, but now I have no job."

Yogi, on the other hand, considered it his patriotic duty to help the FBI. Beyond reimbursement for his expenses, he wanted no money in return.

Yogi impressed both Grogan and Scott as a man who could handle himself well. When O'Keefe asked him to lie, he was able to do it with a straight face and weave in details that lent credibility.

Still, the Air Force was unsure if it wanted him to become a double agent. The Air Force would have to supply actual secret documents for the operation, since Ismaylov, through other sources, might be able to spot fakes. O'Keefe and high-ranking FBI officials convinced the Air Force that the operation would reveal a great deal about what the Russians knew, just from the way Ismaylov asked for documents. With the proviso that Yogi's identity would never be revealed, the Air Force finally acquiesced.

With Zupan posing as Ismaylov, Grogan and Scott put Yogi through his paces at the Ramada Hotel. They wanted him to be prepared for any question.

As Yogi's routine changed, his wife became suspicious. Saying he "had to work," he told her she would have to pick up his relatives at Dulles Airport one evening. When the guests wanted a tour of the J. Edgar Hoover Building, Yogi balked. He didn't want to be seen anywhere near the FBI.

Usually, marital relations are the first thing to suffer during undercover work. Normally close, Yogi and his wife began to argue as tensions mounted at home.

12 *"That's Ron Pelton!"*

Nearly 7,000 miles from Washington, Vitaly S. Yurchenko, one of the KGB's highest-ranking officials, walked out of the Soviet Embassy in Rome, saying he was going to visit the Vatican museums. Instead, on the morning of August 1, 1985, he walked to the U.S. Embassy and asked for asylum.

Blond, dashing, and swaggering, Yurchenko, forty-nine, was one of the most important Soviets ever to defect to the West. At the time, he was deputy chief of the KGB's First Department of the First Chief Directorate, which supervises operations aimed at North America and Americans all over the world. Before that, he was chief of the Fifth Department of Directorate K, the counterintelligence branch of the KGB. From 1975 to 1980, he had been the security officer at the Soviet Embassy in Washington.

Whisked to a safe house on rolling green hills in Fredericksburg, Virginia, Yurchenko told the CIA and the FBI what the CIA had hoped to hear: that there was no KGB mole currently in the agency.

During 1985, CIA officials had become increasingly alarmed as one CIA contact after another disappeared or came under the scrutiny of the KGB. One of the greatest losses was Adolf G. Tolkachev, an electronics expert at a Soviet think tank that does research on military aviation and space-based detection systems. For the past three years, he had been leaving microfilms of classified Soviet documents at "dead drops" serviced by Paul M. Stombaugh, a second secretary in the U.S. Embassy in Moscow. When Stombaugh made a pickup, he was snared by a KGB trap and expelled. Tolkachev disappeared.

There were other incidents—in May 1985, a Soviet military intelligence officer who was giving information to the U.S. on Soviet efforts to infiltrate the Greek military found himself under KGB surveillance; he defected to the West. In England, Oleg A. Gordyevsky, a KGB officer at the Soviet Embassy who was secretly spying for the British MI-6, was placed under surveillance and questioned by the KGB.

Yurchenko immediately established his good faith by warning the CIA that Gordyevsky was about to be arrested. Acting on a CIA tip, the British snatched him from Moscow where he had been called back for "consultations" and smuggled him out of the country.

On August 20, Yurchenko also told the CIA and FBI about two Americans who had been of immense help to the KGB. He could not recall their names, but one had worked for the CIA and had been fired because he was considered a drug addict or alcoholic. He had sold CIA secrets to the Soviets in Austria in the fall of 1984. The other had been an employee of the National Security Agency, the sprawling, super-secret complex north of Washington that intercepts communications all over the world.

According to Yurchenko, the NSA employee had identified for the Soviets those transmissions the NSA was more interested in intercepting. He also told the Soviets about one of NSA's most prized projects, code-named Ivy Bells.

Some years earlier, Soviet military forces had laid an underwater communications cable in the Sea of Okhotsk, between the Soviet east coast and the Kamchatka peninsula near Japan. The NSA man told the Russians that NSA had been able to place a tap on the cable and monitor Soviet military communications. Based on the NSA employee's directions, the Soviets were able to find the tap and remove it.

The FBI immediately began "special" investigations into both cases. Finding the CIA employee proved relatively easy. The CIA was already aware that it had mishandled the case of Edward Lee Howard. Even after the CIA learned that Howard had told a CIA employee he had talked with the Soviets, the CIA failed to notify the FBI.

The son of a career Air Force sergeant, Howard had spent four years in the Peace Corps and worked for the Agency for International Development in Peru for three years before receiving a master's degree in business administration from American University.

In 1980, Howard applied for a job with the CIA. During a polygraph test, he admitted to using drugs, but the spy agency did not consider that a problem. He promised to stop, and in January 1981, the CIA hired him as a probationary staff officer. After being given instruction by the FBI in detecting and evading surveillance, Howard was assigned to Moscow, the CIA's most sensitive post. The rationale: new recruits are more difficult to identify as CIA agents. Just before he was to leave, another polygraph test revealed that he had acute alcohol and drug problems.

Having already learned many of the CIA's secrets and the names of the agency's assets in the Soviet Union, Howard was a walking time bomb. Instead of finding him another job first, the CIA compounded its initial errors by firing him summarily in the summer of 1983, leaving him with no income.

Howard moved to Santa Fe, New Mexico, and found a job with the state legislature. In 1984, he received a five-year suspended sentence for firing a .44 Magnum pistol during a dispute over a woman.

The CIA subsequently gave Howard free psychiatric counseling. During that time, he admitted to a CIA officer that he had entertained thoughts of getting revenge on the CIA by selling secrets to the KGB. Still, the CIA did not report the problem to the FBI. It was too embarrassing.

When Yurchenko disclosed that a former CIA officer had been talking to the KGB, the CIA finally told the FBI what had happened. But Yurchenko's recollections about a man he had never met and whose name he did not know were not enough to lead to an arrest. It was left to the bureau to develop evidence that would hold up in court, a task made more difficult because of the CIA's delay in notifying the bureau.

Meanwhile, the FBI was having difficulty finding the former NSA employee described by Yurchenko. The clues Yurchenko offered were sparse. Nor were they necessarily reliable. He recalled that he had personally met with the former NSA employee when he was working in the Soviet Embassy on Sixteenth Street in Washington. He said he may have taken a call from him initially, but he wasn't sure. Yurchenko believed the call came in sometime between 1977 and 1979. When the American came into the embassy, the Soviets noticed a spurt in the FBI's scrambled radio transmissions around the embassy. The FBI people watching the embassy were apparently frantically communicating with each other, trying to figure out who the man was. The man was so nervous it took him several minutes to begin speaking.

Yurchenko said the man was thirty-five to thirty-eight years old, was married, and had red hair. But then he pointed to teak furniture to illustrate the color. At another point, he said his hair looked like a lamp shade that was wheat-colored. Yurchenko recalled that the man said he wanted to be paid in gold bullion. Because of the language differences, Yurchenko thought he meant chicken soup.

The Soviets immediately recognized him as a valuable spy. He brought with him a document showing he had completed an NSA course, and he told them about the tap on their undersea cable.

Later, Yurchenko learned from other KGB officials that "Mr. Long," as he was code-named, was married and drove a green car. Just like FBI agents who use information gleaned from Soviet defectors, Yurchenko knew the man only by his code name and never learned his real name.

According to Yurchenko, after the man had been in the embassy three hours, the Soviets shaved Mr. Long's beard, dressed him in clothes used by embassy workers, and sneaked him out a side entrance to a van filled with Soviets. They drove him to the Soviet residence quarters at Mount Alto, where he was fed and told how to meet with the Soviets again in Vienna. Then he was taken back to the area where he had parked his car.

As it turned out, the former NSA man had blond hair, and he walked into the embassy in early 1980. But Yurchenko's tips on the NSA man and on Howard were to provide the FBI's counterintelligence program with one of its greatest successes and one of its greatest failures.

On the night of September 20, 1985, Howard and his wife, Mary, drove away from their Santa Fe home. After the FBI and CIA deduced that Yurchenko's information about a former CIA employee pointed to Howard, the FBI Santa Fe office had placed a tap on Howard's telephone and began watching his movements. But the Santa Fe office knew little about counterintelligence work, nor was it interested in learning. An agent there had angrily rebuffed efforts by William Smits, who headed Soviet affairs in the FBI's San Francisco office, to give him some friendly advice on handling the Howard case. Howard, on the other hand, had been trained by retired FBI agents on contract to the CIA to avoid detection.

Howard knew the FBI was watching him and expected that the bureau would follow him as he left the house that evening. It did not. The young, inexperienced FBI agent watching his home on closed-circuit television missed his departure. In the darkness, Howard then jumped out of the car and had his wife drive back home and into their garage with a dummy beside her on the front seat. Seeing the car come back, the agent was relieved that, while he had missed his leaving, Howard had returned.

That night, as instructed by her husband, Howard's wife called the office of his lawyer. When she got the answering machine, she played a tape recording of Howard's voice telling the lawyer he would call him again later.

In fact, Howard had escaped to Moscow, the first CIA employee ever to defect to the Soviet Union. His wife, meanwhile, remained in the U.S.

As reported by David Wise in the November 2, 1986, *New York Times Magazine,* Howard left his wife a note that said in part, "Well, I'm going and maybe I'll give them what they think I already gave them." It instructed her to "sell the house, Jeep, etc., and move [in] with one of our parents and be happy." It said she should tell their son, Lee, "I think of him and you each day until I die."

What is still unclear is what the FBI would have done had it known Howard was leaving the country. It was not until the day after he slipped away that the FBI finally thought it had enough evidence to conclude that it had probable cause to arrest him.

Most likely, the bureau would have come up with something, according to former FBI counterintelligence official Phillip Parker, who arrived on the scene in Santa Fe after Howard left.

"We would have arrested him for spitting on the sidewalk if we had known he was trying to leave," he said.

But whether Howard would have been convicted is another matter. The additional evidence obtained just after his departure was simply an interview with a former colleague who said Howard had told him he sold information to the Soviets. Presumably, if Howard ever returned to the U.S., he would deny ever having said that or claim he had been joking.

According to a former high-ranking FBI official who read an assessment of the case at the time, if the former CIA employee ever returned to the U.S., unless additional evidence was obtained, "Howard might not be convicted."

On August 23, 1985—three days after Yurchenko told the CIA and the FBI about a former NSA employee who had given up secrets to the Soviets—a KGB squad in the FBI's Washington field office located a tape of the man's call to the Soviet Embassy five years earlier.

Since Yurchenko had said the Soviets shipped the man off to the new Mount Alto complex after he came into the embassy, the agents decided the incident must have occurred in 1979 or thereafter, since the Mount Alto complex did not open until September 1979. Then the agents reviewed logs of embassy activity to pinpoint dates when an "unsub"—FBI lingo for an unknown subject—walked into the embassy and did not appear again. During that time period, the only such incident had occurred on January 15, 1980.

As it turned out, Yurchenko had taken the man's call before he walked in. The same American had called the previous day. On the five-year-old tape, Yurchenko suggested that the American come into the embassy. Perplexed, the American asked how.

"Do I just ring the bell and someone lets me in?" he wanted to know. "How do I get in?"

"No, no, you'll enter through the gate directly," Yurchenko said.

"And, okay, they'll let me in?" the man asked.

"Of course, no question," Yurchenko said.

Having gotten a sample of the man's voice, the FBI still did not know who he was. The FBI surveillance team outside the embassy had not gotten a photograph of him, even though some FBI officials believed it should have. While it would be difficult to photograph a person once he has turned to walk into the embassy, the FBI takes photographs of everyone walking down the street in both directions in front of the embassy. It then tries to match up those photographs with those of people leaving the embassy.

The FBI similarly failed to get a picture of Walker when he walked into the Soviet Embassy. Today, thanks to the wonders of videotape, no such slipup could occur because anyone walking near the embassy is on film.

Lacking a photograph, the FBI was faced with the herculean task of identifying the voice on the tape. The NSA has more than 100,000 employees scattered throughout the world. What's more, the FBI had to find out who he was in utmost secrecy. Theoretically, he could have returned to NSA, and he could have accomplices still working there. If they learned the FBI was looking for them, the NSA employee and his accomplices might flee to Moscow, just as Howard had done. (In fact, the NSA employee would later admit, the Soviets had asked him to reapply to NSA, but he feared he would fail the lie-detector test.)

Since the Baltimore field office has jurisdiction over NSA, it had primary responsibility for the case. David E. Faulkner, who was in charge of liaison with NSA, was assigned to be case agent. In addition, agents from the Washington field office conducted investigations in the capital, and O'Keefe from CI-3 coordinated their efforts with Baltimore. Altogether, some thirty to forty agents worked the case each day.

Faulkner was a seasoned agent, at home interviewing bank robbers, car thieves, and white-collar criminals. The fact that counterintelligence agents all started with this experience was considered a plus in the FBI. It meant they could deal with people and could spot con men.

Based on Yurchenko's sketchy descriptions of the man, Faulkner decided the only NSA employees who could be eliminated were those who were bald, unmarried, under age thirty and over age fifty, and didn't work at Fort Meade, NSA's headquarters. Based on the data in NSA's computers, that left about nine hundred suspects. But by getting more current information from personnel files, and by eliminating those who did not have access to information about Project Ivy Bells, Faulkner narrowed the list to one hundred names.

Now the FBI tried to find people at NSA who might recognize the man's voice. In special interview rooms, agents played the tape to particularly trustworthy officials at NSA headquarters. Faulkner was beginning to wonder if they had the right man. For all he knew, the man on the tape was not the NSA employee Yurchenko had described.

Then, on October 15, after the tape had been played to fifteen NSA employees, Donald Bacon recognized the voice of one of his former subordinates at NSA.

"That's Ron Pelton!" he exclaimed.

On Saturday night, November 2, 1985, Yurchenko was dining with a CIA escort at Au Pied de Cochon, an inexpensive French café in Georgetown. In retrospect, the CIA's choice of company and of restaurants was atrocious. The escort was in his early twenties, spoke no Russian, and knew nothing about the Soviet Union—hardly a fitting companion for someone of Yurchenko's stature. And the restaurant was not even on the map of good French restaurants in Washington.

In recent weeks, Yurchenko had grown increasingly uncooperative with his CIA keepers. The CIA has jurisdiction over defectors unless they are developed by the FBI. After giving up Pelton and

Howard, he had lapsed into almost total silence. Did the CIA's choice of escorts signify that the agency felt he was of no further use to them?

"If I walked out of here, would you shoot me?" Yurchenko asked his CIA escort.

"We don't treat defectors that way," was the reply.

"Well, if I'm not back in fifteen minutes, it's not your fault," Yurchenko said.

Yurchenko walked up Wisconsin Avenue to the new Soviet Embassy complex at Mount Alto. When he did not return, his escort called neither the CIA nor the FBI.

Two days later, the Soviets held a press conference in Washington starring Yurchenko. He told how he had been drugged and kidnapped by the CIA in Rome and treated miserably. Next, he showed up on Soviet television to tell the story of how he had escaped the tentacles of the CIA.

Was Yurchenko a genuine defector or a plant meant to lull the CIA into believing the agency had not been penetrated by the Soviets? Just as the defections of Anatoli Golytsin in December 1961 and Yuri I. Nosenko in September 1964 provoked debate about whether their defections were staged, Yurchenko had his supporters and detractors within the intelligence community.

After studying all the evidence, most FBI and CIA officials believe Yurchenko was real. It made little sense to them that the KGB would turn in two of their former spies. What's more, Yurchenko had probably saved the life of Gordyevsky in England. And he had passed CIA lie-detector tests.

Very often, defectors simply become homesick. In Yurchenko's case, it appeared he had hoped to persuade the wife of a Soviet diplomat in Ottawa to defect with him to the U.S. Shortly after she refused, he faded back to Moscow. He was also known to be perturbed that the news of his defection—and the details of what he told the CIA—quickly appeared in the next day's newspapers.

"If you can't keep what I say secret, how can you protect me?" he asked his CIA handlers.

"They would not send a guy who knew all their best secrets on a double-agent mission," said Richard Helms, CIA director from 1973 to 1976. "There would be too big a risk of him saying something he shouldn't."

On the other hand, Yurchenko today is alive and well, having been neither imprisoned nor executed for having spilled KGB secrets, leading to the theory he was a double agent.

"I would be stunned if there were any other explanation," said Senator Malcolm Wallop, a member of the Senate Intelligence Committee. "Yurchenko has been in the KGB all his life. He knows what they do to traitors. Defectors get a bullet in the base of their skull. Yurchenko will get a medal."

But former CIA officials say that's the best way to handle such a sticky situation. If Yurchenko were executed, the KGB could not requestion him about issues that might later become pertinent.

"Today I think he was genuine," said former deputy assistant FBI director Parker. "Tomorrow, I might think he was not."

Privately, many FBI officials blame the CIA for Yurchenko's decision to redefect. An FBI official said there was a grain of truth to Yurchenko's claims at his press conference: the CIA assigned someone to be with him night and day, creating the impression he was under detention.

"Yurchenko felt he was a prisoner," the FBI official said. The FBI approach would have been to give him far more breathing space, according to the FBI official.

A former FBI official said the CIA refused to allow people who were interested in meeting Yurchenko to get in touch with him. One was Alexandra Costa, who defected from the Soviet Embassy in Washington.

"The FBI tried to persuade the CIA to let him interact with individuals, both male and female. But the FBI doesn't have the final say. The CIA doesn't understand people," an FBI official said.

There is ample evidence that Soviet defectors prefer the FBI's treatment of them to the CIA's. In his book, *Breaking with Moscow*, Arkady N. Shevchenko, the former under secretary-general of the United Nations, complains about being pressured by the CIA to remain in his UN job before he formally defected to the U.S. He had no complaints about the FBI.

In her book, *Stepping Down from the Star*, Costa accuses the CIA of misdeeds ranging from sloppy paperwork to insensitivity to her emotional needs. On the other hand, she has high praise for her FBI contacts.

"I'm convinced that Yurchenko didn't feel he had a chance here," an FBI official involved in the case said.

13 "Give Them the Cactus"

The arrest of Walker and the defection of Howard were beginning to have their effect on the U.S. intelligence community. No one likes to snoop on other people, least of all co-workers cleared for access to "top secret" information. But it was clear from newspaper accounts of both spy cases that they never would have happened if fellow workers had been more suspicious.

So when they noticed in early November 1985 that Jonathan Jay Pollard, a thirty-one-year-old research specialist with the Naval Investigative Service, was requesting classified reports unrelated to his duties, co-workers did not hesitate to report him.

Cleared for access to "sensitive compartmented information," a classification level beyond "top secret," Pollard could review information gathered by sensitive technical collection systems like satellites and NSA electronic intercepts. Much of the information could be retrieved through terminals hooked up to secure computer systems. The Navy operated on the "honor" system. Employees were supposed to confine their requests to their own areas of specialization. Supplied with the appropriate codes, Pollard could rummage through classified information about any area of the world, much as Soviet spy Judith Coplon, employed by the Justice Department in 1949, could read a wide range of espionage reports unrelated to her duties.

There was a catch: the Navy computer system kept track of information requests. Pollard, who had been with the Navy for six years, specialized in terrorist threats to North America and the Caribbean. When they noticed that he was requesting voluminous data about the Middle East, co-workers began wondering about Pollard. He had already aroused suspicions because of his fanciful boasts about having been a CIA or Mossad agent. On October 25, one of his co-workers observed him leaving work with what appeared to be classified documents.

When the suspicions were reported to Pollard's commanding officer at the Terrorist Alert Center of the Navy's Threat Analysis Division in Suitland, Maryland, he began looking into Pollard's activities himself. On November 8, Commander Jerry Agee found that a large quantity of "sensitive compartmented information" about the Middle East had been checked out by Pollard but was not in Pollard's office area.

That night, Agee learned from security guards that Pollard had displayed his courier card when leaving work so that he would not be searched. Agee called in agents from the Naval Investigative Service and the FBI.

The FBI set up hidden surveillance cameras in Pollard's work area. The following Monday, November 18, the camera filmed Pollard removing classified documents from a safe and stuffing them in his briefcase. Using his courier card, he left work with the documents. As he was getting into his car at 5:00 P.M., the federal agents stopped him and asked what was in the package he was carrying. When he gave conflicting accounts, they asked him to follow them back to his office, where they opened the package and discovered it contained sixty classified documents, including twenty marked "top secret."

Pollard said he had been taking the documents to another Navy employee in a different part of the Suitland complex. While some of the agents tried to locate the other man, Pollard asked if he could call his twenty-six-year-old wife, Anne Henderson Pollard.

"I'll be late for dinner," he told her at 7:30 P.M. "Go see our friends, take the wedding albums, and give them the cactus," he said.

"Are you sure you want me to give the cactus away? You spent so much time picking it out," she said.

"Yes," he replied firmly.

A few minutes later, he called his wife again to say it was very important that she give away the cactus.

Just the day before, Pollard had told his wife that "cactus" would be a code word: it meant she should remove any classified documents hidden in their apartment in Washington's Dupont Circle area.

Realizing her husband was in trouble, Anne Pollard gathered all the classified documents she could find and stuffed them in a suitcase. She raced downstairs and opened the rear door of the apartment building. There, in the alley, were several cars with their motors running. Not sure who the people were—several were CI-3 agents—she slammed the door and hid the suitcase under a staircase. Then she ran to a friend's apartment and, claiming the suitcase was too heavy, asked if the couple would bring the suitcase to the Four Seasons Hotel, where she would be waiting.

When the couple seemed in no hurry, Anne Pollard said, "I have a feeling something has happened to Jay." Then she blurted out that the suitcase contained classified documents. She said they concerned the People's Republic of China, and she had planned on using them to help with a presentation to the Chinese Embassy on behalf of the public relations firm that employed her.

"I'm going to destroy them instead," she explained.

Anne Pollard waited at the hotel, but the friends never showed up. The next day, they turned the suitcase over to the FBI. There were twenty-five classified documents inside. Just as she had said, the documents included classified FBI reports about China and its embassies. Pollard had given them to her as if he were lending her a bestseller to read.

Meanwhile, back in Suitland, the FBI and Naval Investigative Service agents had found the man Pollard was supposed to be taking the documents to. He said he knew nothing about any documents.

As Pollard began spinning more stories, the agents told him that if he didn't give his approval they would obtain a warrant to search his apartment. Thinking his wife had taken all the documents from his home, Pollard gave his consent. At eleven that evening, as Pollard watched, the agents found fifty-seven more classified documents in a box under his wife's clothing.

Clearly, Pollard had violated Navy security regulations by taking classified documents home, and the agents asked if Pollard would take a polygraph test the next day.

Just before the test, Pollard told the agents that he had given away six or seven classified documents to a friend who was not authorized to receive them. The agents advised him of his right to have a lawyer and to remain silent, but Pollard was not finished. He began admitting to giving away even more documents. Eventually, he signed an eleven-page document admitting that he had given away fifty to one hundred classified documents a month for the past year. Yet Pollard denied that he ever gave any material to agents of another country. According to his statement, the friend who had received the documents was a U.S. citizen. But because of the volume of material involved, the FBI suspected Pollard was working for a foreign power—perhaps the Soviet Union.

That night, CI-3 and other Washington field office agents began around-the-clock surveillance of Pollard. Headquarters wanted no repetition of Howard's escape to Moscow. The agents were under orders to arrest Pollard if he tried to leave Washington or entered any embassy where he could seek asylum.

On Thursday, November 21, the FBI agents followed Pollard as he took his wife to Washington Hospital Center. There, she received regular treatment for a rare stomach disorder—one that left her food partially undigested. After the appointment, instead of driving directly home, the Pollards took a circuitous route. Apparently thinking he had shaken the agents, Pollard fell in behind an Israeli Embassy car at 10:20 A.M. as it drove into the embassy on International Drive NW.

The agents, using aircraft, knew exactly where Pollard was. From wiretaps, they already believed he was working for the Israelis. Several agents had been sent to stake out the Israeli Embassy. But the agents were unable to pursue him when he entered Israeli territory. As nearly a dozen agents waited outside the compound, Pollard and his wife talked with embassy personnel for twenty minutes.

Pollard's Israeli contacts had told him he would be granted asylum if he could shake his FBI tail. Because of the crowd of FBI agents outside, the embassy turned him away. As Pollard and his wife drove out of the compound, the FBI arrested him. The next day, they arrested his wife. Meanwhile, Pollard's current Israeli handler, Joseph "Yossi" Yagur, fled to Israel.

Pollard eventually admitted to stealing over a thousand classified documents, many consisting of several hundred pages, over a period of eighteen months. But his sentencing, less than two years later, would present the Justice Department with some unusual issues.

For months, Robert Fierer had been locked in a Justice Department vault going over secret documents relating to the Koecher case. He was sure he could get his client off, and he told any Justice official who would listen, "You're going to lose this case."

On November 11, 1985, before U.S. District Court Judge Shirley Wohl Kram in New York, Fierer began cross-examining the FBI agents and a CIA official who had obtained his client Karl Koecher's confession a year earlier. His purpose was to show that Koecher's admissions should be "suppressed" or disregarded because they had been made involuntarily—in response to threats and false promises by the government agents.

If Fierer thought he would get any help from his client, he was mistaken. The lawyer had wanted Koecher to testify about his reactions to the agents' statements, but Koecher was supremely uninterested. When Westby, Fierer's then partner, tried to meet with Koecher to prepare him to testify, Koecher said he didn't want to be awakened early to meet with him.

Now Special Agent Geide was on the witness stand in Kram's third-floor courtroom at the federal court in New York's Foley Square. Slowly, Fierer led him through the events leading up to Koecher's arrest—the approach in front of the Diamond Club Building, the ride to the Barbizon Plaza Hotel, and the introduction to Brown, the CIA security official. Then Fierer asked Geide to read out loud some of the statements he had made to Koecher just before Koecher confessed.

As instructed, Geide read the line he had used with Koecher as the Czech sat on a love seat facing a concealed video camera:

" 'What we want to do is talk about a proposition for you and talk about your future, your future and your wife's future. And that future I think is going to depend on what we, what we accomplish today in our conversation with you,' " Geide read.

Turning to Geide, Fierer asked, "[Is that] you speaking when you say, 'We want to talk about a proposition for you?' "

A. Yes, sir.
Q. And you immediately go on and say, you want to talk about the future, isn't that true?
A. Yes, sir.
Q. And it is his future and his wife's future, isn't that true?
A. Yes, sir.
Q. And then you qualify that by saying, "And I think that future, I think, is going to depend on what we, what we accomplish today." Isn't that true?
A. Yes, sir, I said that.
Q. So you have, one, a proposition, two, it is about his future, and three, it depends upon what happens today, isn't that true?

Bruce Green, the assistant U.S. attorney, objected to the question, but Judge Kram overruled him.

Continuing his questioning, Fierer asked, "Isn't that true, sir?"

A. If you are asking me if I said those words that I just read, yes, I did say those words. What I was meaning to convey to Mr. Koecher, if you are asking me that—

Q. I am asking you the words.
A. Yes, I did say those things, yes . . . What I was trying to convey to Mr. Koecher is that I hoped that he would talk with me that day.
Q. But you didn't say that, did you, Mr. Geide? . . .
A. I said those words, yes, sir.

After more questioning, Geide admitted that the only "proposition" he had in mind was that Koecher confess; that, contrary to what he had told Koecher, there were no plans to make him a double agent for the U.S. government and have a "harmonious relationship" with him; that he really had no "attractive proposal" or "other choices" to offer Koecher other than going to jail.

"When I used the terms 'proposals' or 'proposition,'" Geide testified, "I had absolutely no plan or proposal or proposition in mind to suggest to Mr. Koecher, and if he had asked me what proposal or what proposition I had in mind, I was prepared to tell Mr. Koecher at that time that I had no specific proposal or proposition in mind."

Asked by Fierer about Brown's statements to Koecher, Geide said he did not know what the CIA official had meant when he told Koecher his travel plans would not be disrupted. Nor did he know what Brown meant when he said something "terrible" could happen if Koecher left the country.

Fierer asked Geide about Brown's statement that the couple would be free to go on about their business. Did he tell Koecher that was untrue?

A. No, sir, I did not.
Q. And Hana Koecher says, "It sounds great, it sounds really great." And Jerry Brown says, "And I promise." Did you at that time say to Karl Koecher or Hana Koecher that he had no authority to promise, did you say that?
A. No, sir.
Q. Did you tell him that promise was a lie?
A. No, sir.
Q. When he went on to say, "I guarantee you that, that's what I intend," did you tell him that his guarantee was a lie?
A. No, sir. The words on the transcript are accurate.

Geide eventually admitted that several hours into the interview, he realized that some of the things Brown was saying were not a good idea.

". . . I would characterize them as poor interview technique; I would choose not to have said some of those things or done some of those things," he testified.

But Geide also conceded that he and Brown had planned the general approach to the interview for days.

Then Fierer put Special Agent Richard J. Dorn Jr. on the witness stand. Dorn had conducted the interview of Hana in a separate room, yet his line with her bore a striking resemblance to Geide's approach with Koecher.

Reading Dorn's statement to Hana that "You're not going to prison," Fierer asked Dorn, "Do you remember that?"

A. Yes, I do.
Q. And was that part of your attempt to get her to be cooperative with you, the assurance that she would not go to prison?
A. Yes, it was.

Finally, Fierer asked Dorn if he remembered his statement to Hana, made in Karl's presence, that ". . . you can be free to go to Austria in two weeks."

A. Yes, I do.
Q. Was it true at the time?
A. I made the statement.
Q. Was it true at the time?
A. Was what true at the time?
Q. That statement that she would be free to go to Austria in two weeks?
A. I made the statement.

Fierer asked the judge to intercede.
"Can you respond more specifically?" Judge Kram asked.

A. I wasn't in a position to fulfill that.
Q. But you told her that, didn't you?
A. Yes, I did.
Q. And you didn't tell her you weren't in a position to fulfill that, did you?
A. No, I did not.
Q. So you deceived her, didn't you?
A. I told her that in order to induce her testimony.
Q. Right.

It was a skillful performance by one of Atlanta's top criminal attorneys. In a document filed with the court, the government subsequently acknowledged that much of Koecher's confession could not be used at the trial because it was obtained in violation of Koecher's rights. But the government insisted other portions were admissible.

Privately, Justice Department and FBI officials involved in the case conceded that because of the way the agents handled the interview, the charges against Koecher might never hold up in court.

Yet questions remained. James E. Nolan Jr., who was deputy assistant FBI director for operations when the Koecher case began, said the FBI normally would try to recruit an "illegal" like Koecher as a double agent. In that case, he said, the FBI might not inform the Justice Department of the case first, just as it did not inform the Justice Department of the Koecher case at first. The approach would be very similar to the one used with Koecher, he said.

Indeed, the opening remarks used when confronting Koecher were almost identical to those used by FBI agents when they first confronted Josef Zemenek, a Czech KGB officer, in 1977. Posing as a photographer, Zemenek, under the name of Rudolph A. Herrmann, had illegally entered the U.S. from Canada in 1968. His primary mission was to pick up political information in New York, and he never obtained anything classified.

As recounted by John Barron in *The KGB Today,* one of the agents told him, "Rudi, we know who you are. We know who you work for. We know about Inga [his wife]. We know about Peter [his son]. We know everything about you. We have known for years."

Continuing, the agent said, "Knowing your past, I know that in your life you have had to make some big decisions. Now you have to make the biggest one of them all. There are two choices. We can arrest you and turn you over to a federal prosecutor. . . . Your other choice is to join us in a partnership against the KGB. If you honestly cooperate, you and your family may remain in the United States for the rest of your lives. We will relocate you, give you new identities, and guarantee your security."

Zemenek agreed to act as a double agent until the operation was terminated in 1980.

Unlike Koecher, Zemenek came clean and passed polygraph tests. He also had no access to classified material. Koecher appeared to be playing games and eventually failed a lie-detector test. Unlike Zemenek, he had access to classified documents.

Very often Justice suggests ways to recruit spies as double agents, as it did with Zemenek. "You see how long he'll talk," Nolan told me. "You have to decide what you're getting. I think they were trying to find out if he would really tell them anything. He's probably dancing. He would give pieces but nothing substantive. I think it's very possible they were trying to turn him; I don't know of any reason not to turn him. . . . If you can't turn them, prosecute them. The prosecution might not have been very good anyway."

Koecher himself is convinced the agents were genuinely trying to turn him into a double agent. Yet both Brown and Geide testified under oath that they were not—that they had no intention of following up on their promises. Nor was their approach entirely congruent with the one made to Zemenek. The agents in that case did not threaten him. And before he made any admissions, they told him he could be prosecuted.

In Koecher's case, it appears, the agents simply screwed up by making promises they never intended to keep. According to FBI sources, there never was any intention to make Koecher a double agent, because the bureau did not feel he could be trusted. Nor did the FBI have enough hard evidence before his interview to charge him with a crime.

"There was no paper from headquarters to New York saying he should be turned," an FBI official said. "Without that paper, no one could offer to make him a double agent."

In a proceeding after Koecher's arrest before U.S. Magistrate Sharon E. Grubin, Bruce A. Green, the assistant U.S. attorney in charge of the case, said the FBI's primary purpose in interviewing Koecher was "to detect how much damage had been done." This is a classic sign that the FBI is heading in the wrong direction. By handling investigations properly, the FBI can achieve both ends—criminal prosecution and damage assessment. Once they confess and are charged, most spies will provide the details of what they did in hopes of receiving a shorter sentence.

The FBI's Professional Responsibility Office subsequently looked into the handling of the Koecher case and censured the agents for going beyond FBI guidelines in trying to obtain Koecher's confession. However, the fact that Geide is now one of several officials in charge of training other counterintelligence agents indicates the FBI did not take the breach very seriously.

14 *An Unexpected Suicide*

As assistant special agent in charge of counterintelligence for the Sino-Soviet bloc in the Washington field office, Joseph C. Johnson was responsible for spies from any country besides the Soviet Union.

An agent since 1972, Johnson's career in the FBI bore all the notches of a man on the way up in the bureau. After serving in the military and working for a bank in Manhattan, he joined the FBI and worked on criminal cases in St. Louis. But the bureau needed agents to work Hungarian counterintelligence, so he learned Hungarian at the Defense Department Language School. For five years, he was assigned to Soviet-bloc squads in New York. After three years, he became a supervisor.

In 1979, Johnson was transferred to headquarters. He worked in the inspection division, which reviews the work of agents in the field, and then became a section chief over computer operations and an assistant section chief over non-Soviet spies. More recently, he was promoted to section chief over investigative support, which administers the counterintelligence budget, analysis, training, and other functions in headquarters.

When Johnson was in the Washington field office, roughly half of the twenty counterintelligence squads reported to him. Each of the Warsaw Pact countries—Albania, Bulgaria, Czechoslovakia, the German Democratic Republic, Hungary, Poland, and Rumania—operates intelligence services similar to the KGB and GRU. Very often, they get their directions from the KGB. As on the Soviet side, roughly a third of the diplomats from the bloc countries are, in fact, spies.

The squads under Johnson operated much the same way the Soviet squads operated. Sometimes, one squad covered two countries. Because the main threat is the Soviet Union, some agents thought of work on the bloc squads as being not quite as glamorous as working Soviet cases. Yet the Soviets often directed the bloc intelligence services to do their work, and the stakes were just as high.

For several days in the fall of 1985, Johnson was staying at the office until 4:00 A.M. He was helping to direct the investigation of Pollard and of Larry Wu-Tai Chin, a retired CIA translator.

From a defector, according to later newspaper accounts, the FBI had learned that Chin had been spying for the People's Republic of China for thirty-three years—longer than Harold (Kim) Philby had been spying for the Soviets within British intelligence. Chin had been supplying so much material, the defector said, that it took two Chinese intelligence agents two months to translate each shipment, which was sent to the Politburo, the most powerful arm of the ruling Communist Party in China.

Since February 1983, the Chinese squad had followed him and verified that he was meeting with Chinese intelligence agents in China, Hong Kong, and Canada. Other FBI agents developed background information on him by interviewing his supervisors at the CIA, where he was still a consultant. When Chin left for a trip to Hong Kong in May 1983, the agents even searched his luggage at Dulles International Airport before he left.

Now, two and a half years later, they were ready to confront him. The fact that Chin had been meeting with Chinese intelligence agents was enough to give the FBI probable cause to search his apartment in Alexandria, Virginia. But the FBI still had no evidence that Chin had been passing classified documents. The case against Chin might have to hinge largely on the defector, who most likely would not agree to testify. Then again, if Chin confessed, the FBI would have the best evidence of all.

The targets of counterintelligence cases are often quite learned and intelligent. Yet because they are smart, they often think they can handle any problem by talking. So it was with Chin.

Born in Peking, the sixty-three-year-old Chin had majored in journalism at Peking's Yenching University. In 1948, he began working as a translator and interpreter for the U.S. consulate in Shanghai and later in Hong Kong. By 1952, Chin was spying for the Chinese, reporting on the U.S. Army's interrogations of prisoners of war during the Korean conflict.

That same year, Chin got a job as a translator in the CIA's Foreign Information Broadcasting Service in Okinawa. He was later transferred to Santa Rosa, California. Having become a U.S. citizen, Chin was cleared for access to "top secret" information in 1970. He began working for the CIA's service in Rosslyn, Virginia.

198 SPY vs. SPY

Besides translating foreign radio broadcasts and publications for the CIA, Chin had access to reports of clandestine CIA operations in China, handwritten notes of CIA operatives, and intelligence reports presented to the White House.

Very often, compartmentation within the CIA is a joke. If a report came in written in Chinese, it was sent to be translated. Chin thus had access to practically everything the CIA did in the Chinese arena.

Fluent in three Chinese dialects, Chin was considered one of the CIA's best Chinese translators and won the CIA's Career Intelligence Medal just before his retirement in 1981. After the FBI began following him, the CIA fed him phony information for his work as a CIA consultant.

For the past several weeks, three FBI agents from the Chinese squad had been going over the information they had gathered on Chin and discussing what their approach to him should be. Seeking to avoid a repetition of the earlier problem with Koecher's confession, FBI attorneys and Justice Department officials had gone over with the agents what they could and could not say.

Chin had an office in the Watergate at Landmark condominium apartments in Alexandria. To catch him off guard, the agents arranged for another FBI man who lives in the same complex to let them into the building on Friday, November 22, 1985.

From wiretaps, the agents knew Chin was in his office late on the afternoon of Friday, November 22. As it turned out, they did not need a key to get into the lobby: as they walked toward the front entrance, a tenant walked out and held the door for them.

At 4:25 P.M., the agents knocked on the door of apartment 1719.

Chin opened the door, and they showed their badges. They said they were investigating transmittal of classified information and wanted to know if he could help them.

"Why sure, come on in," Chin said affably.

A tall, slim man, Chin was dressed in a white shirt, tie, and dark slacks.

Showing them to the dining area, Chin said, "Won't you please have a seat?"

After verifying who Chin was, Special Agent Mark R. Johnson asked him if he had ever had any contact with any intelligence officers from the People's Republic of China.

"No," Chin said.

To the agents, Chin seemed remarkably calm.

Johnson laid a photo of Zhu Entao, a Chinese intelligence officer, on the table.

"Have you ever met with this person?" the agent asked.

Chin looked at the photo and turned it over. On the back was the man's name.

"No," Chin said. Then he paused. "Well, I think this may be a Bank of China official that I met on my trip to China," he said.

"Did you know Mr. Zhu was a Chinese intelligence officer?" Johnson asked.

"No," Chin said.

Now Johnson laid an index card on the table with the intelligence officer's name written in English and in Chinese. The bottom of the card listed his title with the Ministry of Public Security, one of the Chinese intelligence services.

"Oh, really?" Chin remarked as he read the title.

Johnson proceeded to read a detailed account of Chin's trip to China in February 1982. He recounted how the Ministry of Public Security had given a banquet in his honor. Chin seemed impressed, but he again denied Zhu was an intelligence officer.

"We know you met with Chinese intelligence officers and are working for them," Johnson told Chin matter-of-factly, as if he were discussing the weather.

"Are you serious?" Chin asked incredulously.

"Yes, Mr. Chin, we are very serious," one of the agents said.

Next, the agents showed him an index card for Ou Quiming, Chin's handler. When Chin said he did not know him, Johnson read a detailed account of a trip by Chin in June 1983 to Hong Kong and nearby Macao. During the trip, Chin met with Ou.

Once again, Chin seemed surprised at the amount of detail the agents had.

"Mr. Chin, we are aware of your illegal activities, including your trips to Canada," Johnson said, referring to trips that Chin had made to give photos of CIA reports to Chinese couriers.

The agent paused.

"We have been investigating this matter a long time," Johnson told him. "The reason we were coming by this evening was to offer you an opportunity to explain why you were doing what you were doing. Perhaps there may be reasons you did it. This is an opportunity to explain before we take our case to the Justice Department."

In fact, the agents had already been there.

"Perhaps I should seek a lawyer," Chin said.

"Go right ahead," another agent said, pointing to the phone. "Any time you want to call an attorney, you may do so."

"I'm not an attorney, and I'm not sure what my legal rights are," Chin said.

"Well, Mr. Chin, I am an attorney," Johnson said, "and I want to make it perfectly clear before we go any further that you do not have to talk to us if you don't want to, that anything you say is voluntary, that any time you want to call an attorney you are free to call one. If you tell us to leave, we will go."

But then Johnson added a caveat. If he chose not to talk, Johnson said, besides presenting the case to the Justice Department, the agents planned to continue their investigation and interview all his family members, his business associates, and his girlfriend.

"You mean if I talk to you, no one else will know about this?" Chin asked.

"No, that is not correct," Johnson said. "But there is a possibility that fewer people would have to be contacted if you cooperated fully."

"Well, why should I talk to you?" Chin asked.

Then Johnson told him that if he talked, the agents would tell the Justice Department he had cooperated.

Presenting Chin with a hypothetical situation, Johnson said, "Mr. Chin, you are the Department of Justice. If I come to you with two identical cases—identical set of facts—and I tell you that we went to interview this subject, and he said that he was really sorry for what he did, and he gave you names, dates, places, even gave us trade craft that was used, who would you have more sympathy for?"

Chin thought a moment.

"What would an attorney say if I called him?" he asked.

"If you call an attorney, he will tell you not to talk to us," one of the agents said.

After more sparring, an agent read an account of a September 1983 trip Chin had taken to Hong Kong. The account included the fact that Chin had told Ou how to recruit a fellow CIA employee. Chin had also suggested that if the Chinese were to pay him $150,000, he could divorce his wife and get rehired by the CIA.

Chin was stunned that the agents knew about his proposal.

"Only Ou would know that information," Chin said, thereby

acknowledging that he knew him after all. "Where did you get that information?"

"We are not at liberty to disclose our sources," one of the agents said smoothly.

Chin picked up one of the index cards with Ou's name on it. He scratched out the last part of the Chinese character for "Ou" and left the rest.

"That is the correct character for him," Chin said.

Chin said it would take a long time to tell the agents everything, and he suggested they come back the next day. But the agents said this was Chin's only opportunity to talk before they went to the Justice Department.

"Perhaps I could work for the government," he said. "Maybe I could go back to China and see my Chinese contacts there, and then come back and report to you what they said."

The agents had been prepared for that. They were to tell him they couldn't make such a decision themselves, leaving the door partially open.

"Any decision about that would have to be reached at a level way beyond us," Johnson said. "But before the government would make such a decision, you would have to tell us your whole story," he said.

About fifty minutes into the interview, Chin agreed to provide what he called an "outline" of his activities. He proceeded to corroborate much of the information the agents had already developed, adding some detail as well.

"When I was six I realized that if I learned English I could get out of China and move to the West, and if I moved to the West, I could earn some money," he said.

It was easy to take classified documents from the CIA, he said. He hid them in his briefcase or clothing and took them home, where he photographed them with a Minolta camera. Employees were never frisked. And the only lie-detector test he had ever been given was a perfunctory affair.

He was able to pass the test because "the questions were vague and were not asked in Chinese," he said.

One of the agents sent out for Chinese food. As they ate, they discussed Chin's gambling activities and his jaunts to Las Vegas and Atlantic City, where he played blackjack. At 9:00 P.M., as they finished eating, one of the agents asked Chin if he had a current passport.

Chin went to another room and brought out a passport.

"Oh, that's an expired passport," he said, opening it. He claimed his current passport was in his residence in another building of the same apartment complex.

The agents knew that a warrant to search Chin's apartment had already been approved. But they asked if he would consent to a search. When he declined, one of the agents left the apartment to consult with a supervisor. Meanwhile, the agents discussed the Chinese language with him.

At 10:37 P.M., there was a knock on the door. Four agents came in and arrested Chin.

When Chin was searched at the Arlington County jail, the agents found that he had been carrying a current passport all along.

Chin displayed little emotion during his trial. He testified that he passed information to the Chinese as part of a personal "mission" to reconcile differences between China and the U.S. The only classified report he admitted to giving up summarized President Nixon's intention to normalize relations with China in 1970. The $180,000 he received from Chinese intelligence agents was "only a by-product" of his peace mission, he said.

As expected, the bulk of the government's evidence came from Chin's own admissions to the three FBI agents who visited him on November 22, 1985. While Chin now denied making most of the statements, their testimony about his confession was convincing.

After deliberating a little over three hours, a jury found Chin guilty on February 8, 1986. As he was led away, he paused at the door and looked back sadly at his wife, Cathy, and their three children.

During the course of his spy career, Chin had gambled away most of the money he made, but he parlayed his take into real estate and other investments that were worth $700,000.

To the press, he said he had no regrets. Life in prison was a small price to pay for having played a part in improving the lives of a billion Chinese, who already had benefited from closer ties to the U.S.

But one of his sons sensed that despite his calm exterior, he was depressed. A week after he was sentenced, Chin told a fellow prisoner at the Prince William County Detention Center in Virginia that he would not serve his term if sentenced to life in prison. A diabetic, he said he would induce a coma by eating too much sugar. After being placed briefly on a "suicide watch" in a solitary cell, Chin was returned to a regular cell with another inmate.

On February 21, 1986, Chin ate breakfast in his cell at 6:30 A.M. He reminded a prison worker that the wastebasket in a prison room needed to be emptied. The prisoners earned extra privileges if their areas passed inspections. At 7:15 A.M., the worker emptied the trash can and gave Chin a new plastic trash bag to place in the waste-basket.

At 8:45 A.M., a guard found Chin covered by a blanket with a plastic bag over his head. The bag was tied tightly around his neck with a shoelace. Chin had stopped breathing, and an emergency unit failed to revive him.

Besides Karl Koecher, Chin was the only mole known to have penetrated the CIA at the request of a foreign power.

He was pronounced dead at 9:30 A.M.

15

"You Do Crazy Things"

Now that the FBI knew the voice on the tape of the call to the Soviet Embassy was Ronald W. Pelton's, it took eight days to find him. No longer with NSA, he was renting an apartment in Silver Spring, Maryland, but never showed up there. By tracing his rental checks, Baltimore agents found that Suburban Bank was sending his statements to the address of Ann Barry, a striking, green-eyed brunette who lived in Washington. She turned out to be his girlfriend.

CI-3 and other Washington agents began following Pelton and wiretapping his phones. Yet watching Pelton had produced nothing incriminating. He had not met with any Soviets nor given them any information so far as they could tell. The fact that he had called the embassy five years earlier to say he had information for the Soviets was not a crime. He could have brought them copies of *National Geographic*. Moreover, Yurchenko was by now back in the Soviet Union. Some FBI officials had been considering the possibility of asking Yurchenko to testify against Pelton. Now he couldn't testify against him even if he wanted to—news that O'Keefe had to break to the Baltimore field office when Yurchenko disappeared.

Having exhausted all leads, Faulkner, as the case agent, decided as the agents did in the Chin case to try the direct approach. In going the direct interview route, the FBI takes a chance. If the suspect is still passing secrets, he will stop all contact with the Soviets, depriving the FBI of the chance to apprehend him in the act. If the suspect decides to flee, he places the FBI and the Justice Department in a quandary. Lacking probable cause to arrest the suspect in the first place, the government must decide whether to arrest him anyway and take a chance the case will be thrown out, or let the suspect leave the country and suffer criticism that surely would follow—as it did in the Howard case.

Generally, it is better to have the goods on a suspect before confronting him. Yet proving espionage is one of the most difficult tasks in law enforcement. In a bank robbery, there are usually eyewitnesses, surveillance photographs, fingerprints on the teller's counter, a note demanding money, a getaway car, or money packets that spray red dye on the robber. In white-collar crimes, there are financial records. In espionage, the crime consists of passing information. The foreign power that receives the information will not help out. Usually, there are no accomplices. Even if the FBI sees the suspect communicating with foreign intelligence agents through tree stumps, the case is circumstantial. The FBI must see the suspect leave classified documents for foreign agents. If the information is passed verbally, the case is even harder to prove. For these reasons, a confession is frequently the only way that the FBI can get a conviction in an espionage case.

Over the years, the FBI has developed interview techniques into something approaching a science. With the help of psychologists and psychiatrists, the bureau has compiled profiles of suspects and the best ways to wring confessions out of them. The approach is similar to the FBI's techniques for compiling profiles of suspects in murder and rape cases—an approach that has achieved remarkable success. For example, police in a midwestern city a few years back found the mutilated torsos of a teenage boy and girl floating in a river. They identified the teenagers but had no clues on who killed them or why. The police asked the FBI's Behavioral Science Unit, based at the FBI Academy in Quantico, Virginia, for help.

Reviewing the evidence from the crime scene, the Behavioral Science Unit told the police the person they should look for was a male in his forties who knew the teenagers. He led a macho lifestyle, wore western boots, often hunted or fished, and probably owned a four-wheel-drive vehicle. He was self-employed, divorced several times, and had a minor criminal record.

Armed with this information, the police focused on the girl's stepfather, who knew both teenagers and fit the other characteristics as well. Once they had a suspect, the police gathered enough evidence from eyewitnesses to charge him. In January 1984, he was convicted of murdering both teenagers.

By matching clues from crime scenes with the suspects later apprehended, the FBI had learned that a person who is careful enough to dispose of a body in a river is probably an older person. A body dumped in a remote area means the murderer knows the area and is an outdoorsman. The fact that the slashes on the victim's bodies were vicious and aimed at the sex organs indicated that the murderer knew the victims.

"We believe that in most crime scenes, the killer leaves his signature there," said Special Agent Roger L. Dupue, who heads the FBI's Behavioral Science Unit.

In the same vein, by analyzing many cases, the Behavioral Science Unit knows what personality types respond to which kinds of interview approaches. Based on this knowledge, the unit could tell Faulkner—as it had told the agents handling the Chin case—whether to take a hard or soft approach, whether to interview him in the morning or the afternoon, whether to wear a suit or casual clothes, whether to interrupt him or let him talk, whether to face him toward a window or away from one.

If done right, the interview could elicit a confession without violating a suspect's rights.

Based on the advice from the psychologists and their own instincts, Faulkner and his partner, Special Agent Dudley F. B. Hodgson, decided Pelton was a talker—a man who thought he was smarter than anyone else and would try to explain himself if given a chance. The best approach would be to try to get his help rather than to confront him.

A man with a record would not fall for a con like that, but Pelton would. Nor would Pelton respond to a tough approach. He would simply refuse to talk or ask to see his lawyer. Above all, Faulkner decided, he must never ask a question that could end the interview if Pelton responded negatively.

Much the same approach was taken in 1950 by William Skardon, an interrogator for the British MI5, when he obtained the confession of Emil Klaus Fuchs, who gave the secret of the atomic bomb to the Soviet Union. By "clearing up small points," as he put it, he got Fuchs to admit that he had passed the details of the bomb's design to Harry Gold, an American who promptly turned the material over to GRU case officer Anatoli Yakovlev.

The two FBI agents decided the best time to interview Pelton would be Sunday morning, when he would have few if any other appointments and would be most vulnerable. The best place to interview him would be in a hotel room—neutral ground, less threatening than the FBI's offices.

Together with supervisors in the Baltimore field office and at headquarters, the agents planned the interview for weeks. In several meetings at his office in Washington, John L. Martin, chief of the Justice Department's internal security section, reviewed with them the interview strategy and how to avoid suggesting that Pelton could play double agent and get off the hook. Too many cases had been lost simply because the interview strategy had not been carefully thought out.

In 1981, the Air Force offered immunity to Second Lieutenant Christopher M. Cooke, who had given the Soviets launch commands for the *Titan II* missile, if he would tell what he did and who else was involved. When it turned out no one else was involved, the Air Force tried to prosecute Cooke anyway, attempting to cover up the fact that Cooke had been promised immunity. But the U.S. Military Court of Appeals overturned his conviction.

"Espionage, like treason, is a serious offense against the United States government and the security of the people the government serves," the court said. "An allegation or charge of espionage by itself, however, does not constitutionally justify depriving an accused of due process of law. . . . This is basic constitutional law."

As a result of the Air Force's bungling, Cooke walked away a free man. By handling the case right, the military could have obtained Cooke's confession and prosecuted him, too.

More recently, the military, along with the CIA, again fell down on the job during an investigation of Marine Sergeant Clayton J. Lonetree and Corporal Arnold Bracy and breaches of security at the U.S. Embassy in Moscow. First the CIA interviewed Lonetree for four days without warning him of his rights or allowing him to have a lawyer present. The CIA was hoping to find out how much damage had been done at the embassy. But the CIA neglected to give Lonetree polygraph tests, claiming it had no polygraph operators in Vienna, where he confessed. The result, according to a later FBI investigation, is that the interviews were useless either in terms of assessing damage or bringing a criminal prosecution free of legitimate grounds for appeal.

In a press conference after his release in June 1987, Bracy admitted he had gone to the home of a Soviet woman who worked as a nanny for a U.S. diplomat. But he said the Naval Investigative Service threatened and coerced him into signing a statement saying he had let the KGB run wild in the U.S. Embassy in Moscow—a claim he said they made up. The twenty-one-year-old Marine said the agents told him "my life as an American was over and that I would never have a meal, that I would never have a job."

Lonetree is appealing his conviction, in part because the CIA did not warn him of his rights.

Given the number of espionage cases the FBI handles, its record is quite good. In forty-nine cases since 1975, there has been only one acquittal. Handing an espionage case to the military is like asking a general surgeon to perform heart surgery—he simply doesn't have enough experience. Yet the FBI and CIA went over the line in obtaining Koecher's confession, as they have in several other cases where indictments were never brought. Martin of the Justice Department didn't want a repeat performance in the Pelton case.

Several days before the interview took place, the agents rented a bank of rooms on the fourth floor of the Annapolis Hilton, under the assumed name of A. John Francis. Besides the interview room, the agents rented five other rooms for supervisors, polygraph operators, and "wires and pliers" technicians. For days, the agents rehearsed their roles with another agent who played Pelton.

The night before the interview, Faulkner couldn't sleep. Headquarters was applying incredible pressure on him, sending memos and calling about every step. The bureau had been embarrassed by Howard's abrupt departure for Moscow: he had left after claiming he would talk with FBI agents. Headquarters was afraid Pelton might pull the same stunt.

In case Pelton tried to flee to Moscow, headquarters even ordered CI-3 and other Washington agents to step up their surveillance of the Soviet establishments that they normally watch in the city. Besides the usual locations, they watched the offices of Tass, *Izvestia*, *Pravda*, and Aeroflot, the Soviet airline.

Since September 7, when he first interviewed Yurchenko, Faulkner had been working six- and seven-day weeks. He was assigned to the Baltimore FBI office's only counterintelligence squad, number three. His wife, Carolyn, is an investigative aide in the same office.

Six feet, three and a half inches tall, with short gray hair and an athletic build, he had given up jogging and cutting wood on his Maryland farm since the case began. There just wasn't time, and he was starting to show it around his middle. Hodgson was chosen to work with him because he happened to be the agent who played the tape of Pelton's voice when the voice was identified. "Butch," as he was called, was forty-five, husky, and had a round face. Since being put on the case, he had stopped going on hunting and fishing trips.

The night before the interview, both men slept at the Annapolis Hilton. From his window, Faulkner could see Pelton's Annapolis office across the bay at Safford Marine, a boat showroom. Nervously, he kept getting up and looking out the window as he waited to call Pelton when the former NSA employee arrived at his office on Sunday, November 24, 1985. After trying for ten minutes, Faulkner finally reached him at 9:15 A.M.

"This is Special Agent Dave Faulkner of the FBI," he said. "I need to talk with you about a matter of great importance. Could you meet with us at the Annapolis Hilton?"

There was no mistaking the urgency in the agent's voice. As a former NSA employee, Pelton knew something about the FBI and its responsibilities in the national security field. But he asked if the agent could come to his office.

"Because of the sensitive nature of the national security matter we want to discuss, we need to talk with you in a secure place," Faulkner said.

"Okay," Pelton said. "I'll come over."

By seeking and obtaining Pelton's agreement to come to the Hilton, the agents had already scored a point. Psychologists say people support what they help create. By agreeing to come over, Pelton had taken a small step toward helping the agents.

A beefy man with blond, thinning hair and a mustache, Pelton, then forty-four, stopped at a fast-food store to get a cup of coffee. He arrived at the Hilton at 9:26 A.M. All the while, an FBI surveillance team was watching him.

When Pelton walked into the lobby of the hotel, Faulkner and Hodgson greeted him and showed him their badges. The two agents were dressed casually in sports jackets, slacks, and sports shirts open at the collar. Neither wore a gun or handcuffs. They looked like they were about to go on a cruise. So much the better. The Behavioral Science Unit had said that suits and ties would only make Pelton think he was about to be arrested.

Motioning toward the elevators, the agents took Pelton to Room 409, which had been carefully rearranged. A second bed had been removed, and extra chairs had been brought in. Pelton's chair faced away from the window so he would not be distracted by the sun. Four to eight feet away were two more chairs for the agents. Off to the side was a table, placed so it would not appear to be a barrier between Pelton and the two agents.

A refrigerator stocked with soft drinks had been brought in, along with a coffee machine and doughnuts. Hodgson offered Pelton coffee as Faulkner explained why they had asked him to come.

"We are foreign counterintelligence officers," Faulkner said. "Normally, people expect the FBI to be concerned with bank robberies and stolen cars, but we are here as foreign counterintelligence officers, and our responsibility is to identify and penetrate the hostile intelligence services in this country."

Grinning nervously, Pelton said, "I haven't stolen any cars or robbed any banks. I don't feel I have a problem." Pausing, and looking at the tape recorder on a table, he asked, "Am I being recorded?"

The answer was no. Anticipating the question, Faulkner had decided against taping the interview. In twenty years as an agent based in Baltimore, he had never taped an interview and would feel uncomfortable doing it now. He knew that if Pelton asked about it, he would either have to admit it, and probably have to turn it off, or lie about it, which would not look good to a jury.

"We are concerned with a national security matter," Faulkner told Pelton. "In order to bring you up to date as to the current situation, I'd like to relate a story that concerns a hypothetical individual. I'd like you to just sit back and not make any comments until I am finished relating the story.

"The individual grew up in the Midwest and graduated from Benton Harbor High School in Benton Harbor, Michigan. Because of family circumstances, although he was quite bright, the individual had not been able to attend college and went into the Air Force."

Pelton immediately recognized the individual as himself. Yet because Faulkner had said the story was hypothetical, it seemed he was not directly confronting him. Politely, Faulkner was letting Pelton know the FBI knew all about his activities. There was no need for Pelton to confirm anything. Pelton felt no need to challenge the story because the agent was not accusing him of anything. Indeed, because of the way he related the story, Faulkner seemed sympathetic to him.

"During a four-year tour in the Air Force," Faulkner continued, "this individual took a Russian language course at Indiana University and thereafter received an intelligence assignment with the military. Meanwhile, he began a family. In 1964, he left the Air Force and returned to his home area. He got part-time jobs and, in 1965, he sought and obtained employment with the U.S. government in an intelligence capacity."

By now, Pelton's hands were shaking, and Faulkner noticed his eyes widening and the veins in his throat bulging.

"He was always well regarded by his peers and performed above average in his employment," Faulkner continued. "Toward the end of the 1970s, he began to experience severe financial problems, culminating in his declaring bankruptcy in April 1979. In July 1979, he left his employment.

"On January 14, 1980, he contacted some Soviet officials in an effort to transmit some information to them for money. He talked with Vladimir Sorokin, an aide at the Soviet Embassy," Faulkner said.

Pelton was sweating profusely as Faulkner switched on a tape recorder. He played a recording of Pelton's first call to the embassy:

"Vladimir, yes, ah, I have something I would like to discuss with you I think that would be very interesting to you," the voice said.

"Maybe you can, ah, name yourself?" Sorokin said.

"Uh, on the telephone, it would not be wise. I come from . . . I . . . I . . . I am in . . . with the U.S. government," he sputtered out.

"Uh-huh, U.S. government," Sorokin said. "Maybe you can visit?"

Faulkner related how the individual had called the embassy the next day, spoken with Yurchenko, and then come in and met with Yurchenko and other KGB officials. He showed Pelton a color photo of Yurchenko with two other Soviets at a reception. Pelton shrank from the photo.

"If you're saying that was me, it was not me," Pelton muttered.

"Please don't say anything and let me continue with the story," Faulkner said.

"Subsequently, this individual traveled to Vienna, where he met with the Soviets," the agent said.

Faulkner showed him a photo of Anatoly Slavnov, the KGB officer Pelton had met with inside the Soviet facility in Vienna.

"This is where the matter stands," the agent said. "I would like your assistance in completing the story."

"You have no case," Pelton said. "That was not me. Whoever it was would be crazy to say anything that would hang him."

Hodgson told him it was ridiculous for him to claim that it was not his voice in the conversation, because it clearly was he.

"People have identified you as the voice, and people in the FBI lab have made comparisons indicating that your voice was on the calls," the agent said.

The statement was only partly true. Anyone—including people in the FBI lab—who heard the tape of the call to the embassy and a tape of Pelton's voice from his wiretapped telephone calls thought the voices were the same. But using voiceprints, the lab had been unable to match the voices. Apparently, the lab needed a longer sample, or samples using similar words, to establish a link scientifically.

Even if the voiceprints had matched, a lawyer would have advised Pelton that voiceprints are not admissible as evidence in court. Moreover, his call was not evidence of a crime. But to Pelton, the recording seemed damning. Nonetheless, he told them he would not say anything that would help "hang him."

If the FBI had had enough evidence to arrest Pelton, the agents would have placed handcuffs on him before the interview and advised him he had the right to remain silent and the right to have a lawyer. Because there was no probable cause to arrest him, the agents had no legal obligation to give him any advice. Faulkner knew that if Pelton got a lawyer, the lawyer would almost certainly tell him not to talk to the FBI.

Nevertheless, as instructed by Martin from the Justice Department, Faulkner told Pelton, "You have the right to have an attorney if you so desire." Then he placed an obstacle in the way. He said any attorney would have to have a "top secret" security clearance to delve into the matters Pelton knew about at NSA.

To Pelton, it seemed unlikely he could find such a lawyer. In fact, the law provides a procedure for clearing any lawyer chosen by a defendant.

Then Faulkner gave Pelton another reason for not getting a lawyer.

"If anybody else is involved in these discussions," he said, "the agents here will lose control of the situation, and the options we have would be reduced."

In fact, the agents had only one option: to obtain Pelton's confession. But Pelton was hoping against hope that the agents would somehow give him a way out, perhaps by enlisting him to penetrate the Soviets or helping to assess the damage that had been done.

Using the "good guy, bad guy" approach, Faulkner told Pelton that he and Hodgson didn't believe that Pelton told the Soviets everything he knew.

"However, we have a superior who feels differently and wants a full, overt investigation, which would include interviews with your associates and family. We prevailed upon him to hold off until we got your cooperation in an effort to identify the extent of your activities with the Soviets," he said.

Of course, the agents had already investigated Pelton extensively without talking to people who might have tipped him off that he was a suspect. The embarrassment of being arrested, tried, and convicted would far outweigh any "overt" investigation. But Pelton was in no position to think that through. He had expected to have brunch with his girlfriend in Washington that day, not to be interrogated by the FBI. He was probing, trying to find out if he could make a deal with the agents.

"If I were to talk, I would want guarantees," he said.

"With your cooperation," Faulkner said, "we will make a report of this incident noting your cooperation, and we will provide that to our superiors. They will make a further determination as to the further activities regarding the situation."

"I know it could lead to prosecution," Pelton said.

"That's true," Faulkner said. "However, not all national security matters end in prosecution."

"If I were willing to cooperate and prosecution occurred, what benefit would my cooperation be to me?" he asked.

"You would have two special agents of the FBI testify that you cooperated fully in this matter," Hodgson told him.

Trying to show they sympathized with him, the agents asked Pelton about his finances, which they knew were in disarray. He told them how he had tried in 1979 to build a home in suburban Howard County, but the construction materials had been stolen. The loss was not covered by insurance. His family, meanwhile, had been living in a shanty heated by a wood stove. At the time, he was making a modest $24,500 a year at NSA as a communications specialist.

He had not told his superiors about his financial plight because he had heard about another employee who confided that he was having financial problems. He had been punished—suspended for two weeks without pay. Telling NSA officials had only exacerbated the employee's problem, it appeared.

His experience at NSA was the reverse of that of Sergeant Jack E. Dunlap, a hundred-dollar-a-week NSA messenger who began spying for the Soviets in 1960. The fact that he paid cash for a thirty-foot cabin cruiser and a sleek hydroplane, and drove his Jaguar and two Cadillacs to work, alerted no one at NSA to the possibility he might be leading a double life. It was not until Dunlap applied for a civilian job at NSA and had to take his first polygraph test that the agency caught up with him. Before investigators could find out what he had given the Soviets, he strung a radiator hose from his exhaust pipe into his car and committed suicide in July 1963.

Pelton told the FBI agents he understood Walker had cooperated with the FBI but got a life sentence anyway. Hodgson pointed out that the former Navy warrant officer had not cooperated from the outset of the investigation.

Noting that Pelton had only been trying to get enough money to house his family, the agent said, "We view you differently from Walker."

At 10:30 A.M., Faulkner excused himself to confer with his supervisors in another room. Meanwhile, Hodgson pursued the Walker theme, saying that unlike Walker, Pelton had not given up information that was "life-threatening."

"That's right," Pelton said. "I never gave up anything tactical."

With the other agent out of the room, Pelton felt he could confide more readily. He had made his first tacit admission that he had spied for the Soviets.

Hodgson knew Pelton was about to break, but he didn't want to let on. He brought up his own experiences in the Vietnam War: it seemed the enemy always knew what the U.S. military was planning, perhaps because Walker had let the Soviets know how to decipher the codes, he said.

When Faulkner returned five minutes later, he said his superiors had told him that without more details of what Pelton had done, no decisions could be made. The statement was true as far as it went: no decision to arrest Pelton could be made unless he confessed.

In particular, Faulkner told him, they needed to know if anyone besides Pelton had been involved in the operation.

"No," Pelton blurted out.

He told them that he had been reluctant to continue the relationship with the Soviets. He had moved twice, but each time the Soviets had gotten his unlisted telephone numbers.

The agents told him they knew the Soviets had taken photographs of his home in Silver Spring—a point that heightened Pelton's concern. His reaction was similar to that of Christopher Boyce, the spy who stole codes for the Rhyolite surveillance satellite from TRW Inc. Describing to a Senate subcommittee in 1985 what it was like to work for the KGB, Boyce said, "There was only depression and a hopeless enslavement to an inhuman, uncaring foreign bureaucracy."

Pelton asked if the agents would want him to resume contact with the Soviets under the FBI's supervision.

"No," Faulkner said. "Any decision on that would have to be made at a higher level."

"You can stop with the disclaimers," Pelton said, raising his hands.

Faulkner asked if Pelton would be willing to go overseas to point out where he had made contact with the Soviets.

"There was only one, in Vienna," Pelton said.

Pelton asked if he could go to the bathroom and call his girlfriend, Ann Barry. Then twenty-eight, Barry had grown up in Rockville, Maryland, and attended Catholic schools. After being named Miss Maryland Teenager, she traveled the world and hung out in London gambling casinos. She had sultry good looks and a direct, earthy approach to men. She proudly showed visitors semi-nude modeling pictures of herself.

Barry met Pelton in a Bethesda, Maryland, bar. Temporarily separated from his wife, Pelton paid Barry's $500-a-month apartment rent and gave her ten dollars a day for her expenses. They had been seeing each other for two years.

Dialing her number in Washington, he said, "I'm going to be a little while before I can get out of here."

"That's all right, I'm real sick," she said.

"I had some business this morning, so I'll call you later, about an hour or so, or a couple of hours."

"Okay," she said.

Pouring himself some more coffee, Pelton repeated that he would need "guarantees" before he would talk further, then began pouring out the details of his dealings with the Soviets anyway. At the embassy, he said, the Soviets had asked him to drive to a pizza shop in Falls Church, Virginia, on the last Saturday of each month. There, he was to wait for a call on the pay phone at 8:00 P.M. If the caller said, "We have something for you," he was to fly to Vienna to meet with the Soviets there. For the trip, the Soviets left $2,000 in a magnetic key container at another pay phone.

In October 1980, he flew to Vienna and strolled through the Schönbrunn Palace, the former home of Austria's emperors. Eventually, a Russian driver picked him up and took him to the Soviet Embassy, where he met KGB agent Slavnov from Moscow.

For eight hours a day over a period of three or four days, Pelton told Slavnov about NSA. He returned to Vienna in January 1983, where Slavnov picked his brains some more.

Meanwhile, Pelton was trying to make a living as an independent businessman. He tried to break into international finance but failed. He also split with his wife. Finally, he took a job as a yacht salesman at Safford Marine.

In April 1985, he made his last trip to Vienna. Since the Soviets had not given him money, he told his employer he was on a CIA mission and needed to use his credit card temporarily. Pelton had lost seventy-five pounds since his last trip, and the Russian driver apparently didn't recognize him. He returned to the U.S. without having met the Soviets. When he got back, the Soviets demanded that he fly back to Vienna. After having too many drinks with Barry, he ran out of gas while driving with her to the pizza parlor for the call that would give him instructions. He never got to make the trip.

"He was devastated," she said recently.

Asked how much money he received from the Soviets, Pelton said, "Thirty to thirty-five thousand, plus expenses."

Despite all the details, Pelton still had not told the agents what classified information he gave the Soviets. Without that, a good defense lawyer might convince a jury that Pelton had only been leading the Soviets on.

As the agents pondered how to get Pelton to open up more, he said he needed to leave to make the brunch date with his girlfriend. As he dialed Barry's number at 12:43 P.M. to tell her he was on his way, Pelton agreed to meet with the agents the next day for lunch.

"As long as you're cooperating with us, there will be no overt investigation," Faulkner told him. "But if you do anything to bring in other law enforcement, we can do nothing to help you," he warned him. Then he told him they knew he was using drugs.

Faulkner walked Pelton to his car, where Pelton pulled his passport out from the glove compartment and pointed to the dates of his trips to Vienna.

"Do you mind if I examine this overnight?" Faulkner asked.

"Go ahead; I'm not planning any trips," Pelton said.

With the FBI following him, Pelton drove to Barry's second-floor efficiency apartment at 1525 P Street NW in Washington, where he took a shower, made himself an omelette, and poured himself a glass of Grand Marnier.

As Pelton was lying in bed with Barry and sipping his drink, she suggested that they buy some Dilaudid, an opiate that they injected into their veins three times a week at eighty dollars a shot.

Pelton became angry with her and said she could buy the drugs herself, using his car. He felt she had introduced him to drugs, and now she wanted to make a buy when the FBI was on his tail. He told her he had just met with the FBI—that they wanted him to work with them on a secret project.

All along, something about Pelton hadn't added up, Barry thought. He claimed to be into religion and bought her a Bible. He had grandiose plans for forming his own businesses. And he claimed to be doing undercover work for the government. She never did put it together. Pelton's refusal to tell her any more about the FBI's interest that evening was just one more puzzlement.

Pelton drove her to Eleventh and O streets NW and let her off. As she bought the tablets on a corner, he circled the area. Then he picked her up, and they drove back to her apartment, where they both cooked the drug in a solution and injected it.

As Pelton was sipping a screwdriver made with Stolichnaya vodka at 9:45 P.M., the phone rang. The FBI had been listening to Pelton's conversations and had decided to move. There was a chance Pelton might tell Barry more about his meetings with the FBI. She might convince him not to cooperate.

Pelton picked up the ringing phone.

"Hey, Ron?" Faulkner said.

"Yeah," Pelton said.

"Yes, this is Dave Faulkner. You know I said I wouldn't call you there unless it was important. I've been meeting with our headquarters all day on this thing, and we really need to talk to you this evening. It's quite urgent."

"Umm, Lord," Pelton said. "Jesus, I can but I'm going to have to explain a bit. Boy."

"Well, I understand," the agent said. "But I wouldn't ask you if it wasn't important. Okay?"

"All right," Pelton said.

The conversation provoked an angry outburst from Barry, who demanded to know why Pelton couldn't tell her what was going on.

"Did you kill somebody?" she asked. "What in the world could you do to make this come on? This is Ann you're talking to!"

"They want me to work for them," Pelton said.

"You gave them this fucking number?" Barry said.

"I didn't give them any number," he replied.

"Oh, get out of here. And you have the audacity not to want to tell me a fucking thing," she said.

Pelton drove to Annapolis and arrived at 10:43 P.M. As Pelton sipped coffee, Faulkner suggested that Pelton tell the agents what information he had given the Soviets, since they already knew about it from Yurchenko. In that way, he suggested, Pelton could still avoid giving out new details until he got the "guarantees" he wanted.

It was tortured reasoning, but Pelton fell for it. The agents asked him about Project Ivy Bells and the location of another intercept inside the Soviet Embassy in Washington. Asked why he had chosen to disclose these projects to the Soviets, Pelton said he thought they might already know about them.

Faulkner showed Pelton a paper he had written when he was with NSA in 1978. Entitled "Signals Parameters File," it listed the fifty-seven Soviet communications links NSA was interested in, along with their technical descriptions.

"How much of this did you tell them?" Faulkner asked.

"They were interested in everything," Pelton said.

"Don't you feel this was harmful to the country?" Faulkner asked.

Only to the extent that it costs more to develop other techniques to replace the ones that are compromised, he replied.

Faulkner asked if he would sign a form waiving his right to see a lawyer.

"I have read this statement of my rights and I understand what my rights are," the form said. "I am willing to make a statement and answer questions. I do not want a lawyer. I understand and know what I am doing. No promises or threats have been made to me, and no pressure or coercion of any kind have been used against me," it said.

Pelton signed.

Pelton admitted he had given the Soviets information about improved equipment the NSA was installing. The equipment would process Soviet messages faster. He said he also gave them locations where NSA was intercepting Soviet communications.

Asked again if he thought the information he turned over was harmful, Pelton said, "I guess the bottom line is that it was harmful to the country."

He said walking into the Soviet Embassy was the biggest mistake of his life.

"When you're broke and desperate, your family hardly surviving, you do crazy things," he said.

The questions were coming faster now, and growing ominous. Pelton said he would not give any more details unless he received guarantees that they would not be used against him. At this point, he said, there was no case because "You cannot get your witness back, and there are no documents."

Faulkner called Dana E. Caro, then special agent in charge of the Baltimore field office, and said they had reached an impasse. Caro called back several minutes later and told the agents to place Pelton under arrest.

At 11:50 P.M. on November 24, they placed handcuffs on him, read him his rights, and took him first to the Baltimore field office and then to the Anne Arundel County Detention Center.

At 2:00 A.M., eight agents—including several from CI-3—banged on Barry's door. When she heard it was the FBI, she scrambled to hide any drug paraphernalia that might be in the apartment.

Trying to stall them, she yelled out, "I have a shotgun."

"Open the door or we'll break it down," one of the agents said.

When she opened the door in her skimpy blue nightie, she looked into the barrels of eight drawn guns.

"Can I help you?" she asked demurely. Later, during their search of the apartment, she complimented one of the agents on having "a nice ass."

At 4:00 A.M., Faulkner fell asleep at the Annapolis Hilton, only to be awakened at 4:30 A.M. by a call from the FBI press spokesman in Baltimore. After sleeping for three more hours, he got out of bed for Pelton's appearance before a magistrate.

For the previous week, Barry told me, she and Pelton had argued about who would buy the turkey for Thanksgiving and how the stuffing would be made.

Now there would be no turkey.

16 *Dano*

It would have been laughable had it not been so disastrous. On the afternoon of December 14, 1985, a caller told the person who answered the phone at SMO:

"I have some information I would like to sell . . . I have three documents: two are classified 'secret military,' one is just 'top secret.' I would like to show some, some of it to someone, and see what they would like for them. Very, uh, classified 'top secret' information."

Earlier that day, Randy Miles Jeffries had been asked to tear up extra copies of hearing transcripts marked "secret" and "top secret" at Acme Reporting Co., which transcribed hearings before Congress. At the time, Jeffries, twenty-six, was a $4.50-an-hour messenger. He had no security clearance of any kind.

At first, Kevin Collins, another messenger, had been doing the job, ripping the extra copies into fourths and throwing them in the wastebasket. Now Jeffries, a black man with a long face like a Talmudic scholar, took over as Collins did some delivery runs in Washington, D.C., where the firm is based.

Jeffries noticed the classification stamps immediately. Then he read some of the titles. They were hearings of the House Armed Services Committee and had to do with nuclear weapons and U.S. military strength compared with that of the Soviets.

Only people cleared for "top secret" work were supposed to have access to the documents. What's more, according to Defense Department regulations, any extra copies of classified documents were to be burned or shredded. Yet Jeffries had found in his two months at Acme that the firm frequently did things on the cheap. The copying machine was always on the fritz, yet the company never bought a new one or obtained a service contract. The tapes used by Acme court reporters were used over and over again until they broke in the middle of hearings or court proceedings. And rather than buy a shredder, Acme had messengers tear up documents. A sixth-grader could reconstruct them.

Ironically, Jeffries had come to his job at Acme by way of the FBI. He had grown up in Altoona, Pennsylvania, in a close and supportive family. His father was a foreman for Amtrak. Musically talented, Jeffries played percussion instruments, the bass guitar, and keyboard. He also composed. He had many white friends in school, yet he always felt different, both because he was black and because he was a Jehovah's Witness. As a Witness, he was taught that God's kingdom took precedence over any government. In school, he declined to salute the flag.

Unsure of what he should do when he graduated from high school, he saw an ad placed by the FBI in an Altoona paper. The FBI needed clerks for its Washington headquarters. Jeffries inquired about the job but was daunted by the long form he had to fill out on his background. An FBI recruiter called him and urged him to apply. In 1978, he began working in the FBI's fingerprint section, making sure that real names and aliases were congruent.

"We thought of it as the bargain basement, because it was all blacks from Baltimore who worked there," Jeffries told me. "It was like being in the cotton fields."

Jeffries was eager to become an agent. He impressed people with his intelligence and intuitive grasp of what they wanted. Yet there was a myopic side to Jeffries, a side that impelled him to prove himself by thumbing his nose at authority even when there was nothing to gain from it. He knew, for example, that to apply for a better job at the FBI, he was supposed to talk first with his immediate supervisor. Seeing a notice listing openings for warehouse workers, who were paid at higher rates than clerks, he talked directly with the head of the warehouse department. His supervisor reprimanded him for going over her head, and he never got the promotion.

It was always like that with Jeffries. Headstrong and independent, he was a curious blend of street dude and country boy. While his intentions were often good, his methods got him in trouble.

By 1980, Jeffries was bored with his job at the FBI, and he quit to become a mail handler at the U.S. Postal Service. There he made more money but worked from midnight to 8:00 A.M. He fell in with a crowd that drank and used cocaine and heroin. He began coming to work irregularly. On March 25, 1983, he was convicted of heroin possession and got eighteen months probation. The Postal Service fired him, and he began doing odd jobs at law firms.

Meanwhile, Jeffries had married another Jehovah's Witness. Having a family only added to the pressures. From the time he was a young boy, he remembered being called "nigger." While that did not affect his two brothers, who are prison guards, Jeffries was more sensitive and never overcame the sense of hurt. He wanted to feel accepted, yet it seemed to him that blacks had to work twice as hard as whites to prove themselves. Sometimes even blacks rejected him as being too "white"—imbued with middle-class values. Around his wife, he felt emasculated. Not only was he not providing for her, he was sneaking off to take drugs.

A week before he had been asked to tear up the documents, his wife laid down an ultimatum: get off drugs or leave. Jeffries was wondering how he was going to scrape together enough money to find his own apartment. When he saw the two-foot stack of documents and realized they were classified, he saw the opportunity to make some money.

"The first thing that came to me was the archenemy, the Russians. It was most valuable to them," he said.

When the first messenger returned from making deliveries at 1:30 P.M., Jeffries confided to him that he had hidden some of the documents in the building's parking garage. He asked him for a ride so he could take them home. As Collins held the elevator door on the 2-B level, Jeffries got two hundred pages of documents that he had hidden in the garage and shoved them under his coat. On the way to his apartment at 143 Rhode Island Avenue NW, Jeffries told Collins that he knew where he could get "good money" for the documents. He said he needed to find a Russian to sell them to.

At home, Jeffries opened a Budweiser. He was not scared, just excited and looking forward to making some extra money. He called information and asked for the number of the Soviet Embassy. He was given the number for the Military and Naval Attaché Office, the first listing under "Soviet Embassy."

Jeffries opened a second can of beer as he dialed the number. It was 4:11 P.M.

Identifying himself as "Dano," the name of a character in *Hawaii Five-O*, he described one of the documents he wanted to sell as relating to the "U.S. military and nuclear procedures and funding." He said they were "courtroom, um, straight from the House of Representatives."

Then he read the title of the documents classified "top secret": "U.S. House of Representatives, Department of Defense Command,

Control Communications and Intelligence Programs, C3-1, Closed Session, Subcommittee on Procurement and Military Nuclear Systems, Committee on Armed Services, Washington, D.C." The transcript included testimony by Donald C. Latham, assistant secretary for command, control, communications, and intelligence, and Army General Maxwell R. Thurman, vice chief of staff of the Army. In their testimony, they discussed major military plans and purchases, the strengths and weaknesses of the U.S. as compared with the Soviets, the security of U.S. military communications systems, and secret military locations.

Asked by the Soviet what he was doing, Jeffries said, "I'm trying to sell it!"

Jeffries asked for the address of SMO and said he would be bringing in some of the documents shortly.

At 4:45 P.M., the FBI surveillance team down the street noticed a man getting out of a taxicab and entering SMO. The agents recorded the license number and jotted down a description of the man: a black male, in his thirties, five feet, ten inches tall, weighing 170 pounds, with medium build, black hair, a light complexion, and a mustache. He was said to be wearing a brown leather jacket and blue jeans.

Except for his age, the description fit Jeffries closely. He was twenty-six, five feet, nine inches tall, weighed 175 pounds, and had black hair and a mustache. He was wearing a brown vinyl jacket.

Jeffries brought with him the title page to one of the hearing records and the index to another. The clerk inside pressed a button that opened a second door.

To Jeffries, the Soviets seemed like a bunch of yuppies, wearing Calvin Klein jeans and sneakers. They gave him some books and pamphlets about Russia and asked for his address and phone number. He gave them his phone number but an incorrect address. After half an hour in SMO, the Soviets ushered him out, telling him they would discuss what to do about his offer of more documents. As he walked out the door, a Soviet warned him to walk to his right, away from the FBI's surveillance post.

Because the FBI does not always have Russian translators on duty, it was not until Monday morning that the tape of his call to SMO was transcribed. Up until that point, there had been nothing to arouse the FBI's suspicions. People enter SMO all the time, often to deliver food or fix the heating plant. But once the tape was transcribed, CI-3 agents began a round-the-clock investigation to find out who the man was.

Since he was unknown, no agent had previously been assigned to him. Very often, besides the one or two Soviets that CI-3 agents are assigned to follow, each gets another twenty or thirty other cases to work. For Special Agent Michael Giglia, this was one of his miscellaneous cases. A short, powerfully built man, Giglia was known within CI-3 as "Greaseball" or the "Italian Stallion." He was always telling jokes and enjoying himself, and when other agents went to lunch, they often asked him along because they knew they would have a good time.

After getting the assignment Monday morning, Giglia found out from the House committee who had access to the document the man had cited on the phone. Besides members of Congress and their aides, the list included Acme Reporting Co., which had transcribed the hearing.

Giglia drove to Acme's office at 1220 L Street NW, a modern office building half a mile from the Capitol. Asking to talk with people who had handled the hearings, he found himself interviewing Collins, who had instructed Jeffries in how to tear up the documents two days earlier. Collins told him that Jeffries had taken some of the documents home, claiming he was going to sell them to the Soviets.

That evening, Ramey and Giglia went to the home of the taxi driver whose license number had been taken down by the FBI surveillance team. He wasn't in, but the next evening, the driver told Giglia he had picked up the man whom he later dropped off at SMO in the 200 block of Rhode Island Avenue. That was a block from Jeffries's home.

Meanwhile, Jeffries was becoming impatient. Kevin Quander, a friend who worked as a custodian, dropped by on Tuesday afternoon, and Jeffries decided he would try to speed things up at SMO. As he downed more cans of Bud, he told his friend that he had been to the Soviet Embassy and would call again to find out what was happening.

Dialing the number of SMO, he said, "This is, ah, Dano, from, uh, Saturday evening, and, uh, I wanted to know, if there's been any deposition [sic] been made on the decision. I just wanted to know about their decision."

The Soviet told him to come to SMO the next day between 9:00 A.M. and 6:00 P.M. Instead, Jeffries asked Quander to drive him to SMO. Jeffries got there about 6:00 P.M., bringing with him several more pages of documents and leaving the rest with his friend.

This time, Jeffries got a warmer reception. A GRU officer took him to a small room to the right of the entrance and told him his boss would be coming from his home at the Soviet Embassy complex at Mount Alto to meet Jeffries. When the high-ranking GRU officer arrived, the Soviet was miffed. His subordinates had taken Jeffries to the second floor of SMO, where there was a large conference room dominated by the seal of the U.S.S.R.

Jeffries, however, thought he had arrived.

The boss told them to bring him downstairs, where the attachés informed him his calls had probably been recorded. They said Jeffries had gone about contacting them in the wrong way.

"Did you use your own phone?" one of them asked in disbelief. "You're throwing a lot of heat on us," he said.

The Soviets told him they would get in touch with him in April, after things had cooled down.

Jeffries asked for $100. Seemingly just to get rid of him, they gave him sixty dollars.

Jeffries emerged an hour and a half later with a warm feeling toward the Soviets. They seemed to empathize with his plight. In his confused mind, he realized that people in the Soviet Union are often poor and oppressed, yet he felt the Soviets understood his oppression. The U.S. could easily become just as repressive as the U.S.S.R., he rationalized.

The next day, Jeffries noticed men in his neighborhood who did not belong there. They were white and drove large, four-door sedans. He felt he was being watched by the FBI.

He was right.

On Friday, December 20, Jeffries worked an hour and a half overtime. He got home at 7:30 P.M. Just as he walked in the house, the phone started ringing. The man on the other end had a Russian accent. Identifying himself as "Vlad," he said he was from the Soviet Embassy in New York. Because of the importance of the material Jeffries was offering, he had been authorized by Moscow to deal with him.

Jeffries acknowledged he was Dano but was wary of the caller. He recalled that the Soviets had warned him the phones were tapped, and they had said they wouldn't get in touch with him until April.

"How did you get my name?" Jeffries asked, since he had identified himself to the Soviets only as Dano.

"Don't worry about that," Vlad said. "I understand it's your

Christmas. That's why we decided to speed it up," he said. "My superior was very happy with what you brought. You have something for me, and I have something for you."

Vlad told Jeffries to meet him at 9:00 P.M. at the Holiday Inn at Fourteenth Street and Massachusetts Avenue NW, a seedy area where prostitutes ply their trade.

"I'll be carrying *Time* magazine and wearing a Russian hat. You carry *The Washington Post*," Vlad said.

As he left his apartment, Jeffries noticed that his children were watching *The Pink Panther,* a comedy about a jewel thief, on television. He smiled to himself.

Jeffries took a bus and then walked to the Holiday Inn. Vlad, an agent from another FBI squad, was waiting for him across the street. He suggested they go to his suite on the tenth floor.

Before the meeting, FBI attorneys had gone over with the agent what would and would not be considered entrapment. He could not suggest that Jeffries do anything he had not already offered to do.

As they sat around a table, Jeffries noticed that Vlad was wearing a checkered shirt and striped pants that didn't seem to match.

"Did you bring the documents?" Vlad asked.

"No," Jeffries said.

"I thought you were going to bring the documents. You had something for me; I had something for you," the agent said. "I'm a very busy man. I have important things to do."

Exaggerating to get more money, Jeffries said he had already given the Soviets sixty pages and had asked for $5,000 as payment.

"The first time was just for information. I had to give it to them for them to check to see whether it was worth them being interested in it. Second time I wanted to show that you know, some more, I felt like they needed more information, for validation," he said.

Jeffries said he could get a bag full of "top secret" and "secret" documents which were ripped but could easily be put back together. He said he had three other documents that were not ripped. Each month, he said, he probably could deliver more documents.

Vlad told him he had $5,000 for him if he could deliver the documents. Jeffries called his friend who had the documents, but there was no answer.

"I have to leave and get them and bring them back," Jeffries told Vlad.

The agent gave him ten dollars for cab fare.

From the adjoining room, Giglia, O'Keefe, and Ramey had been monitoring the action. As the supervisor in charge, O'Keefe had to decide whether to wait until Jeffries brought the documents or pop him then. He decided to take him down then.

In the likely event Jeffries was armed, Giglia and six other agents who were there for the arrest were wearing body armor, white vests made of Kelvar which traps bullets in thousands of tough fibers. While the armor protects the heart and lungs, it does not cover the groin, arms, head, or legs.

Since Vlad could not wear body armor without arousing Jeffries's suspicions, Giglia had told the other agents to wait until Jeffries was outside the door of his suite before arresting him. That way, Vlad would be out of danger when they grabbed him.

As the meeting with Vlad appeared to be drawing to a close, the agents blocked off the hallway. Laughing guests coming out of the elevator were horrified to see men wearing what appeared to be white smocks, their weapons drawn.

As Jeffries said good-bye to Vlad, he closed the door and stepped into the hallway. Giglia yelled, "Halt, FBI!" as he and Ramey grabbed his arms and O'Keefe, then head of CI-3, pushed him against the wall. Jeffries tightened up but did not resist as the agents placed handcuffs on him. They advised him of his rights and took him to the Washington field office to be fingerprinted and have mug shots taken.

In the past month, John A. Walker Jr. had pleaded guilty, and Ronald W. Pelton, Jonathan J. Pollard, and Larry Wu-Tai Chin had been arrested by the FBI for espionage.

"How in the world," Ramey asked Jeffries, "could you do this with Pelton, Walker, and Pollard having just been arrested?"

"Who?" Jeffries asked.

The agents did an inventory of Jeffries's belongings. Meanwhile, other CI-3 agents searched his apartment. In the middle of the search, Jeffries's friend Quander returned his call. Jeffries's wife answered the phone and blurted out that her husband had been arrested for espionage.

"Don't say that," an agent said, grabbing the phone from her.

Quander agreed to talk with the agents. He said he had already burned the documents in a wash bucket. Quander later said it was his idea to burn the documents, while Jeffries said it was his idea.

The next morning, Jeffries stood in D.C. Superior Court as a prosecutor read the allegations against him. Each time the prosecutor mentioned a new charge, an elderly black woman sitting at the back said, "Unh-unh! Unh-unh!"

Jeffries thought to himself, "Do they pay her to do that?"

After hearing the evidence against him, Jeffries's court-appointed attorney, G. Allen Dale, got his client's agreement to plead guilty to a lesser charge if the government would drop a count of espionage, which carried a life sentence. Jeffries also agreed to be debriefed by the FBI and take a polygraph test.

The case was not unlike that of Robert E. Cordrey Jr., a twenty-three-year-old Marine private who called SMO and the Czech, East German, and Polish embassies in Washington in April 1984 offering information about chemical and biological warfare. Based on evidence developed by CI-3, Cordrey was court-martialed at Camp Lejeune, North Carolina, on August 13, 1984, and sentenced to two years in the brig.

The difference between his case and Jeffries's was that Cordrey never got beyond making calls and gave away no classified information.

From Jeffries's first call to his arrest, one week had elapsed. Never had CI-3 resolved a case faster.

At Jeffries's sentencing on March 13, 1986, Rhonda C. Fields, the assistant U.S. attorney in charge of the case, called Jeffries's acts "treasonous" and said no one knew how much damage had been done to the national security.

Yet many CI-3 agents privately felt sorry for Jeffries. Unlike other would-be spies they had arrested, Jeffries seemed to care about his family and was acting out of desperation. The material he gave the Soviets was not nearly as damaging as documents others had handed over. They recognized, as did U.S. District Court Judge Gerhard A. Gesell, who sentenced him, that the Acme Company was as much to blame as Jeffries, who had never been cleared for access to "secret" documents and was not being paid to work with them.

Saying Acme had "spewed these confidential documents all over for people to take," the judge questioned at Jeffries's sentencing why the company hadn't been prosecuted.

"Where is Acme?" he asked Fields, who said Acme was being investigated.

Almost immediately, the Defense Department revoked the company's right to transcribe classified proceedings. More than a year later, the U.S. Attorney's office is still investigating Acme and its management. The company is no longer in business, and the former owner had no comment.

Jeffries got three to nine years in prison, substantially less than most of CI-3's targets. He told me he bears no animosity toward the FBI agents who arrested him. They were "just doing their job," and he appreciates the fact that the agents let him keep the ten dollars they had given him. But he is miffed that an agent grabbed the phone away from his wife.

"It's good to have secrets protected," he said. "But by the same token, I believe people are people and governments are governments. Russia is depicted as being very cruel. I'm not sure how much they are. I believe they do repress dissidents. We don't have that here. That's good. But I believe all the basic fundamentals are there [for the U.S. to repress dissidents]. . . . Nothing is all good or all bad.

"I was pretty sure I would be taped [when calling SMO]. I thought it was just words and statements," Jeffries said. "What's in a person's heart when they say these things? As long as I didn't do it—I didn't bring any documents, just a title and index page."

Still, he said, "I realize that what I did was stupid. I regret that. It was based on desperation, ignorance, the fact I had a drug problem."

Because other inmates threatened him, Jeffries was confined to a segregated section of the Federal Penitentiary at Petersburg, Virginia, when I visited him. A guard told me to stay near the front of the visitors' room so he could keep an eye on Jeffries. But when Jeffries came out, he insisted over my protests on moving to the far end of the room. He said the corner offered more privacy.

Predictably, the guard, visibly annoyed, ordered him to the front of the room.

Jeffries lit a Newport.

"Please don't tell my wife I've started smoking again," he said.

17 *Stealing the CIA Blind*

Ismaylov was now ready to play ball with Yogi. For months, he had been doing his homework—watching Yogi, learning his patterns, and selecting remote sites where Yogi could leave secret documents for him.

As they had arranged the first time they met in a bar, Yogi sent the GRU officer a postcard with a view of the Capitol, addressed to him at SMO.

"Dear Dave," it said. "Glad you had a nice vacation. Soon I'll be in Washington, D.C., and hope to get in touch with you. Sincerely yours, Jerry Smith."

That meant Yogi was ready to swap secret documents for cash. When he received it, Ismaylov responded with a card signed "Jerry Smith."

On October 21, 1985, Ismaylov jumped in Yogi's car on Telegraph Road. That rainy October day, he told him to choose a location away from his home where he could bury documents. Eventually, Ismaylov wanted to pick up documents and leave money for Yogi without ever seeing him. That way, it would be harder for either of them to get caught.

Ismaylov set up another meeting for December 20, 1985, at the Belle View Shopping Center in Alexandria. But he was very eager to show his bosses the documents Yogi promised he would bury. So, three days before the scheduled meeting, he again vaulted into Yogi's car while he was driving to work.

"Did you bury the documents?" Ismaylov asked.

"Yes," Yogi said.

"Let's go get them," the Russian said.

Ismaylov got into his own car and followed Yogi's car as it drove along Route 7 to Great Falls, Virginia. There, in a plastic trash bag beside the second post in a split-rail fence on Robindale Drive, the

FBI had buried five technical research and development reports, each consisting of up to one hundred pages and each classified "secret."

As Yogi returned to his car with the package, his hands were shaking so badly he had trouble putting the key in the ignition. With the Russian still stalking him, he drove to the nearby Serbian Crown Restaurant and parked. Ismaylov motioned for him to toss the documents into the coat spread out on the floor of his car. Before Yogi could ask about his money or the next meeting, Ismaylov drove off.

When Grogan told O'Keefe about this latest incident, the two agents shook their heads. A meeting with a spy—called a "brief encounter"—is risky enough without following him in a car sporting diplomatic plates. A car is always a danger. It can be loaded with all sorts of devices to make the other side's surveillance job easier. Once again, Ismaylov had committed a foul.

"It's poor security," O'Keefe muttered, gazing out the window at the Anacostia River. "It shows how interested Moscow is. They want those documents at all costs."

For two hours, Grogan and Scott had been placing dollar bets on whether Ismaylov would show up for the next scheduled meeting on December 20 at the Belle View Shopping Center—the same night other CI-3 agents arrested Jeffries.

Grogan and Scott set up a surveillance post almost an eighth of a mile away in a borrowed office. Invariably, when Grogan, or any other agent for that matter, introduced himself and said he was working on a case, citizens handed over the keys to their home or their office.

Yogi was supposed to meet Ismaylov at 7:00 P.M. in front of the Safeway, but Ismaylov showed up forty-five minutes early. Now he was pacing around the shopping center, peering in the windows of vans and stores to see if the FBI was watching him. Light snow was falling, and the shopping center was mobbed with Christmas shoppers—a better cover than if Ismaylov had met Yogi on some deserted street.

As Yogi got out of his car, Ismaylov walked up to him.

"How is your wife? How is work?" he asked.

Yogi knew that Ismaylov was not making small talk. Ismaylov wanted to know if his wife suspected anything and if he still could remove documents without problems.

As instructed by Grogan, Yogi lit into Ismaylov for brazenly accosting him the last time. After all, anyone could have recognized them. Supposedly, Yogi was risking his job and his freedom, and he should act the part.

Yogi told Ismaylov that his wife wasn't suspicious but was still dissatisfied with his income. This was the excuse Yogi had given for agreeing to become a spy in the first place. He said he was afraid his wife would leave him if he did not bring home more money.

"I don't want the family to be split up," he said.

Ismaylov told Yogi he would find $4,000 as payment for the first batch of documents in a Schlitz beer can next to a tree off Telegraph Road. There would be no preset payments. Ismaylov would give Yogi what he thought the information was worth, but not enough to make him lose his incentive to come back for more.

He arranged to meet him again on January 17, 1986.

As Ismaylov drove off, Yogi tossed some money in a Salvation Army can and bought a record for his daughter at Kemp Mill Records.

All the while, Grogan was filming the scene with cameras that turned night into day. He knew how much O'Keefe liked to watch videotapes of the GRU at work.

When Yogi had trouble finding the Schlitz can later that evening, Ismaylov drove by and yelled, "Over there. Brush away the snow."

This was the first time Yogi used a drop. Ismaylov wanted to make sure he did it right.

"Have a current issue of *USA Today* newspaper in your left hand," Ismaylov told Yogi. "If someone comes up to you and asks: 'Excuse me, sir. Do you know a good lamp shop nearby?' you should answer: 'The best one is the Smith's Lamp Shop on Route One, about four miles from here.' If nobody approaches you, leave the place."

The bizarre instructions were written on cellophane. They became visible when dropped in developer solution. At their January 17, 1986, meeting in front of the 7-Eleven at Huntington and Farmington avenues in Alexandria, Ismaylov told Yogi he had left a half-gallon Shenandoah's Pride skim-milk container for him near a jogging trail in Alexandria. In the carton, Yogi found the instructions written on cellophane along with a treasure trove of spy paraphernalia—a roll-over camera that takes pictures while it passes over documents, thin spy film that crams 130 frames into a standard, 35-

millimeter Kodak film cassette, and other items, including $15,000 in cash to help calm his nerves.

The roll-over camera was of particular interest to the FBI. Made in Russia, it came complete with tiny lights that illuminate documents as the camera passes over them. It was an improvement over previous Soviet spy cameras.

From now on, Ismaylov would pick up his documents and leave cash for Yogi at drop sites. While drop sites had their dangers—someone could pick up the items by mistake—personal meetings were even more dangerous. On the cellophane, Ismaylov laid out a schedule of drops and told him how to signal that he had received his money by leaving a Sunkist orange soda can near a certain stop sign. If Ismaylov had to meet with Yogi urgently—perhaps, he said, to tell him that the U.S. was about to invade Afghanistan—he would draw a vertical line with pink chalk on an electric pole at Telegraph and Farmington roads.

If, for some reason, Yogi didn't hear anything from Ismaylov, no problem. As outlined on the cellophane instructions, he was to show up at predetermined times at the entrance to the Rustler Steak House in Belle View Shopping Center. There, he was to wait for someone to ask him for directions to a lamp shop.

Yogi knew his instructions. Now it was up to Grogan to make his move.

Meanwhile, Karl Koecher was about to prove to his lawyer that he was a very important spy indeed.

On January 23, 1986, the phone in Fierer's mock courtroom in Atlanta rang. It was Bruce Green, the prosecutor in charge of Koecher's case in New York.

"Bob, are you alone?" he asked.

"Yes," Fierer said.

"Are you off the speaker phone?" he asked

"Yes."

"No one is listening?" Green persisted.

"Only if you have the phone bugged," Fierer joked.

"There's going to be a trade," Green said.

Green told Fierer that the Soviets had agreed to a swap of the Koechers and two other spies for Sharansky, two spies, and a Czech who was serving time for helping others leave Czechoslovakia illegally.

For three years, John Martin of the Justice Department had been working on freeing Sharansky and others. Under the agreement he hammered out with East German lawyer Wolfgang Vogel, Koecher technically was not traded for Sharansky, since the U.S. government rejected the claim that he was a spy. But it was clear from the dynamics of the trade that the Soviets were swapping the Soviet dissident for Koecher.

According to the agreement worked out between Fierer and the government, Koecher would plead guilty to espionage. He would be sentenced to life in prison, but the sentence would be reduced to time already served so long as the swap went through. If the swap failed, or if he ever returned to the U.S., he would have to serve the full sentence. He would also have to give up his U.S. citizenship, as would Hana. In theory, Hana could be prosecuted for espionage if she ever returned to the U.S. In fact, the Justice Department had already declined to indict her because she had been denied a lawyer during her confession.

Koecher pleaded guilty and was sentenced in a secret proceeding before Judge Kram at 4:20 P.M. on February 3, 1986. Later unsealed, the transcript shows that Koecher admitted that he was "an agent of the Czechoslovak Intelligence Service when I and my wife entered the United States in 1965, and thereafter I acted in the United States on behalf of the Czechoslovak Intelligence Service.

"On several occasions between 1965 and 1984, both individually and with my wife, Hana, I met with representatives of the Czechoslovak Intelligence Service and provided classified information concerning, among other things, the identities of Central Intelligence Agency agents, of their employees, and operations," he told the judge.

As prearranged, at 11:00 A.M. on February 9, Hana turned herself in to U.S. marshals. Placing handcuffs on Karl, the marshals took the couple to John F. Kennedy Airport at 2:00 P.M. that day.

Fierer suspected that Koecher would throw a last-minute fit, and he did, claiming a lock on a piece of his baggage had been tampered with. In addition, the Koechers say $17,000 worth of jewelry that Hana had on her when she was arrested has never been returned.

"I was ready for a trip to Europe so I took it on me," Hana said. "It disappeared. I had no address so it was sent to my business at Savion. It never arrived."

The Koechers hired a lawyer to try to trace it, but he has taken no action on the case.

The swap took place at noon on Tuesday, February 11, 1986, a dreary, biting cold day. The exchange was to be made on Glienicker Bridge, a 420-foot passage between Potsdam in East Germany and West Berlin. The span has a special place in the history of spydom. It was here, on February 10, 1962, that the first spy swap occurred between the U.S. and the Soviet Union—the exchange of U.S. pilot Francis Gary Powers for Soviet spy Rudolph Abel.

Powers was shot down in May 1960, while flying the U-2 aircraft 68,000 feet over the Soviet Union. In presatellite days, the CIA used the U-2 to take aerial photographs of the Soviet Union. The Soviets sentenced Powers to prison, and the incident prompted Soviet leader Nikita Khrushchev to cancel a summit conference with President Dwight Eisenhower.

The fact that the Soviets were willing to trade Powers for Abel showed Abel was a very important spy. But precisely what he did remains unknown. A Soviet "illegal," he posed as a New York photographer and artist, using the name Emil R. Goldfus. Sent back to Moscow for disciplining, his assistant, Reino Hayhanen, defected to the U.S. Embassy in Paris, denouncing Abel. When FBI agents searched his Brooklyn studio, they found extensive espionage paraphernalia but nothing to show what he had been sending to Moscow. Nevertheless, he was sentenced to thirty years for espionage in March 1960.

Abel's lawyer, James B. Donovan, proposed exchanging his client for Powers and negotiated America's first spy swap with Vogel. Because it has been used for such purposes ever since, the Glienicker Bridge is known as the "Bridge of Spies." To the West Germans, it is known as the "Bridge of Freedom."

To symbolize that Sharansky was not a spy, the U.S. negotiated to have him cross the bridge before the others. A dusting of snow glistened on the stone centaurs that guard the western end of the bridge, where a sign warned, "You are leaving the American Sector." On the eastern side, the Soviet hammer-and-sickle flag and the black, red, and gold banner of the German Democratic Republic flapped in the wind.

The diminutive Soviet dissident was escorted across the bridge by the Justice Department's John Martin and Francis Meehan, ambassador to East Germany. He was met by Richard K. Burt, the U.S. ambassador to West Germany, at the western end of the bridge.

U.S. marshals drove Hana, wearing a mink coat, and Karl, wearing a suit, halfway across the bridge in a van. Vogel and his wife took them the rest of the way in a gold Mercedes.

To Martin, it seemed Hana took the exchange as a "bitter pill."

Since the exchange, the Koechers and the Czech government have refused to pay an additional $110,000 in legal bills, claiming they are excessive. Fierer has obtained a lien on their possessions in New York.

Within the FBI and the CIA, Koecher is looked upon as one of the biggest spies in U.S. history. Yet beyond a story by Rudy Maxa and Phil Stanford reporting on the Koechers' swinging activities in the February 1987 issue of *Washingtonian* magazine, few details about their spying ever came out.

"In the mid-1970s," former CIA officer David A. Phillips wrote in his book, *The Night Watch*, "the CIA has the best record of any intelligence service in history in defending itself against penetration by hostile services."

What he didn't know was that Koecher was stealing the CIA blind even as the book was being published.

"If you look at this operation, you'd be hard-pressed to find anything as professionally done," said James E. Nolan Jr., who was deputy assistant FBI director for operations in the counterintelligence division when the Koecher investigation began.

On the other hand, the FBI's handling of the case illustrates what can happen when it does not check with the Justice Department before confronting an espionage suspect. By obtaining Koecher's confession through outright false promises and threats, the FBI's New York office almost guaranteed that the case would be thrown out if it ever came to trial.

18 *"They Must Be Yours"*

Just over a year after Karl Koecher was traded, I called a relative of his in Czechoslovakia and left a message for him to call me. At 3:08 P.M. on April 2, 1987, he called back. During a ten-minute conversation, he agreed to be interviewed, but only in Prague.

"In view of the whole case, I more or less don't think of traveling to the West for a while," Koecher said. "But I don't think there is any reason why you couldn't come here, provided you get a visa."

Identifying myself as a writer seeking interviews, I got a visa from the Czechoslovak Embassy on the spot. They didn't ask, so I didn't have to tell them, that I was going to interview one of the most successful spies in history, and his spy wife.

Ironically, it was my wife, Pamela Kessler, an art critic with *The Washington Post,* who had the problems. Her request for a visa was delayed two weeks simply because she was affiliated with a newspaper.

The Koechers met Pam and me at the Prague Airport, a modest outpost in the rolling green hills of Czechoslovakia. Koecher fussed with our bags, removing them several times from the trunk of his gray 1986 Volvo to make sure they fit.

There was nothing about the Koechers that would lead one to believe they were spies, at least not at first. He was dressed in Brooks Brothers fashion: gray tweed suit, red tie, blue shirt. Hana wore a tawny leather jacket, a gray tweed skirt, and an expensive white blouse with lace trim.

As Koecher drove us to the Inter-Continental Hotel on Wednesday, April 29, 1987, Pam and I were impressed by the stately, old-world buildings and the huge portrait of Lenin draped on the portal of a stadium.

The Koechers waited for us in the lobby of the hotel as we showered and changed after the long flight from Washington. Later, as I chatted with Koecher in the lobby, he proposed that we begin the interviews the next morning. Then he suggested that I could save as much as two-thirds off the regular price of currency by buying Czech crowns on the black market. Because the Czech government fixes exchange rates at artificial levels, there is a thriving market in foreign money.

Immediately the warnings in a Fodor's guidebook flashed through my mind: "You may be offered a rate of exchange several times better than the official one. But penalties for dealing in this black market are severe and unpleasant. The inside of any gaol is pretty nasty; the inside of an eastern European gaol is very nasty."

"I don't want to create any problems," I said, hoping to brush the suggestion aside.

"It's not a problem," he said. "Everyone here does it."

I took his remark to be more than a helpful tip. His voice and manner betrayed a sense of urgency that was out of keeping with the usual travelers' advisories.

We retreated to the coffee shop of the hotel, and I got a closer look at this CIA mole and his wife. Karl was slight of build but muscular, with graying light brown hair cut short and pale brown eyes. His head was irregularly shaped, as if his ears were pushed into it. His long nose curled down over his mustache. When he smiled, the tops of his cheeks crinkled. He wore no wedding ring.

Hana wore expensive jewelry—a heavy gold chain around her neck, a wide bangle on a wrist, and a large diamond wedding ring. Her hair was streaked blond. Her hands were somewhat pudgy. Her lips were full and sensual.

As Karl began to talk, he appeared to be nothing so much as a disciplined soldier. For all his erudition—he was a brilliant Renaissance man—there was an animal-like quality to him. Nothing escaped his pale brown eyes—or his lips—unless he wanted it to.

When he was asked a question he didn't like, he would wriggle his nose and sniff as he answered.

"I think he really is in command in every situation," Hana said at one point.

The orange light on our table turned Hana's large, widely spaced blue eyes into kaleidoscopes. Her left eye had a black dot, a permanent speck in the iris.

Koecher indicated that he still works for the Czechoslovak Intelligence Service, targeted at the U.S. He indicated later that the meals he paid for—we took turns—were on his expense account. He declined to give his position, saying, "My rank is a sensitive issue. This type of information is classified, at least here. Even the CIA would be clandestine about it. You don't reveal the work you do, even if everyone knows. You say 'no comment,' which doesn't deny it. But I guess you can figure out a lot of things."

"Usually the attitude here is to clam up. I really don't believe in that. Maybe that's also my American experience. I don't hesitate to answer. I try to tell my side of the story. They [the Soviet bloc] do it, but only on the most fundamental issues. It's more conservative thinking. I think I'm more flexible. But of course with the new Soviet leadership, they seem to also believe in public relations in the best sense of the word. So do I. And I think it's also very useful for at least understanding each other more, and maybe we can respect each other more."

Still, he told me, he was taking "a hell of a risk."

"It's far safer not to talk," he said. "Let's say I take it upon myself, and, 'Okay, so Karl go ahead,' " he said, indicating he had gotten approval to be interviewed. "But you know . . ."

Over the next five days, the Koechers picked us up each morning in front of the hotel and returned us each evening.

"Hi, guys," Hana would greet us, demonstrating her appreciation of American slang.

While Koecher clearly wanted to embarrass the FBI, which caught up with him after he had been a mole for twenty years, his approach to providing me with information was sophisticated.

"If I told you that," he said on more than one occasion, "it would look like disinformation, and you would have no way to corroborate it. So what is the point?"

Koecher was sure the FBI had genuinely wanted to make him a double agent, but then reneged.

Referring to the FBI agent on his case, he said, "Geide was offering me a contract [to be a double agent]. That's how I understood it. Certainly Brown [from the CIA] meant it. I assume he had the green light from the director. I don't think he made it up."

To renege is "counterproductive and nonprofessional," he said. "If the FBI or CIA need to deal with someone who works for foreign counterintelligence—the Chinese, the Israelis, the South Africans—and it becomes known that in such dealings the FBI makes promises which it breaks or doesn't mean to keep, then I don't see how they could attempt to turn anyone. They have nothing to offer anymore. Those kinds of things spread like a forest fire. The credibility is ruined."

Koecher talked in complete sentences and paragraphs in a mild, understated way. Occasionally, he punctuated his sentences by letting his voice trail off—a way of magnifying his meaning with a combination question mark and exclamation point. While I had expected he would admit to being a spy, I had not expected that he would reveal his feelings in such an articulate manner.

To be sure, he occasionally dropped some "disinformation"—spy terminology for a carefully planted lie designed to disrupt the other side. But for the fancy name, there is nothing magical about disinformation. A government official or the head of any *Fortune* 500 company may be equally prone to distort the truth to further his own ends. As in any interview, it would be necessary to weigh what Koecher said against any corroborating evidence that could be obtained.

Koecher was as proud of his own professionalism as any doctor or lawyer. When I mentioned that the FBI learned of his spying activities by seeing him engage in "brief encounters" with Czech intelligence agents in Washington, he took it as a personal affront.

"Do they have pictures?" Koecher asked.

"I don't know."

"How can you not make pictures?" he asked. "In other words, every counterintelligence organization takes pictures, and it's no problem with remote-controlled cameras and infrared. . . . It would be totally nonprofessional not to take photos. It's simply not so. I've never seen any pictures, and there are none."

Having thrown out the red herring of whether the FBI had taken pictures of his contacts with the Czechs, Koecher would return several more times to the subject over the next five days. Clearly, he was annoyed by the implication that he might have slipped up. He preferred to believe that the FBI had learned of his activities from someone else—perhaps a defector from the Czechoslovak Intelligence Service or the KGB.

Koecher's comments about the way the FBI had discovered his activities led inexorably to other questions: Did he know the FBI was following him? Why did he decide to leave the U.S.? Did the CIA suspect him? Just what kind of information did he give the Czechs and Soviets? And what connection, if any, did his swinging activities have with spying?

Koecher suggested that we drive to Old Town Square in the heart of Prague to see some sights. In some ways, the city was like Disneyland, with Cinderella's castle towering over it, and normal traffic prohibited from downtown streets. To Western eyes accustomed to bustle, the people seemed mildly drugged: their pace was slow, steady, controlled. There were no "street people," no blacks. There were no pretty girls in advertising on the backs of buses. Instead, many of the corners sprouted loudspeakers. Koecher said they were seldom used.

Using his official government card, Koecher was allowed to park even in the most sacrosanct areas. Nonchalantly, he explained that the "A, B, C" imprinted on the card means he can drive in each of these three restricted areas. In addition, a red stripe on the card gives him access to still other prohibited areas.

As we approached the square, Koecher pointed out the Old Town Hall, scene of the defenestration that started the Thirty Years' War, when Hapsburg representatives were thrown out a window. The famous fifteenth-century astronomical clock there was being repaired. Koecher described how, when the clock is working, Christ and the twelve apostles show themselves at two little windows above the clock face, and a skeletal Death tolls the hour. We happened to pass there at 6:00 P.M., and a crowd of tourists was gathered just in case it miraculously worked. A few doors down was Franz Kafka's boyhood home, a six-story building decorated with elaborate Florentine graffiti, figures in relief parading above, below, and between the windows. A block or two away was Tyl Theater, a pale green building with sweeping curves—someone once called it "frozen music"—where Mozart's *Don Giovanni* was first performed in 1787. In the square, we slipped into the chill sanctuary of Tyn Church, which is Gothic outside and baroque inside. An evening service was going on.

Besides the astronomical clock, many of the buildings in the square were being renovated, and we ducked under scaffolding to enter a wine bar that served regional offerings from casks. As we sipped a white Burgundy, I commented on how laid back the people seemed to be. Koecher attributed it to the personalities of wine drinkers.

That night, we were to dine at the Three Ostriches, an inn dating to the Renaissance, when it was the home of an ostrich-feather merchant. Killing time before our 7:30 P.M. reservation, we walked near the magnificient castle where Gustav Husak, then the president of Czechoslovakia, lived. From the square in front of it, we had a panorama of Prague, spread before us like a pastel picture postcard.

The restaurant turned out to be nearly deserted. I wondered if it had been emptied so Koecher's superiors could better listen to our conversations. But Koecher explained that it is common for restaurants in Prague to be half empty. Like everything else, the state owns them. There is no monetary incentive to have a quick turnover. Each table is held for only one party during the evening, even if the people never show up.

When the waiter began reciting the specials, Hana Koecher stopped him.

"*Prosim, Anglitsky,*" she said. In this and other restaurants, the waiters would then reel off the specials in quite good English.

I had a crisp duck with sauerkraut ringed by sliced dumplings with herbs.

"If you eat Czech food, you'll get fat," Hana said.

Hana talked far less than her husband, and her accent was more pronounced. But she had a way of cutting to the heart of an issue with very few words. Clearly, she was Koecher's intellectual equal and was well-acquainted with spy terminology and lore—tradecraft, as it is called. Presumably, Koecher discussed his true political views with her during their twenty years in America. I asked if the FBI might have picked that up while they were bugging their New York apartment.

"We didn't discuss these things in the apartment," Koecher said. "We usually took a walk."

They both laughed.

Reflecting on his reasons for being a spy, Koecher said, "If you want to make an impact, you don't have that many opportunities. You want to distinguish yourself; you want to set yourself from the crowd somehow, even if it's in secret. I wanted to shape the course in a way. But modern times here and in the West don't give you that much opportunity. The whole way of life is standardized. There is a system, and you work as a cog in the system."

Koecher said he felt an obligation to perpetuate the Czech culture.

"This is a lifestyle that makes life worthwhile," he added. "This is my idea of living life to the hilt: challenging the powers," he said. "I probably like that [danger]. It makes you feel more alive. To face danger and cope with it and overcome it.

"You have to be cool. That requires some discipline. I think you can develop discipline. Let's say education and learning require a lot of discipline. It's like being a good musician. That would require it, oh God, yes. I get scared afterwards. I don't panic."

When asked if he had compared himself with other spies or intelligence officers, Koecher said he admires the most famous Soviet spies—Rudolph Abel, Gordon Lonsdale, and Richard Sorge.

The most successful spy of the World War II era, Sorge was a GRU officer who learned through German Embassy sources in Tokyo that Japan did not plan to attack the Soviet Union through Siberia in 1941. This allowed Stalin to pull back enough troops to save Moscow from the invading Germans. On the eve of his arrest he dispatched a message that the Japanese were about to strike Pearl Harbor. He was hanged by the Japanese in 1944. His handsome features were immortalized on a Soviet postage stamp.

"The courage and the sense of moral obligation the man had were very impressive," Koecher said of Sorge.

Koecher seemed to identify most with Lonsdale, a KGB officer who entered Great Britain illegally in 1955. After uncovering atomic secrets, Lonsdale, whose real name was Konon T. Molodi, was arrested by the British MI5.

"To any questions you might ask me, the answer is: 'No.' So you needn't trouble to ask," Lonsdale told the British.

His arrest was a disappointment not only to his wife in the Soviet Union but to his many girlfriends. Eventually, he was traded for Greville Wynne, the British businessman involved in the Penkovsky affair.

Of Lonsdale, Koecher said, "He had a total lack of any fanaticism, combined with the personal sacrifice he made. He had to be brilliant. He could have succeeded at anything, and he chose intelligence work, where you really have no visible rewards. He had to think in broad historical terms, feeling he had to carry a broad obligation. He was very sophisticated, very mild."

Saying Lonsdale was one of the most successful KGB officers of his time, Koecher added, "I like the way he handled it when he was arrested, with a sense of humor. He tried to protect everybody he took advantage of. He inspired respect . . . I think an intelligence officer could well be a gentleman and an officer as well."

"Are you like Gordon Liddy?" I asked.

"Perhaps I am like a Gordon Liddy," he said. "I have a sort of liking for him. He really bungled the whole [Watergate break-in] thing. He really overdid it. There is something nice about him too. All this Nazi thing is too much. Or burning himself with a match is silly. I read his book. I have a certain amount of understanding for him."

Later, he corrected his comments, saying he only admired the Watergate burglar's determination.

When Koecher asked the waiter about dessert, he was told there was only one choice—malakoff, a dense, rectangular slab of almond cream topped with whipped cream and dribbled with chocolate.

Dessert was a subject near and dear to Koecher and his wife. He loved cakes and had once unsuccessfully tried his skills to obtain the recipe for the chocolate apricot cake made by Eclair, a New York pastry shop.

"They're more secretive than the CIA, in effect," he said.

Since returning to Czechoslovakia, Hana had begun baking for him because of the paucity of desserts in Prague. She was concerned that he had not fully gained back the weight he lost while in prison.

After each dinner, he would ask the same question: "What's for dessert?" And always the same answer: ice cream, malakoff, or palacinky, a crepe filled with jam, whipped cream, and chocolate. Whatever the waiter would utter, Koecher would bow slightly to cover his irritation, maybe sit back and sigh, looking down at the table and then up at the waiter. He would then resignedly order something, or shrug, and ask for the check.

When I paid, he would admonish me not to leave too large a tip. Even Hana got into the act. "Ooh," she would say if too many korunas were put down, "that's too much."

Driving back to the hotel at 11:00 P.M., I asked Koecher what he thought of *Amadeus*. The film about Mozart had won an Academy Award and had been filmed in Prague by Milos Forman, who was born in Czechoslovakia. Yet I had heard that Koecher considered it terrible. I wondered why.

"They portrayed Amadeus as an asinine drunk who knew how to write music but was otherwise incompetent," Koecher said.

"Did you identify with him?" I asked.

"He wants to know if you are crazy, Karl," Hana said.

"It's an attempt to put down a genius, which is something certain kinds of people enjoy," he said.

Despite his vehemence about some subjects, Hana never seemed shy about expressing differing views.

"It's historically untrue," she said. "But I liked it."

Before going up to our hotel room, I suggested to Pam that we take a stroll in the hotel lobby. There, I told her about Koecher's suggestion earlier that day that I buy currency on the black market. She thought that perhaps he was trying to test me, to see if I might be susceptible to bribes. The next evening, Pam was the one who wanted to take a walk in the lobby. Despite my negative reaction, Hana had made the same suggestion to her while they were out shopping.

The next day, I went over Koecher's background, filling in holes in the job applications and other records I already had. But he did not want to talk about his recruitment by the Czech Intelligence Service.

"It's probably the sort of information that the service itself would like to keep a secret, no? That's vital information, basically. Because then you narrow down the kind of man who could be recruited," he said.

I asked if the CIA could have done a better job of screening him. He called lie-detector tests "useless" and bragged, "They couldn't have done anything better. I believe if I went back and started it over again, I would use the same ways."

But he allowed that the FBI's and CIA's view of the type of person who should be considered suspect was too rigid. Noting that he had posed as a right-wing reactionary, Koecher said, "They think there's a method and you go by the book. You develop it as the situation develops. You respond to their prejudices. You do it by not fitting into any of their preconceived ideas."

"Like what?" I asked.

"That changes. They have a profile of what a drug smuggler is like. So you don't fit into it. I came across as a reactionary guy. Now they might be wary of that."

What was still unclear was the precise nature of Koecher's activities in the 1980s, before he was arrested.

Koecher said he had continued as a CIA contract employee until he was arrested. While he undertook few specific projects for the CIA, his status gave him access to a number of U.S. government officials in sensitive positions—even some in the White House. Because of the CIA connection, they trusted him and disclosed details of operations targeted against the Soviets and U.S. allies alike, he said. In spy jargon, these people are known as unwitting agents—unaware they are being used by an intelligence service.

"You live in Washington, you meet people. The fact you worked for the CIA gives you a certain standing and credibility so that people who wouldn't talk to you normally would. You become a part of the club," he said.

It appeared from what Koecher was saying that the operations against allies consisted primarily of intercepting their communications. I told him that did not seem particularly shocking. But Koecher said, "Those operations . . . would embarrass the U.S. in any number of countries badly. They would harm relations even with allies because the U.S. doesn't trust its allies. It spies on them."

Koecher said he saw no point in disclosing the details simply to embarrass the U.S. If the Soviets wish to embarrass the U.S., he said, they will do it for a specific reason. When I asked him how much the FBI knows about what he gathered and conveyed to the Czechs, he said the bureau knows only a portion of it.

"It's surprising how inept they were," he said. "They just talked about what they knew."

"Like Ogorodnik?" I asked, referring to the CIA asset in Moscow who committed suicide after Koecher revealed his identity.

"Yes, Ogorodnik," he said. "And they asked the same questions on the polygraphs over and over again."

"Have you heard of any specific people besides Ogorodnik?" I asked.

"If they don't know, I won't tell them," Koecher said.

"Are there others [moles] who have done that but haven't been found out?" I asked.

"You don't expect me to answer that," he said.

"Or were found out but haven't been publicized?"

"Not to my knowledge," he said.

"You're the only one who penetrated [the CIA]," I said.

"At least that's the claim," he said.

"Besides Chin who worked for China. And you did it for the KGB."

"It's really a different service," he said, glossing over the fact that the KGB and the Czech intelligence service work together—that, in fact, KGB officers known as "advisers" sit at every level of the Czech service.

Just as an FBI or CIA agent would not disclose his methods, Koecher said he would not disclose his.

"That I won't reveal," he said, referring to how he got material out of the CIA. "It's like providing a spy manual. Again, it's a true secret. How do you really get hard-core intelligence? I don't think any intelligence officer would speak about that, especially for a successful operation when the opposition doesn't really know."

I did not press him, but after a few days of interviews, Koecher dropped some hints. For one, he noted that he has a photographic memory and did not need to physically remove documents. He also talked about his ability to travel to other countries to pass information to his handlers.

Koecher said the FBI and CIA know a good deal more about the damage he did than they want to reveal.

"Let's say that they may know more about it than you think, except that they wouldn't charge me with it because it would compromise their sources of information," he said. "But what was the purpose of dragging this on? I think it indicates that there are very sensitive issues which were never mentioned. They know and I know that I could, if I really started talking, compromise people in very high positions in the White House and Pentagon. I'm not saying I will not. I may well decide when the moment is right or when sufficiently provoked. I don't think it's worth doing it right now."

Koecher had a Machiavellian theory that the FBI was trying to edge out the CIA politically. He said the FBI had used him to try to embarrass the CIA by publicizing the fact that it had been penetrated by a mole. To support his theory that the two agencies are engaged in a power struggle, he said that the FBI has been secretly sending its agents overseas under diplomatic cover—a function normally reserved for the CIA.

"Simply embarrassing an intelligence agency is a questionable thing to do in the eyes of professionals, if it involves a foreign-born person," Koecher said. "If it's an American traitor who sells secrets, that's reprehensible, just as if it's a Russian who takes action against Russians. If it's a foreign-born person, professionals on both sides regard those people as professional intelligence officers doing their job. They then settle the matter in a gentlemanly manner—by trading off. Certainly the publicity doesn't serve the prestige of the organization."

Of course, Koecher much preferred the gentlemanly ways of the CIA to the FBI's penchant for putting people in jail. He found it hard to understand the open way things are done in the U.S. The fact that the FBI had lied to him about making him a double agent had opened up all kinds of possibilities about what the FBI's motives really were.

To be sure, there was more friction between the FBI and CIA than either agency likes to admit. Yet, in this particular case, there was no basis for believing the FBI wanted to embarrass the CIA—a charge that could put the bureau on the defensive. Quite the contrary, the FBI had kept the Koecher case under wraps, disclosing far fewer details than it normally does about spy cases.

On the other hand, when I got back to Washington, I was surprised to find that the FBI had been secretly sending agents overseas under diplomatic cover. For years, the FBI openly stationed legal attachés in friendly countries to help gather information needed for cases in the U.S. Now, I was told, the bureau was sending covert agents to help keep track of American spies who meet with their handlers in Communist countries. In addition, the FBI agents watch Americans who might be recruited overseas to spy for the Russians. The recent security breaches by Marine guards at the U.S. Embassy in Moscow provided a clear example of the need for such surveillance.

Since these are counterintelligence functions involving Americans, I was told, the CIA did not mind the bureau stepping in. In fact, the CIA had welcomed the move because it freed up its agents to gather intelligence. However, I found the new arrangement had been kept so secret that even the House Judiciary Committee, which has oversight responsibilities over the FBI, did not know about it. On the other hand, the Senate Intelligence Committee knew about the arrangement and approved of it.

Earlier, Koecher mentioned the article in *Washingtonian* magazine about his swinging activities, dismissing it as "trash." But now, as we settled into two leather chairs in the hotel lobby after lunch, he confirmed that he and Hana had frequented several sex clubs.

"I went to Plato's Retreat a few times and the Washington club [Capitol Couples], but not Virginia's In Place," he said. "I went to sex parties afterwards. I wouldn't say people went exclusively for sex. It was chic to go to bars like that. It's a lifestyle."

Just then, Koecher noticed three rather swarthy young men listening to our conversation from their chairs nearby.

"They're not mine; they must be yours," he said quite seriously.

In my hotel room, he sipped a Pilsner beer as he talked about what he perceived as his obligation to preserve Czech culture against encroachments by an all-powerful United States.

"We are as a nation, and as a specific central European culture, different from the French, Russian, and Yugoslav culture," he said. "It's very specific and disappearing. We are neither part of the East nor the West. We have an obligation to continue it. Generations have tried to preserve it. It should not disappear. If people don't do it, it will go to hell and become a hamburger culture."

I commented that Hana likes hamburgers, but Koecher went on:

"I feel a strong obligation to defend against American aggressiveness. I really believe that. I believe the ideology of both political parties has a very strong aggressive tone . . . I think the American influence is really pernicious. It's very alien to Europeans. It's commercial and money-oriented. To the extent they want to control, I think they have to be opposed.

"Even John Kennedy was not defensive," he maintained. "He was aggressive as hell. He paved the way for the war in Vietnam. He didn't go through the Congress."

While the Soviets went through a period of violence under Stalin, he said, "this [the Soviet Union] is a young regime. America was not a very nice country to live in some sixty years after it was founded. You had racial zealots, or the massacre of the Indians. It became a decent, nice civilized country much, much later."

I mentioned the Soviet invasion of Afghanistan.

"Privately, the way I see it, although I am convinced the current Soviet leadership is determined to end the conflict and pull out, I don't find it an aggressor against Afghanistan," he said. "There's a traditional Russian interest in the area.

"You can pass out leaflets on Fifth Avenue," he said, referring to the freedoms enjoyed in the U.S., "and nobody will mind. It really doesn't matter. But it doesn't matter because it doesn't matter. Nobody gives a damn. It's worthless. In Russia and here, too, incidentally, a written word has a terrific impact. Everybody says, 'My God.' So therefore they handle it differently. In the U.S., it's a free country and so what?"

Yet occasionally, Koecher expressed admiration for some aspects of American culture—an objectivity that he felt was a key to his success.

"A good intelligence officer is a reasonable man with a strong moral sense—not a fanatic," he commented. "If you're a fanatic, you don't operate well, period. You are unable to relate to people who are your enemies or the opposition. I prefer the word 'opposition.'

"You have to understand them," he continued. "You have to have a broad understanding of humanity, for Christ's sake. You cannot be a narrow, dogmatic ideologue. . . . We can learn from them and admire their achievements."

Friday was Labor Day, a holiday that Koecher said got its start in the U.S. From every building flew pairs of Czech flags and modified Soviet flags. At some buildings, small flags fluttered at every window. Because of the crowds heading for the all-day rally, Hana came on foot to the hotel to take us by subway to the outskirts of the city. There, Koecher would meet us with their car. The charge for the subway was ten cents, and no one checked at the exit to make sure we had purchased a ticket.

I wanted to buy a Czech fashion magazine at a newsstand for my daughter, but Hana said, "What do you want to buy that for? You'll find better ones in Paris [where we were going after Prague]." But should Hana return to work, it would be with one such fashion magazine. She told Pam that in order to get the quality she would like, she has to have her clothes custom-made—$250 for a leather suit, the nuisance of five fittings, and then if you didn't like it you were stuck with it.

On the subway, I moved to take my camera from its case, but Hana said it wouldn't be a good idea to take pictures. When a bearded man got on and opened a book, I suddenly realized no one else on the train was reading a magazine, book, or newspaper.

Koecher took us to see a young artist named Rona whose home and studio were inside the New Jewish Cemetery. Hana explained that artists have to go through a difficult selection process to get into art school, but after going through their formal schooling they've got it made. Painters can work at home and make a living. The state guarantees them three exhibitions a year, and it will buy their work if no one else does. But artists who are not official artists had better change careers; they will not make it.

Some contemporary artists are reluctant to explain their work, but Rona was not one of them. He said every painting of his had a story behind it, which he enjoyed telling. He favored droopy looking monsters, and his palette was rust. He laughed about the lumpy fossils and shells that appear on a few of his canvases. A natural history museum had inspired them.

Koecher asked Pam what kind of art instruction she had before becoming an art critic for *The Washington Post*.

"On-the-job training," she said.

I noticed that Koecher was vaguely dissatisfied with her answer.

She was not feeling well that day, and the last thing she wanted to talk about was work. That night, I told her that I thought Koecher was becoming suspicious of her, but she couldn't believe he would question her identity.

Leaving Rona's studio, we followed a wooden sign to Kafka's grave. Saying the cemetery authorities required it, Koecher had brought along yarmulkes to wear on our heads.

After visiting another, more accomplished artist, we headed for Koecher's new home outside of Prague. Koecher was scheduled to move from his apartment to the new home within a week. Out past factories and apartment complexes, there was a sudden decrease in population, and we were driving through farmlands.

The house was at the end of a road—a white stucco house with dark brown trim, standing out as tidier and a little bigger than the other houses in the village.

As a rooster crowed, we walked inside the house and were surprised at how light and airy it was. A huge aquarium had been built into the wall between the living room and Koecher's workout room. Hana took us upstairs, which had three bedrooms. A fourth, smaller room had been turned into a walk-in closet. The workmen were stunned at the novel suggestion, but they followed Koecher's design. The Koechers were pleased with the result.

Most of their belongings had not yet arrived, but the living room was already furnished with a soft brown leather sofa and two chairs. On the mantel over the raised fireplace was a seven-candle Jewish menorah, its branches symbolizing the seven days of creation.

Hana complained that they can't get the newspaper delivered. By the time it arrives in the mail, it's too late. In Czechoslovakia, she said, there is no such thing as a kid having a paper route. It is not considered proper to have monetary incentives. Once she suggested to Koecher's mother she have two neighborhood boys help her with vacuuming.

"You don't want to make them servants!" she had said.

By now, there was a pattern to our interviews. Koecher would begin by interviewing me, reviewing any item that raised a question about my identity. Usually at these times, he would tape me and I would keep my tape recorder off. Once he was satisfied, he would relax and turn off his tape recorder. Then I would begin my questioning.

This time, Koecher wanted to know more about Pam's background. I had already sensed that he was suspicious of her, and I took the opportunity to tell him exactly where her art reviews appeared under her byline.

Koecher was satisfied, and he later commented to me, "Pam seems to be really relieved that this is basically a normal type of interpersonal relationship. She was probably expecting really something awful."

We took a short walk before dinner in the woods where Koecher jogs. He recalled jogging in the Washington area, at Great Falls, Maryland, and along the C&O Canal.

Back at the house, we settled into chairs on a deck overlooking a cherry tree in the backyard. Beyond it was a rabbit hutch and a pottery kiln, in the muddy yard of the Koechers' poorer neighbors. Koecher poured slivovitz into small Moser crystal glasses. He gulped his drink, while I was barely able to let the strong plum brandy touch my lips.

"In my opinion," Koecher said, "the Soviet Union and the United States have much more in common than not—culturally, their size, their natural resources, the fact they each have different types of populations that have to be integrated, their admiration of technology.

"We don't fanatically hate America," he said, referring to the Soviet bloc. "We happen to have a conflict. There is a cold war still going on. We are threatening each other with mutual annihilation. That's a very serious matter. You have to defend yourself and know what the other side is doing. The only way to find out is to gather intelligence."

Perhaps in ten years, the Soviets and Americans will become friends, he said, just as the U.S. and the People's Republic of China have overcome their hostility.

I mentioned a theory that the more both sides know about each other, the more secure both sides are.

"I do believe it's desirable to know as much as possible," he said. "It would be the other way around if we were preparing for a war. We're not; I think it's obvious. I believe myself that the United States is preparing for a war. The belligerent people are in charge—Caspar Weinberger is in charge, more so than [George] Shultz."

Hana brought out pirogi, ground meat wrapped in triangular-shaped dough. I asked what Koecher liked about the U.S.

"It's a sort of combat zone," he said, referring to the forces of competition there, "but it's a hell of a challenge. That's one thing I like about it. It forces you to squeeze everything out of yourself. It's like a combat situation, competition. That's really how things get done."

Then, very softly, he said he likes the way Americans do "things in a grand style." And he said he misses Thanksgiving turkey.

By now, I knew that Koecher almost whispered when he said things he felt deeply about and didn't really want to say.

"I like many things about America also," Hana said. "I like the easiness that somehow gets people together. They are not formal at all. In Europe they are much more formal. And of course all the good things about supermarkets and the easy life you can have there."

"Well, supermarkets aren't specifically American," Koecher interjected. "There are the West Germans, the Swiss. So I wouldn't include the standard of living."

It was permissible to cite American plusses as long as Koecher was doing it.

"Do you feel you made a lot of personal sacrifices?" Pam asked.

"I certainly do," Koecher said. "I liked going there [to the U.S.]. It's exciting in many ways. Intellectually you can hardly know our century without knowing the United States. The sacrifice is, if you really can't come home. Leading a double life you certainly don't enjoy, and your friends and people you like thinking you're something you're not. I really don't like that part. Certainly by following a career that is secretive, if you are a success nobody knows about it, as compared with an academic career," he said. "Perhaps it would have been successful or not, but if it were successful, it could be very glittering."

I was learning that this was Koecher's way of being modest.

Koecher popped the cork on a bottle of Czech wine and poured it into our glasses. He continued to drink slivovitz, but Hana removed the decanter and his glass.

"I think Hana doesn't want me to drink any more slivovitz," he said. "Maybe she thinks it is not good for my health, which very often is true."

The question of Koecher's religious orientation had been bothering me, and now I asked about it. There was the Jewish candelabrum on the mantle. And he seemed much more emotional when talking about Judaism than when talking about Catholicism, which was his father's religion. When he talked about his grandparents being killed in a Nazi concentration camp, his face contorted. What's more, he seemed to know more about Judaism than most Jews. Yet some people thought he was anti-Semitic. He refused to be photographed wearing a yarmulke next to Kafka's grave. When applying for a job at the CIA, he had listed his religion as Roman Catholic.

Koecher said he called himself Roman Catholic because it would look better on his application than "atheist," which is what he really is. He dismissed the menorah as a decoration without religious significance to him. As for posing at Kafka's grave, he said, "I don't want to appear in a picture which may be taken out of the context of my taking you to a cemetery. Do you know what I mean or not? If someone is wearing a yarmulke, it's religious. I don't want to appear to be religious one way or the other."

"We happen to have some Jewish friends, and sometimes we wear a yarmulke with them on Jewish holidays," Hana said.

"You have these Jewish strains and feelings but—" I began.

"I wouldn't say even feelings," Koecher interrupted. "You extract your heritage as such." Referring to his grandparents, he said, "The fact they were killed is a very significant consideration."

"Is there any ambiguity in your mind?" I asked.

None, he said.

"I'm not a champion of Jewish causes," he said. "I'm a Czech who happens to have a Jewish background. I think the Jewish contribution to European culture has been extremely significant. It's really Judeo-Christian civilization. It's certainly a heritage to be proud of."

Perhaps, he said, the idea that he was anti-Semitic arose from his views about Zionism.

"I don't make the conclusion I have to go to Israel," he said. "I think you believe—which is common in the U.S.—that religion is significant to your value system. I don't," Koecher said. "I philosophize . . . I don't have any question about which religion I should choose. I don't choose any of them. That resolves any questions."

I thought back over how committed and geniune he had seemed when talking about Judaism. Since I was Jewish, Koecher probably wanted to emphasize his Jewish side with me. Yet others—including Robert Fierer, his lawyer—were convinced he was anti-Semitic because of denigrating comments he had made.

In fact, Koecher was a chameleon, just as effective at projecting himself as Jew, anti-Semite, or Christian as he was at posing as a capitalist when he was a Communist.

By now, the sun had slipped behind the cluster of houses nearby. Outside on the deck, Hana served what she called chicken and vegetables. Because fresh vegetables are so scarce, the vegetables were the frozen kind; the chicken, too, had been frozen. But this was typical: even the best restaurants in Prague served canned peas.

"How do you feel about Ogorodnik's death?" I asked him.

"I'm deeply sorry about that," he said. "But the people who did him in were the CIA and he himself. They recruited him in such a clumsy manner. . . . I'm not denying I gave them the document [that compromised him], and I'm not confirming it. I sure do know I worked on the case. I confess it."

"What was clumsy?" I asked.

"Let's put it this way: what makes it incompetent is the very fact the other side knows he was there," Koecher said.

"But that's because the CIA gave the material on him to you," I said.

Koecher explained that the CIA should not have given the document describing Ogorodnik's defection to anyone to translate. The CIA officers who dealt with the matter should have known Russian themselves, he said.

He called Ogorodnik "a vain man" and a "careerist." But he said, "I didn't want to see him dead."

Did the CIA suspect him after Ogorodnik's death? I asked.

"They didn't suspect me," he said. In fact, he said, he subsequently got access to more classified information than before. As a contract employee, he was perceived to need information on many different areas.

"If you do projects," he said, "you can look into a lot of things. It was more commensurate with my education."

While he refused to specify what projects he did, Koecher said that he learned "embarrassing information, like Colonel North's actions are embarrassing to President Reagan. . . . The American allies would be offended."

Listening to Koecher talk, I was impressed by his erudition and sense of history. I welcomed our friendly exchanges and the lip service he paid to peace. And I believed that from his point of view, his intent was noble. But there was no question in my mind that if I were his professional opponent, he would not hesitate to do me in.

As we finished dinner, I asked Hana about her comments when the FBI confronted her. For the first time, she began to open up, describing how she had asked for a lawyer and been told by the agents that she didn't need one.

As Koecher made a fire in the fireplace, he and Hana argued about whether a condiment made with rose hips and served with game at a particular restaurant was a marmalade or a sauce.

"Are you crazy?" Hana said when Koecher insisted it was a marmalade.

"There is a debate," he said, trying to appear calm.

I asked Koecher whether he thought Yurchenko, who had abruptly left the U.S. after dining at a Washington restaurant, was a genuine defector. If he was genuine, why hadn't he been executed upon his return?

Koecher said he did not rule out the possibility that the CIA originally kidnapped him, as he claimed.

"It's a wild theory, but I don't quite rule it out," he said.

More likely, he said, Yurchenko genuinely defected and changed his mind.

"My personal opinion, if that were the case," Koecher went on, "is that the KGB response to that would be, 'We'll just bite the bullet, we hate that creep, and let him live, go, give him a decent existence.' First of all he admitted he betrayed his country; that is something. Thinking in broader terms, it's better to have a defector who reconsiders than to have a defector who doesn't, and for that sake, 'Let him go.' "

"There were rumors he was executed, remember that?" Koecher said to Hana.

"Yes," she said.

"The Soviets produced him. You have to be a fool to do that anyway, to defect. In terms of recognition, in terms of anything, he wouldn't have a better life over there than in the Soviet Union," he said.

As we left the house that night, Koecher said there was no need to douse the fire with water, while Hana insisted that the house would burn down otherwise.

"I will pour water over it," she said.

No, Koecher insisted. The fire is safe. Let it be.

Each night, Karl and Hana alternately abstained from drinking. In Czechoslovakia, even one drink was enough to revoke a driver's license for a year. This night, it was Hana's turn to drive. As she backed up to turn around at the end of the street, the car lurched into a ditch.

"Hana!" Koecher said with some feeling. He got out from the

backseat and climbed into the front. She said she had had little need to drive in New York.

Koecher put the car in gear and roared out of the ditch.

As we drove away, he began talking to her, not realizing that he had left her behind in the dust. He backed up, got out, and then let her get behind the wheel again.

On the way back to the hotel, Koecher joked that the house probably would not be there the next day, since the fire was still burning in the fireplace. It was symbolic of the chances he likes to take.

At lunch on Saturday, I said I had heard that Koecher could become quite abusive to Hana.

"Sometimes we fight. You get upset," she said.

"But he doesn't beat you?" I asked.

"Beat me?" she said.

"Or do you beat him?" I asked.

"I don't think either. Why beat him? If he beat me I'd kill him, all right," she laughed.

Both Koechers complained that as a condition to being traded, they had to voluntarily give up their U.S. citizenship. I pointed out that they did not want to be U.S. citizens anyway, nor could they ever return to America. Yet they still insisted they had been abused. It was a bizarre contradiction.

After lunch, we toured the Sternberk Palace, now a museum devoted to the works of Picasso, Renoir, Degas, Cézanne, and Gaugin. As the sun began to set, we strolled across the Charles Bridge, a grand pedestrian promenade begun in 1357. Thirty baroque statues lined the sides, each a saint or a Christian vignette.

Koecher seemed particularly fascinated by the one of St. John of Nepomuk, who was thrown off the bridge and into the river at a point near where his statue stands. The legend goes that when he was thrown off, five stars appeared on the water. And somewhere on the bridge—Koecher was sure of it—a plaque of five stars commemorated it. Koecher was delighted when, after a few minutes' search, he found the plaque.

Koecher said King Wenceslas IV, who completed the bridge after it was commissioned by his father, Charles IV, was a shameless philanderer. He had the symbol of his mistress's profession—a masseuse—carved on the bridge. It was a rolled towel tied in a knot to form a wreath with a bird inside.

On the other side of the old bridge tower, Koecher pointed to another bit of ribald whimsy—a priest with his hand under a nun's habit, carved into the stone trim during the same era.

Later, we sat against fur-backed chairs as Koecher translated the menu at the Gamekeepers Place.

"There is wild pheasant breast, pheasant Czech style, deer sausage, venison pâté," he said. "The deer run wild. Usually they're shot on some military territory. You have to control the herds."

He continued: "Breast of deer in cream sauce, venison goulash, hare in cream sauce, hare in cherry sauce, wild boar leg with rose hips. That is excellent. I recommend that. Then there is wild boar roast. The pheasant comes with stuffing, dumplings, sauerkraut, and red cabbage, and another red cabbage."

Koecher mentioned that his mother lives nearby, and Pam asked if Koecher told her the truth about his defection after he left Czechoslovakia.

"No," Koecher said. "But she knows me, and she might have wondered how this guy suddenly turned so radical."

Hana pointed out that Koecher's mother came to visit them in New York.

"How did you talk when you saw her?" I asked.

"As an émigré," Koecher said.

We invited Koecher's mother to lunch the next day at the Golden Prague, the restaurant atop our hotel. Her eyes lit up when she heard Pam's name. While she doesn't speak English, she explained through Hana that she knew the name "Pamela" from having seen *Dallas*. She saw the show on West German television while visiting a relative in Pilsner.

During lunch that Sunday, Koecher said, "You know one thing. You never asked me why did I want to move from the United States."

"You said because you were going to retire," I said.

"I said. But why particularly would one want to move in the middle of surveillance which they think was not detected by me? What I'm saying is why did you never ask me why we decided to move?"

"I should have," I said.

"I probably would have 'no commented' on it. But think about it for a while and maybe you'll come up with something, even if I don't comment on it."

I recalled that Koecher had told a relative he still might go back and forth between the U.S. and Austria.

"I said I might come back and forth. That's what I said. Perhaps I didn't want to alert the FBI and make it look suspicious. Certainly if somebody decides to leave under those circumstances, he might well be aware or maybe have been warned," Koecher said, laughing. "I didn't have anything lined up there. I opened a bank account and made arrangements to move my household goods there," he said.

"I did wonder about it," I said. "So presumably the tip-off came from a defector."

"It could be. You could speculate that. You could also reason that the FBI surveillance was not that good, or had been unable to conceal the fact that the lines were being bugged." He added, "I think it's obvious that I had to find out one way or another."

"When did you find out?" I asked.

"I had been getting ready for quite a while before June [1984]," Koecher said, referring to the date when he put his co-op up for sale.

"How did you find out?" I asked.

"It's part of the business," he said. "You can deduce quite a few things."

As we finished lunch, Koecher finally got an opportunity to have some cake, and I took a picture of him eating it.

"Say 'spy,' " I said as I snapped the shutter.

While Koecher took his mother home, I sat with Hana in the hotel lobby and asked her about her husband.

"He is considerate and a nice person, even when he gets bursts of anger and is impatient," she said. "Basically, he's a very, very considerate man and mild even, which is kind of strange to imagine. But he is. If someone gets him angry, he is an explosive person. I don't get angry that fast. Also I don't get as cheerful. He's more outgoing than I am.

"I was afraid to come back here because I knew almost nobody," she said. "Karl had no problem. It's like Karl was away for three weeks instead of twenty years. They pick up like that. They're interesting people involved in TV, radio—artists, teachers."

I asked her what she feels strongly about.

"Karl," she said.

"What about Communism?" I asked.

She said her commitment to Communism is related to Karl.

"It's his philosophy," she said.

I had heard that Koecher had become interested in swinging first, and that once she tried it, she found she liked it even more than he did. Now I asked who had started it.

"Well, I don't know," she said. "It was just the thing to do at that time. All our friends somehow went to a little club or something. So we went there too to see how things are. I should say friends instigated it. The atmosphere in those years somehow elicited that."

Now we were going to visit the Old Jewish Cemetery, an astounding sight. Because Jews were crowded together in the Prague ghetto, space in the cemetery was at a premium. It was necessary to layer graves one on top of the other—as many as twelve deep. The headstones had to be lifted each time. And so they are crowded together helter-skelter, the earliest headstone dating to 1439 and the most recent to 1787. The site has an estimated 12,000 headstones, and many more graves. In the light rain, it was a mystical place.

Koecher explained that many of the symbols on the headstones go with the decendents' names. A fish, for example, denotes "Fisher."

"These are grapes denoting fertility if it's a woman," he said, pointing to one tombstone. "If it's a man, it means genius."

Each Jewish tribe has a symbol as well, Koecher said. The Cohens have a jar of oil on their tombstones.

He pointed to the grave of Rabbi Löw, who died in 1609 and was the creator of the Golem, a mythical figure who became part of Jewish folklore. After making wishes on them, visitors had placed small stones in the crevices of his tombstone. Pam and Hana each picked up a small stone and placed it atop the headstone. They didn't share their wishes, but Pam imagined Hana's had something to do with being in the West again.

Koecher pointed to the lion on the rabbi's gravestone.

"It's a lion because 'löwe' means lion in German," he said.

Hana said the cemetery scares her, and we left to see the nearby Old-New Synagogue. Built in Gothic style around 1270, it is still used for worship.

Koecher wanted to show that he knew as much about Catholicism as he did about Judaism. The day before on the Charles Bridge, and in the Church of Our Lady the Victorious, he had regaled us with tales of local miracles. On this day, we drove to the Loretto, a shrine that houses an impressive collection of a monastery's jewels—on monstrances in which the priest would carry the body of Christ, said Koecher. We saw the Wallenstein monstrance, which dates from 1721 and is encrusted with amethysts and diamonds, and the spectacular "diamond monstrance," which looks like a sun mounted on a tree trunk and is encrusted with 6,222 diamonds, each weighing up to twenty-two carats. One reason Karl knew so much about the place is that he had worked in the Loretto as a guide when he was fifteen.

Then we drove on to the castle. Within its walls, we passed the St. Vitus Cathedral, whose construction spans six centuries. It has gargoyles of animals and armless men that stretch out from the side of the cathedral like bulkheads on a ship, their mouths open as if retching.

As we toured the nearby National Gallery, I asked Koecher if he had found out that the FBI was onto him because he saw agents following him.

If he had, he said, that was not enough reason to leave the country. He said he was reluctant to say how he did find out, noting that I would have no way to corroborate the information anyway.

"Just think about it," he said. "If I start giving you all kinds of stories, I could be making it up."

"It's a problem I would try to confront after I hear it," I said.

"An FBI agent could have been indiscreet, talking to a girl in a bar, for example," Koecher said. "In that case, you have to consider the possibility that the way I found out could further embarrass the FBI without our compromising or giving up more information."

"You could have a bug also," I said, referring to the possibility FBI offices were bugged.

"There could be a bug, or an indiscretion even if he doesn't do it that often. We don't always come across it. It's not the normal thing. Maybe that's what I was also hinting at—that we may embarrass people in higher positions. It doesn't have to be in a lower position. But as I said, we don't embarrass for the sake of embarrassment."

Koecher said he would seek approval to disclose exactly how he found out about the FBI investigation. He later wrote to me: "Okay, I knew about the FBI surveillance of me and Hana, and you may quote me on that. But I have no comment about how I found out—sorry about that."

I later interviewed the Koechers' favorite swinging couple, and they told me about the man watching them with binoculars from across the street. Could the man have been an FBI agent? Other agents said it was very possible the surveillance was indiscreet. In another letter, Koecher confirmed that the incident had tipped him off that he was being watched.

Koecher said that if he had left the U.S. abruptly, it would only confirm that he had been a spy, and the FBI would begin investigating all the people he had dealt with.

"You have to choose how fast you react. You don't want really to allay their suspicions. You still want them to worry, so you try to make it appear as natural as possible. There's a certain risk involved. You have to figure it out. You don't want to resolve their problems. That would be the logic behind it," he said.

"By disappearing," he continued, "it confirms their suspicions. I don't want to confirm them. I want to keep them worried. On the other hand, how did I find out? Perhaps there is a possibility he learned this from a mole in their service. But we don't want them to think we have a mole. So again you do not want to make it appear as an escape. I'm not saying this is the way it happened. I'm just giving you a line of reasoning."

Why would he allow himself to be caught? I asked.

"You don't know if they have enough information on you. You may conclude that if they had a suspicion, they would try to turn you and maybe you can play that game to get out. It would be logical. It would be asinine to arrest me. I have to admit I wouldn't have expected them to be that stupid. They haven't gotten anything, and they destroyed the credibility of the American intelligence community.

"I'm not unwilling to admit the opposition is competent," he added. "Absolutely not. But Geide [the case agent] is not very bright."

"I can't see why anyone would take all those chances," I said.

"That's the business. You have to. It's the line of business we are in," he said. "You have to risk in order not to give information to the opposition. You don't know to what extent they are informed. Suddenly they would start looking at people around me and maybe discover something I wouldn't want them to discover."

By now, we were having coffee in the coffee shop back at the Two Swans, a short walk away, where we had eaten dinner a few nights earlier.

"Could it all be a hoax?" Hana asked.

"Whose?" Koecher said.

"Somebody's?" she said.

"What? All what?" I said.

"All this," she said.

"Hardly," Koecher said.

"Who are you referring to? Him or me or what? Me? Pam? Karl?" I asked.

"That they came up with a story," she said.

"Who came up? Us?" I asked.

"No, no. The way how we speak here. We are trying to find out different things," she said.

"True," I laughed.

Hana had been playing games, trying to see what my reaction would be. Koecher didn't think it was funny and later upbraided her for it.

After dinner that night, I suggested we talk about our reactions to one another.

"There have been times when we've been suspicious," I said.

"I would say it's steadily improved, though," Koecher said.

"Yes, every day it's more relaxed. Hana is the most relaxed today," I said.

"Hana was much more suspicious," he said.

I said I had wondered why Koecher suggested that I buy black market currency.

He said trying to set me up would be "out of the question even if I hated you. I wouldn't do that. Once you're here? Ridiculous."

"He shouldn't have even talked to you about it," Hana said. "But everybody's doing it here."

"Already somebody might have told you about it," he said. "If I say the same thing, it confirms the advice you already got before. You might have known that the possibility exists and wondered about it."

"Is there anything that stands out in your mind that you were suspicious about?" I asked.

"One always wonders, of course, when someone makes a suggestion like that or wants to come, whether you might be, let's say, an FBI guy," Koecher said.

"Of course," I said.

"On the other hand, I realize that as an author, you'd be finished. It would be most unreasonable," he said. After reading my previous book and a reference in *Who's Who in America*, Koecher said he was satisfied about my identity. His only other question had to do with why I had won a journalism award from the Freedoms Foundation. I explained that it was for a series of articles that resulted in the erecting of a memorial in downtown Boston to the Revolutionary War Liberty Tree. Koecher could identify with that. Several times, he said he liked what I had done.

Turning to Pam, Hana said, "We thought maybe you worked for the FBI."

"Uh-huh, oh really?" Pam said, shocked that anyone would think she was someone she was not.

"Sure," I said.

"Well, why not?" Koecher said.

"It's not that surprising," I said.

"There's always the possibility," Koecher said.

"But it was mainly that she wasn't talking about art?" I asked, recalling that I had told Pam they were suspicious.

"Mainly, yes," Koecher said.

"And?" Pam asked.

"Nothing more," Hana said.

"If you were to do that," Koecher said, "we started thinking what a smart thing it would be to do to protect your identity, even at the cost of delaying approval of your visa application [because she listed her employment with *The Washington Post*]. In that way, you sort of suggest that you really should be checked a little bit. It's like saying I would walk over to the FBI office [to avoid suspicion]. Making myself suspicious in order to escape suspicion.

"I would ask and develop enough to resolve the questions," he said. "The fact is the suspicions and paranoia didn't cultivate.

"You've done something very unusual by coming here and having these interviews," Koecher continued. "It's never happened. Not to my knowledge. Not as far as the Soviet Union and allied countries are concerned. Not while the man is still in active service. So I think the opportunity was important."

Koecher picked us up at 9:00 A.M. on Monday to go to the airport. As Pam and Hana went to a shop to buy a doll for the daughter of a friend of Pam's, Koecher and I talked in the car.

Koecher said Hana was concerned about the description of their swinging activities. Perhaps, he said, they could be described as rumors rather than fact.

"It might be possible to describe what you learned about an orgy place and say maybe they went there as some people claim," he said. "Certainly in Washington it was chic. It is a fact some people in sensitive positions went there. It was certainly desirable to find out about that," he said.

Referring to Plato's Retreat, he said, "It's a spectacle where we were twice maybe. It was a matter of curiosity about the bizarre, like wax figures in a museum, more or less. In principle you don't have to be a part of such a crowd that indeed engages in things like that. Neither Hana nor I denies that it was something we found of interest to watch sometimes, among other things."

"You did it [swinging] with your friends also," I said.

"Who says that?" Koecher asked.

"It was on the FBI bugs for one thing, when they were bugging your apartment," I replied.

"I think that would be very strange," he said. "They never mentioned anything like that. They could just as well make it up. There's no way I would confirm that. I'll ask our friends and see what they say. You'll probably find the same answer."

Looking up through the windshield, he said, "Incidentally, just to turn the leaf for a moment, this house has been standing here maybe four hundred years. On the top floor is where Johannes Kepler lived and discovered the laws of the motions of the planet. The plaque is there. If you walk up you follow his footsteps. That's the beautiful thing about Prague, that you indeed are in intimate touch with history. If you walk up the steps a few times and read his books, you almost have the feeling you know the man."

He added, "Kepler is my favorite figure in the history of science. I admire him far more than Galileo. I think he is the central figure in modern [scientific] thinking. That's where the scientific revolution began. Others claim it was Bacon or Newton."

There was no more talk about swinging.

As we drove to the airport, we had mixed emotions. The previous night, Koecher had said we could become quite good friends if Pam and I stayed in Prague for any length of time. It was easy for him to talk about friendship, since I was not a spy. As a matter of principle, being friends with someone who had done collective damage to one's own country would be unthinkable.

As I stepped off the plane in Paris, I felt a tremendous surge of relief. The people were so much more alive and spontaneous, and we could say what we pleased.

Pam showed me a U.S. penny Hana had taken out and given her just before we left. With perhaps a tinge of regret, Hana had said she would not be needing it.

Why did Koecher agree to talk?

"The fact I'm talking must be embarrassing," he said at one point.

James E. Nolan Jr., who was deputy assistant FBI director for operations when the FBI first got onto him, agreed.

"One thing he wanted to show is he's alive, well, and well-treated," he said when I interviewed him after returning to Washington. "So anyone else who's out there knows the heroes are welcomed. You served your twenty years in the West, and you come back and have the good life."

"We are very comfortable," Koecher had said.

Beyond that, I believe Koecher agreed to talk for the same reasons anyone submits to an interview—ego gratification, a desire for recognition, a belief that he will come across well, a desire to shape discussion of an issue, even a diversion from the routine.

Nolan thought Koecher's claim that he found out that the FBI was watching him was probably true. The fact that Koecher was leaving the U.S. at all was a tip-off. Usually, he said, the KGB would want an "illegal" to remain in a country for as long as possible.

Yet Nolan was puzzled that Koecher hadn't left more abruptly.

"I would have thought that after all those years, if he thought he was under surveillance, he ought to be thinking about leaving [quickly]," Nolan said. "But the Rosenbergs did the same thing. I guess it's hard for people to believe that it's really come unglued."

Why was Koecher so sensitive about his offer to become a double agent for the FBI?

"Maybe he doesn't want to admit that he was directed to do it," Nolan said. "This is one technique for establishing credibility. How does he establish he's a loyal American of Czech descent? He reports an approach and offers to cooperate. Maybe he doesn't want to say it was our plan that the [Czech] mission should contact him and that he would report it. He doesn't want to disclose a method."

In the end, Nolan said, the FBI had very little evidence that it could use in court beyond Koecher's own statements. The fact that he was engaging in "brief encounters," and Hana was servicing "dead drops," was not enough to produce a conviction.

"If you think of a Herrmann, a Koecher, or an Abel, and you find him, what do you do with him?" he said. "The most you can do is get him deported if you don't have a violation of the espionage act. It's conceivable you have nothing else. That's very tough. I've got nothing to hold him on. How can I interview him? He can walk away tomorrow."

19

"Halt, FBI!"

The State Department tried to convince the Justice Department to go easy on Jonathan Pollard. Israel was not only a staunch ally but a country the U.S. had an interest in supporting and protecting. Yet the espionage statute does not draw any distinctions between hostile countries and allies. Pollard's wholesale approach to spying was a shocking security breach to be dealt with firmly.

When Israeli officials refused to cooperate fully in the ensuing investigation—returning only 163 of the more than 1,000 documents Pollard had compromised—the Reagan administration decided to show no leniency.

Having agreed to plead guilty, Pollard sought to portray himself as a savior of Israel and of the U.S. In a memo introduced at his sentencing hearing in U.S. District Court in Washington, Pollard described his upbringing as a Jew and a Zionist, his family's assistance to the Israeli Army in 1948, and his belief that Jews must support Israel as a refuge in the event of another Holocaust.

Pollard said he spied for Israel because he became convinced the U.S. was not sharing with that country all the intelligence information it could provide about Arab and Soviet security threats. A stronger Israel meant a stronger U.S., he said.

During the sentencing hearing on March 5, 1987, Assistant U.S. Attorney Stephen S. Spivack said Pollard had damaged U.S. intelligence efforts by delegating to himself the authority to determine what should or should not be given to a foreign power. Many of the documents pinpointed U.S. ship positions and aircraft stations, and described tactics and training operations. They also included analyses of Soviet missile systems.

Because the sources of much of the information were evident or could be inferred, Pollard jeopardized the sources, Spivack said.

Contrary to Pollard's assertions that his motives were ideological, Spivack told Judge Aubrey E. Robinson Jr. that the Pollards' income from the Israelis equaled their annual disposable income of $29,200 from their salaries. During the year before their arrest, he said, the Pollards had eaten out at restaurants almost daily, purchased $2,000 in jewelry in Israel, and traveled to Marseilles, Saint Tropez, Cannes, Florence, Rome, Venice, Vienna, Zurich, Paris, London, Tel Aviv, and Munich.

By the spring of 1985, Pollard was receiving monthly cash payments of $2,500 from the Israelis, plus additional lump-sum payments of up to $30,000.

What's more, Spivack told the court that Pollard had shown no remorse. In fact in an interview with Wolf Blitzer, a correspondent for the *Jerusalem Post*, Pollard had likened himself to an Israeli pilot who got shot down over enemy territory. And he apologized for not having done a better job of spying.

Referring to Israel, he said, "As far as I am concerned I am as much a loyal son of that country as anybody has been. I did my best. I am sorry if it wasn't the most effective thing from a long-range standpoint, but I really did my best."

Pollard appeared to be expecting a slap on the wrist from the court. His memo, introduced at the hearing, is full of scholarly touches, as if he thought he were writing a college term paper.

"At times I feel as if I have metamorphosed into a twisted Zionist version of Alcibiades, never again to know the comfort of a homeland and spiritual refuge," he wrote. "I would seem to have strangled my dreams on the altar of unbridled hubris."

Most of all, he asked for mercy for his wife.

"By far and away the most serious loss I've suffered from throughout my imprisonment has been the separation from my wife, without whom my life ceases to have any importance or meaning," he wrote. He asked the court to spare her further imprisonment, so she might "reconstitute her life in preparation for our reunion."

Pale and solemn, Pollard stood with his arm around his frail, red-haired wife as Judge Robinson pronounced the sentence. When the judge sentenced him to life in prison, his wife collapsed to the floor, crying out "God!" and "No! No!"

Helped to her feet, she sank to the floor again as Robinson sentenced her to two concurrent five-year prison terms as an accessory.

When the judge denied her request that she remain free on bond until a prison could be located where her stomach problem could be treated, cries could be heard from her father in the rear of the courtroom. Robinson hurriedly recessed the hearing and ordered the courtroom cleared.

Marshals led the Pollards to a holding cell at the front of the courtroom. As the door closed behind them, Anne Pollard's piercing screams filled the court, and there was a thumping sound from within the cell.

Saying it is for the U.S. to decide what information to give to friend or foe, Joseph E. diGenova, then the U.S. Attorney in Washington, told the press, "It is likely he will never see the light of day again."

From jail, Pollard wrote to a friend to express regret that he had shown any remorse for his actions.

"Needless to say, our experience at the sentencing was cruel beyond comprehension," he wrote in a letter that wound up being published in the *Jerusalem Post* in May 1987. "Although I would have preferred to have gone down flying my 'true colors,' the attorneys stressed the fact that I had to show remorse if Anne were to stand any chance at all of receiving probation. Accordingly, I agreed to say things which burned my soul with shame, hoping that any such contrived regret the court's apparent need for a moral victory over my convictions would be satisfied. In hindsight, this recantation, which fooled no one, was reprehensible and debased the memory of those Jews who had found the courage to endure such torment, unsullied by submission to either their prosecutors or despair."

If finding Ronald Pelton had been an impressive feat, getting the NSA to agree to testify against him was even more impressive.

In 1980, Congress passed the Classified Information Procedures Act, which set up ways for prosecuting espionage cases without revealing classified information. Known as the "graymail" statute because defendants had used the threat of exposure to win dismissal of the charges against them, the law permits judges and lawyers for defendants to examine classified information relating to their cases outside of public view.

But the law was not good enough for the NSA, which for years had refused to acknowledge publicly that it even existed. Now the Justice Department wanted the agency to admit in court that it intercepts communications.

After months of negotiations, John G. Douglass and Robert N. McDonald, the assistant U.S. attorneys assigned to the case, and

Justice Department attorneys from the internal security section, got NSA to agree to supply several officials who would describe at Pelton's trial the damage that had been done.

William P. Crowell, the chief of the NSA group that intercepts and studies Soviet communications, testified at the trial that the undersea tap disclosed by Pelton to the Soviets "gave us an insight into [Soviet] military forces, the relative sizes, [and] their plans for maneuvers. . . ." David Bacon, Pelton's former boss at NSA, said the fifty-seven communications channels NSA was concentrating on intercepting had given NSA access to "the highest levels of the Soviet government down to the next-level echelon."

On June 5, 1986, a federal jury in Baltimore convicted Pelton of espionage. Despite the former NSA employee's confession to the FBI, Pelton claimed he was not guilty and had not been adequately apprised of his rights when he spoke with the FBI. In letters to his girlfriend, he boasted he would, be out of prison in two months. Chiding him for leaving her with only twenty dollars, she told him to stop writing to her and found another boyfriend.

During thirty-five sessions after his conviction, Pelton briefed NSA officials on what he had told the Soviets. At his sentencing, attended by his wife, he pleaded for a sentence that would give him "some glimmer of hope" of spending the final years of his life outside of prison.

Saying he had done "inestimable damage" to U.S. security, U.S. District Court Judge Herbert F. Murray upheld the legality of Pelton's confession and sentenced him to life in prison. While Murray took note of the fact that Pelton ultimately had cooperated, he decided the damage he had done was so great that only life in prison was an appropriate punishment.

Under a life sentence, a prisoner technically becomes eligible for parole consideration after ten years, but the average life sentence in the federal prison system runs about thirty years. Pelton could well be into his seventies by the end of his term.

Most legal experts thought his conviction would hold up on appeal. Unlike the FBI agents involved in the Koecher case, Faulkner and Hodgson had managed to avoid promising Pelton anything while leaving the impression that he would help himself by talking—a fine distinction that has been upheld by the courts. Recently the Fourth Circuit Court of Appeals upheld his conviction.

Yogi had told Ismaylov that he was about to be promoted, which was true. He also told him that because of his promotion, he would have to take a lie-detector test, which was not true. Grogan had wanted to see what Ismaylov would do if he thought Yogi would be polygraphed.

Sure enough, at the next drop on March 21, 1986, in Lorton, Virginia, Ismaylov left Yogi *How to Beat the Box,* a booklet on how to outsmart polygraph examinations. The GRU didn't want one of its star performers to be compromised by a polygraph. But the book got yawns at the FBI, relating tips that were already well publicized in the U.S.

Besides the booklet, Ismaylov left another $10,000 and cellophane instructions foreshadowing the end of the operation. The Soviet had noticed the decline in the quality of material Yogi was giving him.

"Dear Friend," the message began. "Please keep in mind . . . I'm interested only in up-to-date classified stuff concerning advanced and prospective weapons systems such as being developed under SDI program, cruise missiles, TAV [Trans-atmospheric vehicle], Stealth technology, etc. The highest payment for such info is guaranteed."

When Nicholas J. Walsh heard about Ismaylov's latest demand, he decided the sting had served its purpose. The assistant special agent in charge of counterintelligence in the field office, Walsh, forty-three, was another former CI-3 supervisor. Soft-spoken, with blue eyes and boyish good looks, he felt there was no point in continuing to devote manpower to an operation just so the FBI could boast that it was fooling another Russian.

From the way Ismaylov had specified the reports he wanted, the FBI and the Air Force had already learned a good deal about what the Russians knew. The relationship between Ismaylov and Yogi was settling into a routine, and the Air Force would soon have to give up more information than it was getting.

On May 14, 1986, the Soviets expelled U.S. Embassy attaché Erik Sites for alleged spy activity. It was the second such expulsion that year. The State Department decided it was time to retaliate.

After then FBI Director William H. Webster approved it, the Ismaylov case was offered for the purpose. Usually, such expulsions—well over a dozen a year—are not publicized. In this case, the FBI was surprised to find that the State Department had no objections to publicity. Eventually, President Reagan was informed of the plans to apprehend Ismaylov and to publicize it.

———

Fort Foote Road in Fort Washington, Maryland, is only a few minutes from the Woodrow Wilson Bridge into Washington, but it's as rural as a cow pasture. Ismaylov had chosen this site, at the base of Potomac Electric Power pole No. 198329-2242, as the place for Yogi's next—and last—drop of documents.

At noon on June 18, 1986, Grogan and Scott drove their four-wheel-drive Broncos into the woods near the pole. With eight other FBI and OSI agents dressed in camouflage, they pitched camp a hundred yards from the drop site. To make sure they didn't get lost, Grogan laid branches end to end from the camp to the drop site.

Meanwhile, a mile and a half away, two female agents from the CI-3 squad began monitoring a second site where Ismaylov was supposed to leave more money for Yogi. In a field four hundred yards across Fort Foote Road, O'Keefe and two other agents set up a command post in a mobile trailer. There, they could watch all the sites on TV monitors and keep in touch with other agents watching Ismaylov's movements in Washington.

So that Ismaylov didn't suspect anything, Grogan and Zupan had shown up at his apartment a week earlier, business as usual, and openly filmed him as he left for work.

Linking all the FBI agents hidden in the woods were FBI walkie-talkies as well as cellular phones. In case they didn't work, Grogan had strung a rope from the main drop site to the campsite. When the agents at the drop site pulled the string, it rattled some ball bearings inside a Campbell's Soup can at the campsite.

While they waited, the agents in the command post played gin rummy and Trivial Pursuit. The agents at the drop site placed bets on when Ismaylov would show up and debated the merits of the freeze-dried barbecue supplied by Andrews Air Force Base.

By Friday, many of the agents had been bitten by ticks or chiggers, and most of them had slept only a few hours in the eighty-five-degree heat. And, rather than being deserted, Fort Foote Road had suddenly turned into a subway platform. Bicyclists, tennis players, kids dribbling basketballs, and people enjoying the sunny weather meandered down the road. Grogan and the five other agents stationed four feet from the pole had to keep ducking down and lying flat in the thick bushes.

A jogger stopped at the bushes and pulled down his pants. He stooped down and defecated. Grogan and Zupan looked at each other in horror. He had missed them by three feet.

At 9:50 P.M. on Friday, June 19, Grogan noticed the light blinking on his cellular phone. It was one of the agents calling from the other drop site on Riverview Road.

"He just buried the package," she said.

O'Keefe and the other agents from the command post had already converged on the drop site. Other agents began fanning out along the road.

At 10:10 P.M., they saw headlights piercing the night. Then they heard the scraping of gravel as a car pulled onto the shoulder. The door of a Chrysler LeBaron slammed, and a man with a mustache hurried out. Crouching on his hands and knees, he began digging up the package buried behind the Potomac Electric Power pole.

"Halt, FBI! Halt, FBI!" O'Keefe shouted.

Zupan turned on his video camera and bathed the scene in light. More agents from the campsite came crashing through the woods. Up the road, FBI cars with flashing red lights sealed off the street in both directions.

Ismaylov hit O'Keefe on the chin and smashed his walkie-talkie. The terrified Soviet struggled to get back up the incline to his car. When he refused to lie spread-eagle on the hood of his car, O'Keefe handcuffed his hands behind his back.

Regaining his composure, Ismaylov protested, "I am diplomat. What are you doing?"

He said he was lost and was looking for a fishing hole.

"There is no fishing hole where you were digging," O'Keefe said.

In his pockets, they found a four-inch folding knife and twelve dollars in cash.

Grogan rode with Ismaylov to the field office, where he told him his diplomatic status would be verified. Most of the time, they said nothing to each other.

When they entered the glass doors of the FBI's reception room on the eleventh floor, Grogan reached over and pulled a tick from Ismaylov's neck.

Grogan let Ismaylov call his office, which dispatched two men from the embassy to pick him up. Meanwhile, in interview room 11411-B, Grogan and Ismaylov postured, Grogan telling Ismaylov he was shocked he would try to steal documents, while Ismaylov demanded to see his comrades.

An hour later, CI-3 agents leaving the office noticed two white men looking out of place in a 7-Eleven on South Capitol Street, a mostly black neighborhood. Dispatched to fetch Ismaylov, the Soviets had gotten lost trying to find Buzzard's Point. The FBI agents escorted them to the field office. Grogan turned Ismaylov over to the two Soviets.

Operation Jai-Aflai—a play on words chosen by Grogan for the fast-paced Latin game of Jai-Alai and a poem called "High Flight" by a U.S. military pilot—had come to an end.

The next evening, Grogan called Yogi at home.

Affecting his best Russian accent, he said, "I guess you know who this is. It's your friend Vladimir. I just want to thank you for everything you did to me."

Yogi's wife—who had by now been apprised that her husband was engaged in a secret project—reported that Yogi turned white.

On June 21, 1986, Dana E. Caro, the gruff-talking head of the field office, announced that Ismaylov had been apprehended. He displayed some of the items Ismaylov had given Yogi. In his last message to Yogi, the Russian had expressed disappointment that not all of the documents from the last drop were "Grade A."

Meanwhile, the FBI credited Ismaylov's latest $8,000 payment to the general fund of the U.S. Treasury. Altogether, the Soviets had kicked in $41,100 to help defray the costs of apprehending Ismaylov.

Declared *persona non grata* by the State Department, Ismaylov boarded an Aeroflot flight for Moscow with his family on Tuesday, June 24, 1986. Because of his accomplishments, he had been promoted to air attaché just weeks earlier.

So far, the State Department has refused to allow the Soviets to replace him. Nor can Ismaylov ever return to the U.S.

On July 2, the fifty FBI and OSI agents who had worked on the case met at the Officers Club in the Washington Navy Yard for drinks and hors d'oeuvres. Choking up, Yogi spoke about the bravery of the agents. Then his wife read a poem she had written:

There are some American heroes who caught
a Russian spy.
Their patriotic effort gave them a natural high . . .

Trading secrets for money on nights that
were more than cool
Must have convinced comrade Vladimir that
he had an American fool!

When the "commie" fell for the sting, it
was even better than pay.
And to cuff the Russian diplomat made the
agent's day!

So let's raise a glass of vodka and have
a memorable toast
To the unsung American heroes who should
be praised the most!

Afterword

Today's FBI is quite different from the one J. Edgar Hoover headed. The symbols of the Hoover era—the fedora, the white shirts, and the stiff manner—are gone. So are the files that Hoover kept on the personal lives of members of Congress—political blackmail to preserve his power. Illegal wiretaps and break-ins are a thing of the past, replaced by official reminders that the FBI's sole purpose is to investigate violations of law.

Nowhere are the changes more evident than in the FBI's training program at Quantico, Virginia. There are new courses in organized crime, white-collar crime, and computer crime. In the gym, male and female agents frisk and flip each other. To acquaint agents with what they can expect to encounter in court, there are mock trials where defense attorneys eviscerate new recruits. There is a new emphasis as well on the mental attitude and physical well-being of agents. To maintain their weight and composure, they are taught to eat a good breakfast and to avoid sugar and white flour, which can wreak havoc with blood-sugar levels. They are told they are not Batman or Batwoman and cannot solve all the world's problems.

"When you mow the lawn, you're still the FBI," a teacher told one class. "If someone cuts in front of you in traffic, you should not yell at the offender. You're federal officers. You have no right to react that way," he said.

"Our concern is not physical strength only," said FBI Assistant Director James D. McKenzie, until recently in charge of the academy. "The first way to solve a problem is with your brain. The defensive tactics [boxing, wrestling, and judo] are next. The last resort is deadly force."

As the emphasis has changed, so has the FBI's effectiveness. The FBI under Hoover was bogged down investigating car thefts. Hoover wanted to impress Congress with the number of cases solved. Now the FBI undertakes massive investigations that take years to complete and have put members of Congress, judges, top Mafia leaders, and heads of major corporations in jail.

Yet the greatest change has not been in the criminal side of the FBI but in the counterintelligence area. For all his genius at building a great law enforcement organization, Hoover confused espionage with lawful political dissent. His career began in the radical division of the Justice Department, which became the general intelligence division of the FBI in 1920. Established in 1908, the FBI was then a small unit of the Justice Department, rife with corruption and political patronage.

As chief of the new intelligence division, Hoover set about compiling information on 60,000 "radically inclined" individuals. Like investigating car thefts, this exercise produced impressive statistics but no spies. By casting such a wide net, the bureau wasted its resources by vacuuming up gossip. Meanwhile, the bad guys got away.

Attorney General Harlan Stone put a stop to the practice in 1924, telling Hoover the bureau should confine its investigations to violations of law.

"The bureau," he told him, "is not concerned with political or other opinions of individuals. It is concerned only with their conduct and then only with such conduct as is forbidden by the laws of the United States."

But Hoover, besides being incorruptible and a good administrator, was a master at using his position to enhance his own power. If he could enshrine himself as the nation's conscience, no President could replace him. By 1936, he had convinced President Roosevelt that there was a need to resume the investigations of "subversives." Using tenuous legal justification, Roosevelt ordered a resumption of the investigations. Soon, Hoover was sharing with Roosevelt juicy bits of gossip that the President could use against his political opponents.

Hoover continued the investigations until he died in office in 1972, even expanding them into what was known as the Cointelpro program. Under it, the FBI resorted to the most unprofessional, foolish, and useless tactics in its history—sending poison pen letters to people like Martin Luther King. In doing so, the bureau became no better than the KGB, the organization whose tactics it was fighting. So engrossed did the bureau become in trying to control political dissent that it lost sight of its real purpose in the counterintelligence arena—catching spies.

The Soviets were not about to send their agents to the U.S. to become members of radical groups, where they would be easily spotted. As far back as 1957, Reino Hayhanen, the assistant to Soviet spy Rudolph Abel, told the FBI that Moscow had ordered Soviet agents to have as little to do as possible with the Communist Party.

"[Hayhenen] stated that in Moscow he was told that an agent would be better if he is not a CP [Communist Party] member, and that if an agent is a CP member he should be told to make some move which would cause him to have his membership in the CP terminated," a June 1957 FBI report says.

According to John L. Martin, chief of the Justice Department's internal security section, "During the height of the investigation of domestic groups, they caught a couple of spies, who were merely expelled with no trial. They were not particularly successful at turning them and had no significant trades."

When the FBI's abuses came to light during the Church Committee hearings and the Watergate investigations of the early 1970s, the bureau rethought its approach. Under guidelines developed by Attorney General Edward Levi, the FBI no longer is permitted to investigate groups because of their political leanings. Under the classified guidelines governing counterintelligence, the FBI may begin an investigation of an American only if he may be engaged in hostile foreign intelligence activities or may be a source of information or assistance in an ongoing counterintelligence investigation.

The fact that the Justice Department has brought cases against forty-nine spies caught by the FBI since 1975 is impressive evidence that the bureau has learned to keep its eye on target. Nevertheless, the FBI's equilibrium is fragile, threatened by pressures within and without.

Nowhere is this better illustrated than in the views expressed by retired intelligence officials and other experts in a book published by the National Strategy Information Center Inc., a Washington think tank. In a preface to the book, *Intelligence Requirements for the 1980s: Counterintelligence,* Frank R. Barnett, president of the center, defined the issues addressed in the book as that of "intrusive investigative techniques versus privacy, of CI [counterintelligence] versus civil liberties."

"Effective CI necessitates sometimes and under rigorous self-imposed professional discipline engaging in activities that from a purist, civil libertarian perspective are simply not 'nice,' " he stated.

Elsewhere in the book, another writer said, "Today, the Soviets are prepared to use the 'new left,' the drug culture, the radical chic activitists. . . . The FBI is hamstrung by the fact that collaborating with a hostile intelligence service may not be a crime in this country. It isn't even a crime to reveal classified information, if the person revealing it does not have authorized access in the first place."

The author is quite right that if a person "collaborates" with the KGB by taking notes on TV shows, he has committed no crime. But the idea that giving classified information to the enemy is not a crime if the individual is not authorized to have it in the first place will be news to Randy Miles Jeffries, who sits in prison for doing just that.

Implicit in these views is the idea that somehow enforcing the law cannot be done lawfully—that investigations involving the national security are too important to be done according to the book and the Constitution. This same ends-justify-the-means mentality led to the scandal known as Irangate. And just as surely as Irangate failed to release U.S. hostages, the sloppy thinking that confuses traitors with dissidents will fail to catch spies.

Fortunately, efforts by some members of Congress to impose these views on the FBI have met with little success. However, the FBI reflects the political climate. In less tranquil times, under a different director, and aided by the secrecy that shrouds the subject of counterintelligence, such views could well be adopted. To do so would not only impinge on our civil liberties but impair our security as well.

Again and again when one examines the recent spy cases, one finds not left-wing groups or Communists but greedy military and intelligence officers abetted by lax security practices at intelligence agencies. Instead of pointing fingers at political dissidents, the Naval Investigative Service should be asked why it permitted Jonathan Pollard to have access to classified material anywhere in the world, when his duties entailed activities in North America alone. The CIA should be asked why thirteen copies of the spy satellite manual codenamed KH-11 could not be found during the prosecution of William Kampiles. The Navy should be asked why it never reinvestigated John Walker during the twenty years he held a "top secret" security clearance. The FBI should be asked why it hired an incompetent like Richard Miller as a counterintelligence agent and gave him access to classified information. The CIA should be asked why it misread the results of a polygraph exam of Karl Koecher. Why it permitted TRW Inc. to maintain such lax security that Christopher Boyce partied in the vault where codes to the Rhyolite spy satellite were kept. And why it hired Edward Howard when he had a history of drug use, then trained him for Moscow and fired him without permitting him to find another job first. Finally, the CIA should be asked why it did not tell the FBI about Howard until a year after CIA employees knew he had considered getting in touch with the Soviets.

Determined spies will find a way to obtain classified information with or without good security. But giving "top secret" documents to a $4.50-an-hour messenger like Randy Jeffries is like leaving a bank unlocked overnight.

Removed from jail temporarily to testify at a Senate hearing in 1985, Boyce said the government's background investigation of him never uncovered the fact that he used drugs. His sister had to take a lie-detector test when she took a job with a convenience store, yet he did not.

"I suppose most people view security regulations as something that should be held in awe by employees," Boyce said. "That was clearly not the case at TRW. A number of employees made phony security badges as pranks. My immediate supervisor once made a security badge with a chimpanzee's face on it, and to everyone's amusement, used it to come in and out of the building. . . . Aside from badges, there was almost no supervision over access to the building and the vault. Although my comings and goings at building M4 were logged by the security guards, there was nothing to stop me from entering the building during the day or night. On occasion, I returned to the [code] vault late at night without being questioned or even arousing suspicion," he testified.

It was during these late-night visits that Boyce said he photographed or removed documents classified SCI, the government's highest security classification, compromising the Rhyolite satellite surveillance system to the Soviets.

If the government's security is lax, so are its standards for classifying material in the first place. During a hearing on government security, Senator Sam Nunn said he was at a military briefing where each chart was classified.

"There was one chart [that] had up there these words: 'We must not fail.' And it was classified as secret. Of course, we asked the question why," Nunn said. "Nobody could give an answer, but the answer is, when you are classifying a whole lot of things, you tend to classify everything."

In writing his book, *Secrecy and Democracy,* former CIA director Stansfield Turner said the CIA made more than one hundred deletions. Presumably, as CIA director when the events he was writing about took place, he should have been in the best position to know if those items should remain classified.

"These [deletions] ranged from borderline issues to the ridiculous," he wrote.

To this day, the FBI refuses to admit that it wiretaps the Soviet Embassy—even though transcripts of the recordings have appeared in court cases, and the Soviets are well aware that their conversations are monitored. Openly admitting to wiretapping the Soviets could lead to charges the U.S. is violating rights protected by international treaties.

On the other hand, protecting secrets known to the other side can be just as harmful as too little security, because it breeds cynicism about the classification system. When everything is classified, nothing is classified. That, combined with the fact that too many people have security clearances—incredibly, 2 percent of the American population—means background checks cannot be done properly, reinvestigations are never done, and the real secrets are not safeguarded.

"Quite simply, the classification process is out of control," according to the *Preliminary Staff Study on the Protection of National Secrets,* prepared for the House Judiciary Committee's subcommittee on civil and constitutional rights. Because of a revision by President Reagan in the executive order on classification, even more documents are being classified than ever before, the report noted.

"Much material is classified to protect diplomatic relationships, hide bargaining positions, or prevent premature disclosure," according to the subcommittee's report. "All too often, documents are classified to protect politically embarrassing information or to hide government misconduct," the report said.

"There are too many classified documents and too many people—some four million—with access to classified information," former FBI director Webster has said.

The subcommittee recommended classifying only codes, operational plans, high-technology products, and sources and methods for gathering intelligence. Nine-tenths of the information now classified would not fall within this definition. The remaining sensitive information would be "administratively controlled."

Presumably, no criminal sanctions would apply when this kind of information is disclosed. As it now stands, government officials leak classified information to the press every day. In his book, former CIA director Turner noted that the "White House staff tends to leak when doing so may help the President politically. The Pentagon leaks primarily to sell its programs to the Congress and the public. The State Department leaks when it's being forced to follow a policy move that its people dislike. The CIA leaks when some of its people want to influence policy but know that's a role they're not allowed to play openly. The Congress is most likely to leak when the issue has political ramifications domestically."

As CIA director, William J. Casey regularly leaked to the press, according to government sources. He then demanded that the Justice Department prosecute members of the press who got leaks from other government officials. Retaining criminal sanctions for behavior that is accepted only breeds more contempt for the law.

Because it lacked a royal license, the first American newspaper, Boston's *Publick Occurrences Both Foreign and Domestick,* was suppressed in 1690 after one issue. The last thing the Founding Fathers wanted to do was create an official secrets act that would censor the press. In drafting the espionage statutes, Congress used language so broad that it could be interpreted to prohibit even the publication of Defense Department listings in the phone book. But other parts of the law and its legislative history make it clear that Congress never envisioned prosecutions over material that appears in the press.

Nevertheless, the Justice Department has seemingly confused the issue by prosecuting Samuel L. Morison. A two-headed monster, Morison was a government official who was also a member of the press. As an analyst with the Naval Intelligence Support Center, he had access to "top secret" photos taken by the KH-11 satellite. Yet in an incredible blunder, the Navy also permitted him to serve as an editor of *Jane's Fighting Ships,* an annual review of the world's ships.

In his latter role, he gave three photos taken by the spy satellite to *Jane's Defense Weekly,* a sister publication. The photos showed a Soviet carrier under construction. Similar photos had already appeared in *Aviation Week* and other publications. Because of this fact and because Kampiles had already given the Soviets the manual to the satellite, Roland Inlow, a CIA official involved in the development of the satellite, has said the damage to the government was "zero." Nor did Morison receive any special compensation for providing the photos. *Jane's* paid him for all his contributions.

Nevertheless, tipped off by Naval investigative agents, the FBI arrested Morison in October 1984, and he was convicted of espionage. Joined by media organizations such as *The Washington Post,*

The New York Times, the *Chicago Tribune,* and CBS Inc., Morison is appealing the case. But meanwhile it could set a dangerous precedent. Certainly, Morison should have been fired. Whether his actions are viewed as selling secrets for money, or simply abusing his trust, he did wrong. But he did not give the photos to a foreign power. While Morison's was not a leak case, it was also not an espionage case. By choosing to prosecute someone who doesn't quite fit into either category, the Justice Department took a chance that leakers could, in the future, be prosecuted—a possibility that appears more ominous in light of the Reagan administration's attempts to cover up its actions during Irangate.

A questionable focus if carried into the FBI's work can be even more disastrous. Few fields of endeavor are as difficult and important as catching spies. Within the FBI, there are constant tensions between those who want to make a quick arrest and let a jury decide the case—as happened in the "Cruise Missile Case" of 1977—and those who put in the extra effort to make the charges stick.

"Probably nothing is harder than being a counterintelligence officer in the U.S.," James E. Nolan Jr., the former deputy assistant FBI director for counterintelligence, told me. "It's an open society. You have to obey the laws. You deal with the right to privacy. You have to err on the side of protection of rights. After all, that's what it's all for. And that's very hard. It makes a lot of things very frustrating. There are always tensions."

Other pressures come from those who become caught up in the mystique of the spy business; they see it as a glorious game. A month before he died in 1987, I met with James J. Angleton, who formerly headed the CIA's counterintelligence program. Angleton had spent his career looking for KGB moles in the CIA. Now, for the first time, there was evidence of one—Karl F. Koecher. Angleton had heard that Koecher had done tremendous damage. Yet he showed no interest in him. Sitting on his living room sofa, he rambled on lucidly about other moles, real or imaginary. Clearly, what captured his interest was the chase, not whether a spy was ever caught. In fact, for all his brilliance and good intentions, Angleton never did catch a spy.

The same almost amateurish approach led Peter Wright, former assistant director of the British MI5, to suspect that the head of his organization was a mole. As described in his book, *Spycatcher,* Wright suspected there were leaks to the KGB and decided by the process of elimination that the so-called Fifth Man Soviet spy was none other than Sir Roger Hollis, the longtime head of MI5. In the real world of law enforcement, cases are made through hard investigative work, not by the process of elimination. Wright never proved his case but generated enough paranoia within his agency to temporarily cripple it.

The fact that the CIA often prefers to turn spies into double agents instead of arresting them is but another manifestation of this naïve attitude. It is highly unlikely that most spies would genuinely change their allegiance. As Koecher told me, he would have taken off for Czechoslovakia if the FBI had allowed him to become a double agent. By failing to make an arrest, the FBI loses sight of its goal—to stop spying. As in an organized-crime investigation, the FBI's purpose should be to arrest or expel, not to play games. Under this umbrella, the FBI is still free to develop informants, recruit the other side, and run reliable double agents. Some FBI supervisors see this goal clearly.

"Our investigations are directed at violations of law. The driving force is to bring investigations to the courts," according to Donald Stukey, chief of the FBI's Soviet section.

But others allow counterintelligence investigations to take on a life of their own, much as police departments in the 1960s ran intelligence divisions that picked up gossip without producing any evidence of criminality.

According to Nolan, "The ideal FBI supervisor would do both—he would be somebody who would say there's no further we can go with this case, what can we get out of it? 'He isn't recruitable so let's get him out of here.' There are others who would probably watch the spies until they die of old age. Is he someone who couldn't recruit his mother, in which case put him on the back burner. Or is he an active agent recruiter and good at it? Then you ought to find some way to curtail his tour. If you don't have a prayer of discovering who his agents are, you better throw somebody at him [a double agent] and get rid of him. Whoever replaces him may be less skilled. What you want in a supervisor is someone who can blend those approaches."

To minimize some of these pressures and make counterintelligence more efficient, some have proposed combining the counterintelligence functions within the government. Although the FBI has primary jurisdiction for counterintelligence, the CIA and the military both try to weed out spies in their midst. The other agencies are supposed to coordinate their activities with the FBI but often don't.

Despite the problems, the solution is not to create a single monolithic agency divorced from the FBI. The FBI's law-enforcement orientation is a healthy one. The business of catching spies is too important to be carried out without constant scrutiny by the Justice Department and the courts. Retaining several agencies helps to keep them accountable.

Despite the Church Committee hearings and the subsequent Rockefeller Commission report criticizing the CIA for becoming involved in domestic operations, the CIA to this day violates its charter by running double agents in the U.S., according to present and former FBI officials.

"They [the CIA] get involved in double-agent operations," says a former FBI official. "I've spent an awful lot of time fighting with them. They always say they're sorry and it won't happen again. Then it happens again. It's always a battle."

A current FBI official said these incidents are rarely reported to the FBI director. The CIA had no comment.

Theoretically, the FBI could arrest CIA employees engaged in such operations. It never does. But the existence of two agencies watching each other introduces a form of accountability that would be missing if only one agency had counterintelligence authority.

"Ideally, you might have centralized counterintelligence, but I don't think the American people will buy it," Robert B. Wade, assistant chief of the FBI's Soviet section, told me. "The checks and balances we have now are very frustrating from an efficiency standpoint sometimes, but that is the secret of what makes a democracy a democracy." Indeed, he said, "One of our strengths is secrets aren't kept. That's one of the bennies of being a democracy."

In this area, as in others, the existing laws and regulations are sound. The problems arise when the rules are not followed, either because of jurisdictional rivalries or the hysteria that national security investigations can provoke. It is easier to question loyalty than to do the difficult investigative work necessary to bring a conviction.

Yet all the investigations and security would be unnecessary if the Soviets were unable to recruit Americans to spy for them. Toward that end, the FBI runs a program known as DECA—Development of Counterintelligence Awareness Program—which briefs employees of defense contractors on how the Soviets try to develop American agents.

The same approach should be used to educate the public as a whole through advertising, just as ads are effectively used to help combat drug use and the spread of AIDS.

In his Senate testimony, Boyce said the government had failed to impress upon him the personal consequences of spying. He suggested that strict security is "next to worthless if each of the four million Americans with security clearance do not have a grasp of how espionage could affect them personally."

Counterintelligence is too important to remain a secret. In one experiment in Detroit, the FBI found that bank robberies plummeted when banks publicized their use of video cameras. Would-be spies should know that they will be photographed and their conversations monitored if they contact a Soviet establishment or meet with a Soviet intelligence officer.

While it makes mistakes, the FBI overall has gotten very good at what it does. People need to know that. Because it has gotten so good, it has also become more powerful than before—even more reason to keep it in check. Protecting our freedoms and snaring spies go hand in hand.

Author's Notes

Many people gave of their time and knowledge in interviews, or helped in other ways to make this book possible. My thanks go to each of them:

The late James J. Angleton, Joseph J. Aronica, Fred Asselin, Thomas J. Baker, William M. Baker, Ann Barry, Jerry J. Berman, Leakh Bhoge, Barry A. Bohrer, Lane M. Bonner, Donald F. Burton, Leo D. Carl, Dana E. Caro, A. Brent Carruth, Thomas Patrick Cavanagh, Daniel M. Clements, William J. Colligan, Dr. William R. Corson, Sharon Credit, Robert T. Crowley, G. Allen Dale, Richard J. D'Aleo, Nicholas Daniloff, Joseph E. diGenova, Lisa D. Dillman, Robert Dunn, John T. Elliff, David A. Faulkner, Robert G. Fierer, Nick Gage, James H. Geer, Steven Gittelson, Culver Gleysteen, Dr. Loren Graham, Bruce A. Green, Theodore Grish, Michael D. Grogan, H. Russell Hanna Jr., Naomi Jeffries, Randy Miles Jeffries, and Joseph C. Johnson.

Also Brian Kelly, James R. Kirkpatrick, Dr. George Kline, Karl and Hana Koecher, Dr. George Kukla, Martin Lobel, John L. Martin, Rudy Maxa, Robert N. McDonald, Lawrence McWilliams, Kathy L. Morse, James E. Nolan Jr., Frank O'Keefe, William P. O'Keefe, Sam Papich, Phillip A. Parker, Robert A. Peter, David D. Queen, J. Stephen Ramey, Benjamin T. Rome, Dean Rusk, John K. Russell, Joseph Savion, Michael D. Scott, Michael Schatzow, Richard W. Shear, Joan Shoemaker, Carl Shoffler, Richard Craig Smith, William Smits, Stephen S. Spivack, Phil Stanford, John L. Stine, Donald Stukey, Malcolm Toon, William E. Trible, Robert B. Wade, Nicholas J. Walsh, W. Raymond Wannall Jr., John C. Warnecke, John C. Warnecke Jr., Dr. Armand B. Weiss, Peter F. Weslow, Steven A. Westby, Judge Richard L. Williams, George D. Wiltshire III, Norman A. Zigrossi, and Al Zupan.

Chapter 1

Interviews with O'Keefe, Frank O'Keefe, Johnson, Walsh, Caro, Grogan, Zupan, Ramey, Parker, Wade, Koecher, Martin, Geer, Kirkpatrick, Elliff, Daniloff, McWilliams, Johnson, and confidential sources.

Also, *Meeting the Espionage Challenge: A Review of U.S. Counterintelligence and Security Programs,* U.S. Senate Select Committee on Intelligence; *Taking Care of the Law,* by Griffin B. Bell with Ronald J. Ostrow; *KGB Today* by John Barron; and articles in *The Washington Post.*

Chapter 2

Interviews with Weiss and confidential sources.

Chapter 3

Interviews with Nolan, Karl and Hana Koecher, Angleton, Graham, Kline, Wiltshire, Weslow, Colligan, Savion, and confidential sources.

Also, documents filed in *U.S.* v. *Koecher* in U.S. District Court in New York and in *Robert J. Eyman* v. *Country Squire Realty Inc.* in Fairfax County Circuit Court, Virginia; correspondence, diaries, and job applications of Karl and Hana Koecher; FBI reports on Koecher's attempt to become a double agent; and articles from *The New York Times, The Washington Post,* the *New York Daily News, Washingtonian,* and the *New York Post.*

Chapter 4

Interviews with Stine, O'Keefe, Ramey, Parker, Walsh, Grish, and confidential sources.

Also, instructions from Pavlov to Stine and articles in *The Washington Post* and *Life* magazine.

Chapter 5

Interviews with Weiss and confidential sources.

Chapter 6

Interviews with Smith, Aronica, Carruth, Smits, Williams, Shoemaker, and confidential sources.

Also, documents filed in *U.S.* v. *Smith* in U.S. District Court in Alexandria and articles in *The Washington Post, Regardie's,* and *U.S. News & World Report.*

Chapter 7

Interviews with Cavanagh, Grogan, Zupan, Geer, Shear, Toon, Rusk, Nolan, Warnecke, Credit, Dunn, Hanna, and confidential sources.

Also, documents filed in *U.S.* v. *Cavanagh* in U.S. District Court in Los Angeles, articles in the *Los Angeles Times* and *Defense Security Institute Security Awareness Bulletin,* and documents relating to Shear's efforts to sell Tregaron to the Soviets.

Chapter 8

Interviews with Parker, Smits, Martin, and confidential sources.

Also, documents filed in *U.S.* v. *Whitworth* in U.S. District Court in San Francisco; opinion by the U.S. Court of Appeals for the Fifth Circuit in *U.S.* v. *Wieschenberg; Breaking the Ring,* by John Barron; *Family Treason: The Walker Spy Case,* by Jack Kneece; and articles in *The Washington Post* and *Defense Security Institute Security Awareness Bulletin.*

Chapter 9

Interviews with Karl and Hana Koecher, Cavanagh, Kukla, Kline, Fierer, Dillman, Stukey, Johnson, Westby, and confidential sources.

Also, documents filed in *U.S. v. Koecher* in U.S. District Court in New York; diaries of Karl and Hana Koecher; and articles in *The Washington Post* and *The New York Times*.

Chapter 10

Interviews with Cavanagh, Parker, Smits, and confidential sources.

Also, documents filed in *U.S. v. Cavanagh* in U.S. District Court in Los Angeles and in *U.S. v. Whitworth* in U.S. District Court in San Francisco; *Breaking the Ring,* by John Barron; *Family Treason: The Walker Spy Case,* by Jack Kneece; and articles in *The Washington Post, Los Angeles Times,* and *Defense Security Institute Security Awareness Bulletin.*

Chapter 11

Interviews with Richard and Ann D'Aleo, Bhoge, Grogan, Scott, O'Keefe, Parker, Zupan, and confidential sources.

Also, articles in *New York* magazine and *The New York Times Magazine.*

Chapter 12

Interviews with Faulkner, Parker, Nolan, and confidential sources.
Also, documents filed in *U.S. v. Pelton* in U.S. District Court in Baltimore.

Chapter 13

Interviews with Fierer, Dillman, Westby, Green, Nolan, Karl and Hana Koecher, Martin, and confidential sources.

Also, documents filed in *U.S. v. Pollard* in U.S. District Court in Washington and *U.S. v. Koecher* in U.S. District Court in New York.

Chapter 14

Interviews with Aronica and confidential sources.
Documents filed in *U.S. v. Chin* in U.S. District Court in Alexandria, Virginia.

Chapter 15

Interviews with Barry, Dupue, Faulkner, and confidential sources.

Also, documents filed in *U.S. v. Pelton* in U.S. District Court in Baltimore; opinion by the U.S. Military Court of Appeals in *Cooke* v. *Orser;* and articles in *The Washington Post.*

Chapter 16

Interviews with Randy and Naomi Jefferies, Dale, and confidential sources.

Also, documents filed in *U.S. v. Jeffries* in U.S. District Court in Washington and in the court-martial of Robert E. Cordrey Jr. by the U.S. Marine Corps.

Chapter 17

Interviews with Grogan, Zupan, Ramey, O'Keefe, Scott, Fierer, Green, Walsh, Karl and Hana Koecher, Nolan, and confidential sources.

Also, FBI documents from the Ismaylov case.

Chapter 18

Interviews with Karl and Hana Koecher and with Nolan.

Also, documents filed in *U.S.* v. *Koecher; Strangers on a Bridge,* by James B. Donovan; and articles from *The Washington Post, The New York Times,* and *Time* magazine.

Chapter 19

Interviews with Caro, Walsh, O'Keefe, Ramey, Scott, Faulkner, Grogan, Zupan, diGenova, and confidential sources.

Also, documents filed in *U.S.* v. *Pollard* in U.S. District Court in Washington and *U.S.* v. *Pelton* in U.S. District Court in Baltimore.

Afterword

Interviews with Nolan, Faulkner, Parker, Ramey, Martin, Elliff, Geer, Stukey, McWilliams, Wade, Schatzow, Berman, and confidential sources.

Documents filed in *U.S.* v. *Morison* in U.S. District Court in Baltimore; *Intelligence Requirements in the 1980s: Counterintelligence,* edited by Roy Godson; *Meeting the Espionage Challenge: A Review of U.S. Counterintelligence and Security Programs,* U.S. Senate Select Committee on Intelligence; *The Preliminary Joint Staff Study on the Protection of National Secrets,* House Judiciary Committee's Subcommittee on Civil, and Constitutional Rights; and *U.S. Counterintelligence and Security Concerns—1986,* U.S. House of Representatives' Select Committee on Intelligence.

Also, *The Reform of FBI Intelligence Operations,* by John T. Elliff; *Secrecy and Power: The Life of J. Edgar Hoover,* by Richard Gid Powers; *Federal Government Security Clearance Programs,* hearings and report of the U.S. Senate's Governmental Affairs Committee's Permanent Subcommittee on Investigations; and *Keeping the Nation's Secrets: a Report to the Secretary of Defense by the Commission to Review DOD Security Policies and Practices.*

Glossary: FBI Foreign Counterintelligence Terms

Accommodation Address   an address used to receive mail or other communications held for pickup, forwarded to, or relayed to a member of an intelligence service. Sometimes called a mail drop or live-letter box (LLB).

Agent   an individual other than an officer, employee, or co-opted worker of an intelligence service to whom specific intelligence assignments are given by an intelligence service. An agent in a target country can be operated by a legal or illegal residency or directly by the center. An agent can be of any nationality.

An agent who is operated by an illegal residency or directly by the center is termed an *illegal agent*.

An agent who, under the direction of an intelligence officer, is responsible for the operational activities of other agents is termed a *principal agent*.

An agent whose dual role has been discovered by the service on which he is reporting and who is used, wittingly or unwittingly, voluntarily or under duress, to serve the purpose of the latter service against the former service is termed a *redoubled agent*.

An agent who serves three services in an agent capacity but who, like a double agent, wittingly or unwittingly withholds significant information from two services at the instigation of the third service is termed a *triple agent*.

An agent of some stature who utilizes his position to influence public opinion or decision making to produce results beneficial to the country whose intelligence service operates him is termed an *agent of influence*.

An agent who furnishes information without knowing the ultimate recipient is an intelligence service or is unaware of the true identity of the government receiving it is termed an *unwitting agent*.

An individual under development or being considered for development as an agent by an intelligence service is termed a *potential agent*.

Agent net   an intelligence-gathering unit of agents supervised by a principal agent who is operating under the direction of an intelligence officer. An agent net can operate in either the legal or illegal field.

Agent of influence   see *Agent*.

Alias   an assumed name, usually consisting of a first and last name, used by an individual for a specific and often temporary purpose.

Alternate meet   a prearranged meeting that takes place in the event a regularly scheduled meet is missed for any reason.

Asset   any human or technical resource available to an intelligence or security service for operational purposes.

Backstop   an arrangement made to support a cover story.

Bogie   a visitor to an official establishment whose identity is not known. See *Stray*.

Bona fides   documents, information, action, or codes offered by an individual to establish his good faith, identity, dependability, honesty, and motivation.

Briefing   preparation of an individual for a specific operation by describing the situation to be encountered, the methods to be employed, and the objective; presentation, usually orally, of information.

Brush contact   a discreet, usually prearranged momentary contact between intelligence personnel when information or documents are passed. Also known as a brief encounter.

Build-up material   see *Feed material*.

Cache   see *Dead drop*.

Carbons   paper that produces secret writing through the use of chemicals.

Case officer   intelligence officer with closest responsibility for the direction of an operation or subordinate intelligence personnel either at headquarters (headquarters case officer) or in the field (field case officer).

Center   intelligence service headquarters.

Cipher   a method of concealing the meaning of a message either by replacing its letters or numbers with other letters or numbers in a predetermined manner (a substitute cipher) or by changing the order of the letters or numbers according to certain rules (a transposition cipher). See *Cryptosystem*.

Cipher pad   a small, thin pad of paper sheets printed by machine with a nonrepetitive key for use in sending code. Also known as a one-time pad.

Code word   a prearranged word used in communications or conversation to disguise the identity of an individual or object or to convey a meaning other than the conventional meaning.

COMINT   see *Communications intelligence*.

Communications intelligence (COMINT)   technical and intelligence information obtained from foreign communications.

Communications security (COMSEC)   provision of codes and ciphers to any department of the government or military forces requiring them.

Compartmentation   management of an intelligence service so that information about the personnel, organization, or activities of one component is made available to any other component only to the extent required for the performance of assigned duties.

COMSEC   see *Communications security*.

Concealment devices   innocuous objects designed or adapted as containers for secreting any selected material or equipment. Also called containers.

Containers   see *Concealment devices*.

CONUS   continental United States.

Co-opted worker   a national of a country who assists foreign intelligence services. While in most circumstances, a co-opted worker is an official of the country, he can also be a tourist or student. Sometimes referred to as co-opted agent or co-optee.

Co-optee   see *Co-opted worker*.

Counterintelligence actions undertaken to counter the intelligence, espionage, and sabotage operations of foreign governments.

Cover guise used by an individual, organization, or installation to prevent discovery of intelligence activities.

Cover story plausible account of background, residences, employment, activities, and access furnished to an individual who is operating in our behalf in order to substantiate whatever claims are necessary to successfully carry out an operation. The difference between a cover story and a legend is that a legend is furnished to an illegal or agent by a foreign intelligence service. See *Legend.*

Covert activities activities conducted in a concealed manner that make it difficult or seemingly impossible to trace the activities back to the intelligence service or government that sponsors the intelligence service.

Cryptoanalysis conversion of encrypted messages to plain text without having knowledge of the key used.

Cryptology the science of secret communications.

Cryptonym code word or symbol used to conceal operations, organizations, projects, and individuals. See *Pseudonym.*

Cryptosystem the associated items of cryptomaterial and the methods and rules by which these items are used as a unit to provide a single means of encryption and decryption. It embraces the general cryptosystem and the specific keys essential to the employment of the general cryptosystem. See *Cipher.*

Cultivation apparently casual but actually deliberate and calculated effort to gain control of an individual, induce him to furnish information, and agree to recruitment. Cultivation can extend over a considerable period of time.

Cutout an individual whose services are used to avoid direct contact between members of an intelligence service.

Dead drop a location where communications, documents, or equipment can be left by an individual and picked up by a second individual without any meeting. Also called dead-letter box (DLB) or simply drop. Sometimes called a hiding place. A long-term drop is sometimes called a black cache.

Dead-letter drop (DLB) see *Dead drop.*

Debriefing a nonhostile interview of an individual who has completed an intelligence assignment or who has knowledge of operational or intelligence significance.

Deception material information passed in any form to an intelligence service or government to mislead. See *Disinformation.*

Defection abandonment of loyalty, allegiance, duty, or principal to one's country.

Defector a national of a country who has escaped from the control of such country or who, being outside such jurisdiction and control, is unwilling to return to that country and is of special value to another government because he is able to add valuable new or confirmatory information to existing knowledge of his country. In intelligence operations a defector is, in most instances, an official of his country.

Disinformation carefully orchestrated misinformation prepared by an intelligence service for the purpose of misleading, deluding, disrupting, or undermining confidence in individuals, organizations, or governments. See *Deception material.*

Documentation documents, personal effects, equipment, or anything that will lend authenticity supplied to intelligence personnel to support a cover story or legend. See *Cover story* and *Legend.*

Double agent an agent who is cooperating with a foreign intelligence service on behalf of and under the control of an intelligence service and/or security service of another country.

Drop See *Dead drop.*

Dry cleaning any technique used to detect surveillance; a usual precaution engaged in by intelligence personnel when actively engaged in an operation.

Dry run rehearsal of an operation, or an operation which produces no results.

EEI see *Essential elements of information.*

Electronic intelligence (ELINT) information derived by intercepting and studying electromagnetic radiation from noncommunications sources, such as radar.

ELINT see *Electronic intelligence.*

Employee an individual, other than an officer, employed by an intelligence service. He may be serving in the home country or abroad as a member of a legal or illegal residency. He is usually employed in a service capacity such as stenographer or radio monitor.

Espionage intelligence activity aimed at acquiring classified information from a hostile intelligence service.

Essential elements of information (EEI) the critical items of information about the enemy and his environment needed to complete an assessment. See *Target.*

False-flag recruitment occurs when an individual is recruited believing he is cooperating with an intelligence service of a particular country. In fact, he has been deceived and is cooperating with an intelligence service of another country.

Feed material information that is usually true but unimportant given to an individual to pass to another intelligence service to maintain or enhance his value to that service. Sometimes called build-up material. See *Build-up material.*

Generated key numerical key sequences, derived through complicated cryptographic manipulation of key phrases and numbers.

Handler see *Principal.*

Hiding place see *Drop.*

Human intelligence (HUMINT) intelligence collected by humans.

HUMINT See *Human intelligence.*

Illegal an officer or employee of an intelligence service dispatched abroad with no overt connection to the intelligence service which sent him or the government operating the intelligence service. An illegal is operated by the center, not by a legal residency.

Illegal agent see *Agent.*

Illegal net an intelligence-gathering unit operating under the control of an illegal residency.

Illegal operations intelligence operations conducted by intelligence officers, employees, and agents under the control of an illegal residency or under the control of the center.

Illegal support officer an intelligence officer assigned to a legal residency whose primary function is to support illegals by supplying them with anything that is needed in their daily lives. A secondary function is to gather information and documents that will help illegals avoid detection.

Intelligence community   all components of a government that produce intelligence and counterintelligence.

Intelligence officer (IO)   a professionally trained member of an intelligence service. He may serve in the home country or abroad, as a member of a legal or illegal residency.

IO   see *Intelligence officer.*

Legal operations   intelligence operations conducted by intelligence officers, employees, co-opted workers, or agents under the control of a legal residency.

Legend   a coherent and plausible account of an individual's background, living arrangements, employment, daily activities, and family given by a foreign intelligence service by an illegal or agent. Often the legend will be supported by fraudulent documents. See *Cover story.*

Lippman   a special high-resolution emulsion used in preparing microdots and mikrats.

Live-letter box (LLB)   see *Accommodation address.*

Mail drop   see *Accommodation address.*

Meet area   the area surrounding a meeting site.

Microdot   photographic reduction of documents to three by six millimeters.

Mikrat   Smaller than a microdot.

Notional   fictitious; most commonly used to refer to a nonexistent agent but also used to refer to fictitious organizations, individuals, or sources of information.

Official establishments   any offices in this country controlled by foreign governments.

Officials   aliens assigned in this country to official establishments or to the United Nations and its organizations.

One-time pad (OTP)   see *Cipher pad.*

One-way radio link (OWRL)   transmission of voice, key, or impulses by radio to intelligence personnel who, by prearrangement, can receive and decipher the messages. See *Two-way radio link.*

Open code   seemingly inocuous messages that, by prearrangement, convey a different message.

OTP   abbreviation of one-time pad.

Overt activities   activities that may be openly attributed to the government responsible for them.

OWRL   see *One-way radio link.*

Parole   a prearranged verbal exchange used by intelligence personnel to identify themselves to each other.

Persona non grata   the official act of declaring a foreign national unwelcome in this country.

Picket surveillance   placement of surveillance personnel at locations that encircle an area being watched. Also known as perimeter surveillance.

Positive intelligence   interpreted intelligence.

Potential agent   see *Agent.*

Principal   intelligence officer or co-opted worker directly responsible for the operations of a principal agent or agent. Also known as a handler. See *Case officer.*

Provocation   activity designed to induce an individual, organization, intelligence service, or government to take action damaging to itself.

Pseudonym   a false name that looks like a true name. See *Cryptonym.*

Recognition signals   prearranged visual signals used by intelligence personnel to identify each other.

Recruitment   the process of enlisting an individual to work for an intelligence or counterintelligence service.

Recruitment in place   a foreign official who overtly continues to work for his government and covertly provides the U.S. with information of intelligence value.

Redoubled agent   see *Agent.*

Referentura   a Soviet term referring to rooms inside Soviet establishments that are protected from outside surveillance and periodically swept for bugs. Inside the rooms are classified correspondence and files, and ciphering and radio transmission personnel.

Residency, illegal   an intelligence establishment in a target country consisting of one or more intelligence officers and possibly one or two other employees with no overt connection to the intelligence service that operates it or to the government operating the intelligence service.

Residency, legal   an intelligence establishment in a target country composed of intelligence officers and employees assigned as overt representatives of their government.

Resident   the head of a legal or illegal residency who supervises subordinate intelligence personnel.

Residentura   a Soviet term that refers to the personnel and activities of an overseas residency and the space occupied by the residency.

Safe house   a location controlled by an intelligence service that provides a secure place for individuals engaged in intelligence operations to meet.

Sanitize   alteration of information to conceal how, where, and from whom the information was obtained.

Secret writing (S/W)   invisible writing.

SIGINT   see *Signal intelligence.*

Signal   a prearranged visual or audio sign that a dead drop has been filled or emptied or that an emergency meeting is needed.

Signal intelligence (SIGINT)   intelligence obtained by monitoring foreign radio transmissions from any source including missiles, satellites, and spacecraft.

Signal vicinity   the area surrounding the place where a signal is located or transmitted from.

Sign-of-life signal   a signal emitted periodically to signify that an agent is safe.

Singleton   an illegal who lives in a target country and operates alone. He does not become involved in the operations of agents or illegal residencies.

Sleeper   an illegal or agent in a foreign country who does not engage in intelligence activities until told to do so.

Soft film   the gelatin emulsion of a film that has been removed from the film base so the film can be rolled or folded and secreted in a small place.

Source   an individual who occasionally furnishes information to foreign intelligence representatives but is not an agent.

Spotter   an agent or illegal agent assigned to locate and assess individuals who might be of value to an intelligence service.

Staging   sending an illegal or illegal agent to another area of the home country or to another country before he is sent to the target country so he can establish a legend and receive training.

Sterile funds   money used by intelligence personnel and obtained so it cannot be traced to an intelligence agency.

Sterilize   removal of signs that would connect material or devices to an individual, intelligence service, or country using them.

Stray   see *Bogie.*

Surface   public disclosure of an intelligence operation or the identity of intelligence personnel.

S/W   see *Secret writing.*

Target   an individual, organization, or intelligence service against which intelligence operations are conducted. Also refers to documents or instruments which an intelligence service is trying to obtain, or to the subject of a surveillance.

Third-country operation   an operation conducted by an intelligence service in one country but based in a second country and aimed at a third.

Tradecraft   specialized techniques used in intelligence operations.

Triple agent   see *Agent.*

Two-way radio link (TWRL)   transmission of radio messages between intelligence officers and their command centers. See *One-way radio link.*

Unwitting agent   see *Agent.*

Walk-in   an individual who voluntarily offers his services or information to a foreign government.

SOURCE: Edited version of the FBI's *List of Terminology Used in Foreign Counterintelligence and Counterespionage Investigations.*

Index

co